THE SHIFTING LANDSCAPE OF WORK

THE SHIFTING LANDSCAPE OF WORK

Norene Pupo
York University

Dan Glenday
Brock University

Ann Duffy
Brock University

NELSON | E D U C A T I O N

NELSON EDUCATION

The Shifting Landscape of Work
by Norene Pupo, Dan Glenday, and Ann Duffy

Associate Vice-President, Editorial Director:
Evelyn Veitch

Editor-in-Chief:
Anne Williams

Acquisitions Editor:
Maya B. Castle

Senior Marketing Manager:
Amanda Henry

Developmental Editor:
Liisa Kelly

Permissions Coordinator:
Debbie Yea

Permissions Researcher:
Sandra Mark

Senior Content Production Manager:
Anne Nellis

Copy Editor:
Erin Moore

Proofreader:
Manikandan

Indexer:
Kevin Broccoli

Senior Production Coordinator:
Ferial Suleman

Design Director:
Ken Phipps

Managing Designer:
Franca Amore

Interior Designer:
Joanne Slouenwhite

Interior Design Modifications:
Peter Papayanakis

Cover Design:
Jennifer Stimson

Cover Image:
© ETTORE FERRARI/epa/Corbis

Compositor:
Cadmus

Printer:
RR Donnelley

Library and Archives Canada Cataloguing in Publication

The shifting landscape of work / edited by Norene Pupo, Dan Glenday, Ann Duffy.

Includes index.
ISBN 978-0-17-650065-8

1. Labor—Social aspects—Textbooks. I. Pupo, Norene, 1952- II. Glenday, Daniel, 1948- III. Duffy, Ann

HD4901.S45 2010 331
C2010-904419-3

ISBN-13: 978-0-17-650065-8
ISBN-10: 0-17-650065-0

To the women and men of the Canadian labour movement whose struggles and sacrifices on behalf of workers, in and out of the paid labour force, are an inspiration to all who aspire to social justice.

CONTENTS

PREFACE

Work and uneasy prospects about employment now figure prominently in the consciousness of many Canadians. As the financial costs associated with higher education steadily inch upwards along with education requirements and as the social safety net is increasingly frayed, there is growing frustration with what the future holds. "Good" jobs appear to be increasingly scarce and competition for even entry level and low-paid jobs seems to be intense. Yet, the individualistic rhetoric of more education, more savings for retirement and, over all, more personal effort speaks to the continued enthusiasm for the traditionally framed "good life." Finding secure, interesting, and fulfilling employment with opportunities for advancement remains very much the popular dream.

The selections in this text are intended to "wise up" the reader as to the dynamics of the labour market, the pressing realities of unpaid work, and the impact of structural shifts in societal power relations. The popularization of neoliberalism, the struggles of organized advocates, the intensification of paid and unpaid work, the upsurge in "rights" movements, the concentration and national externalization of corporate rule, along with growing demands from anti-consumerists and reduced work advocates all speak to a dynamic and tumultuous period of change in Canadians' experience with and relationship to paid employment. The following selections provide accessible, timely, and challenging invitations to enter into these debates and struggles.

ACKNOWLEDGMENTS

The editors would like to thank the very patient and supportive Nelson staff. Specifically, Liisa Kelly, Laura Macleod, and Maya B. Castle have been absolutely key to bringing the book to completion. Additionally, we would like to acknowledge the contributions of Anne Nellis, Ferial Suleman, Franca Amore, Debbie Yea, and Sandra Mark of Nelson's Manufacturing and Production Services team, and of Amanda Henry, who has managed the marketing of the book.

We would also like to thank the reviewers, some of whom have asked to remain anonymous, whose thoughtful suggestions and guidance were very helpful:

Carolyn Bassett	*University of New Brunswick*
Donna Harrrison	*University of Victoria*
Larry Savage	*Brock University*
K. Wayne Taylor	*University of Manitoba*

Finally, but most importantly, we would also like to acknowledge the pivotal support provided by our partners and families whose presence in our lives makes the work both meaningful and possible—John, Jennifer, and Gregory; Rick; and Dusky, Mayra, and Hermana.

Norene Pupo

Dan Glenday

Ann Duffy

ABOUT THE AUTHORS

Ann Duffy is a Professor in the Department of Sociology and is affiliated with the M.A. in Social Justice and M.A. in Critical Sociology at Brock University. She also teaches in Brock's Women's Studies Program. She has authored and co-authored a variety of books, chapters, and scholarly articles. Most of these publications concern some aspect of employment, women, violence, and aging. In addition, she has co-edited several texts that have become popular sources in the sociology of Canadian society, sociology of the family, and work and employment. Professor Duffy is currently, under the auspices of a SSHRC grant, collaborating on an exploration into the impact of worker displacement on workers' communities and their families.

Dan Glenday is Professor of Sociology and past Director and Founder of the Labour Studies Centre at Brock University. The recipient of three SSHRCC awards, his research and published interests over the past three decades covered the social, cultural, and political impacts of new information technology on working men and women. His present research project takes him into the colourful world of independent professional wrestling and its cross-cultural expressions.

Norene Pupo is an Associate Professor in the Department of Sociology and former director of the Centre for Research on Work and Society at York University. She has researched and published in the areas of women, work and social policy, part-time employment, call centres and shifting employment practices in the public sector, and unions and economic restructuring. She has been the Principal Investigator of a project entitled "Restructuring Work and Labour in the New Economy." Under this grant she has studied changes in worktime and in work processes within a globalized economy. Out of this grant she has recently co-edited (with Mark Thomas) *Interrogating the New Economy* (UTP, 2010), a collection of articles exploring changes in the structure of work and labour processes.

ABOUT THE CONTRIBUTORS

Kate Bezanson is an Associate Professor in the Department of Sociology and in the graduate program in Social Justice and Equity Studies at Brock University. She works in the areas of gender, social policy, political economy, and family change. She is currently exploring the rise of neoconservatism in Canada in relation to family and social policy, and is beginning a research project on class, motherhood, and infant feeding. She is involved in local food sustainability initiatives and is past president of the Rosalind Blauer Centre for Child Care.

Nel Coloma-Moya has a Master's degree in Adult Education from OISE/UT and has recently completed another at York University in Geography. Currently she is at Queen's University in a Ph.D. program in Geography. She has a broad range of interests from feminism to post-modernism but her focus continues to be on migration, especially in relation to the Filipino diaspora.

Angelo DiCaro is a national staff representative working in the communications department of the Canadian Auto Workers union. He completed his Master's of Industrial Relations from the University of Toronto, and holds an undergraduate degree in labour studies and sociology from York University. He began his affiliation with the CAW as a retail worker in CAW Local 414.

Alan Hall is currently the Director of the Labour Studies Program at the University of Windsor, a position he has held for eight of the last 11 years. Dr. Hall's main areas of research are occupational health and safety politics, the policing of labour and social protest, and legal reforms in labour and environmental law. He has co-authored a book on the policing of public order and is completing a book on restructuring and the production politics of health and safety. He is currently doing research on ethnicity and workplace injury reporting.

Gerald Hunt is a Professor of Organizational Behaviour at the Ted Rogers School of Management, Ryerson University, in Toronto. His research focuses on the experience of minorities in the workplace, and he has a particular interest in the response of labour unions to a more diverse workforce.

Chad Johnston works as a national representative in the Pensions and Benefits Department at the CAW. Chad graduated from the University of New Brunswick with a Bachelor's of Business Administration, and Queen's University with a Master's of Industrial Relations. He developed his interest in labour relations while working on behalf of CAW members at Air Canada.

Arlo Kempf teaches in the Initial Teacher Education Program at the University of Toronto. His latest book is the edited collection *Breaching the Colonial Contract: Anti-Colonialism in the US and Canada* (Springer, 2009).

Srabani Maitra is a doctoral candidate in the Department of Adult Education at the Ontario Institute for Studies in Education of the University of Toronto. Her doctoral research examines the active ways in which South Asian immigrant women, running small businesses from home, negotiate their exclusion from the Canadian labour market to create a niche for themselves in the new country. She has also published and presented on adult learning, contingent work, and transnational telework.

Kiran Mirchandani is an Associate Professor at the Ontario Institute for Studies in Education of the University of Toronto. She has published on home-based work, telework, contingent work, entrepreneurship, transnational service work, and self-employment. She is the co-author of *Criminalizing Race, Criminalizing Poverty: Welfare Fraud Enforcement in Canada* (2007) and co-editor of *Crimes of Colour: Racialization and the Criminal Justice System in Canada* (2002) and *The Future of Lifelong Learning and Work: Critical Perspectives* (2008). Her articles have appeared in journals such as *Gender & Society*, *Global Networks*, *Qualitative Methods,* and *Gender, Work and Organization*. She teaches in the Adult Education and Community Development Program (workplace learning and change focus), and offers courses on gendered and racialized processes in the workplace; critical perspectives on organizational development and learning; and technology, globalization, and economic restructuring.

Roxana Ng is a Professor of Adult Education and Community Development at the Ontario Institute for Studies in Education of the University of Toronto. Her primary empirical research focuses on the varied and multidimensional experiences of immigrant women in Canada. She has published extensively on this topic. Her recent investigations explore the changing working conditions of immigrant garment workers, and how professional immigrant women navigate the tension between family and paid work. Based on these studies, her theoretical work is concerned with how gender, race, class, and other axes of difference intersect with globalization in transnational contexts.

Trudy Rawlings is a doctoral candidate, Department of Adult Education and Counselling Psychology, OISE/University of Toronto. Her research interest is in information and communication technology access and training. As a researcher, she participated in the working group, Democratizing Workplace Learning (DWL), which is part of the Centre for the Study of Education and Work located at OISE. Also, as a director and researcher, she participated in the eCommons project, which was a national not-for-profit organization devoted to closing the digital divides by providing public access and citizen engagement.

Peter H. Sawchuk is a Professor of Sociology & Equity Studies in Education at the University of Toronto. He specializes in the area of learning and labour studies. His books include *Adult Learning and Technology in Working-Class Life* (Cambridge University Press, 2003) and *The Future of Learning and Work: Critical Perspectives* (Sense Publishing, 2008).

Hongxia Shan recently obtained her doctoral degree from the collaborative program of Adult Education and Community Development and Women and Gender Studies hosted at the Ontario Institute for Studies in Education (OISE) of the University of Toronto. Currently, she is a postdoctoral fellow with Saskatchewan Population Health and Evaluation Research Unit, University of Saskatchewan. She specializes in immigrant studies, gender and work, and adult learning, and her work falls in the areas of settlement studies, sociology of education and work, lifelong learning, and women and gender studies.

Khaleda Siddiqui is an independent researcher in Toronto. She holds a doctorate from Germany.

Bonnie L. Slade is a SSHRC Post-Doctoral Research Fellow at York University working in the Centre for Feminist Political Economy with Dr. Leah Vosko. Her research broadly addresses the deskilling of immigrant professionals in Canada. Her doctoral research, undertaken at the University of Toronto, focused on immigrant volunteering for "Canadian work experience" and how adult education programs are implicated in the deskilling of immigrant professionals. Her post-Doctoral research analyzes the impact of provincially funded employment programs with volunteer work placements on the labour market integration of immigrant professionals.

Jim Stanford is an economist with the Canadian Auto Workers union, and a regular economics columnist for *The Globe and Mail*.

SUPPLEMENTS PACKAGE

For Students

Sociology on the Web

http://www.shiftinglandscapeofwork.nelson.com

The Shifting Landscape of Work features a companion website designed for both students and instructors. Features of the website include study resources, links to news sites, search engines, a dictionary, and career information, all specific to sociology.

InfoTrac

InfoTrac® College Edition is automatically bundled FREE with every new copy of this text! InfoTrac College Edition is a world-class on-line university library that offers the full text of articles from over 500 scholarly and popular publications—updated daily and going back as far as 20 years. Students (and their instructors) receive unlimited access for four months.

For Instructors

Combined Instructor's Manual and NETA Test Bank

Available specifically for instructors is a combined Instructor's Manual and Test Bank, designed to help you work through the material in the text with a group of learners. The test bank portion of this resource has been created in line with our NETA—or Nelson Education Teaching Advantage—program.

The **Nelson Education Teaching Advantage (NETA)** program delivers research-based resources that promote student engagement and higher-order thinking and enables the success of Canadian students and educators.

Nelson Education Ltd. understands that the highest quality multiple-choice test bank provides the means to measure *higher-level thinking* skills as well as recall. In response to instructor concerns, and recognizing the importance of multiple-choice testing in today's classroom, we have created the Nelson Education Testing Advantage program (NETA) to ensure the value of our high quality test banks.

The testing component of our NETA program was created in partnership with David DiBattista, a 3M National Teaching Fellow, professor of psychology at Brock University, and researcher in the area of multiple-choice testing.

All NETA test banks include David DiBattista's guide for instructors, "Multiple Choice Tests: Getting Beyond Remembering." This guide has been designed to assist you in using Nelson test banks to achieve your desired outcomes in your course.

INTRODUCTION

"Work" is one of those words loaded with emotions and images. When you hear the word, it immediately evokes associations—hard work, no work, looking for work. As Sigmund Freud noted more than a century ago, work (along with "love") is one of the central pillars of our lives. Children in the earliest grades are routinely asked, "What will you do when you grow up?" and the taken-for-granted answer is not along the lines of being an environmental activist, an animal rights proponent, or a loving mother or father. From the beginnings of our consciousness, we are socialized to think of our lives in terms of paid employment and to formulate our identities around work. Indeed, the question to young people is often framed, "What are you going to be?" and the clear implication is that paid work and personal identity are inextricably linked. Once adults, "where do you work" or "what do you do" are prevailing themes[1] in the most casual conversations.

As with many aspects of our shared social realities, the taken-for-granted centrality of "paid work" is rarely scrutinized. The prevailing social assumption is that we will inevitably build and live our lives around the contours of employment and the personal and societal implications of these patterns are routinely not examined. Despite the centrality of paid work to almost every aspect of our personal and social experiences, we are rarely encouraged to question its primacy in our lives. Although our most intimate and personal experiences—from sexual relations to child rearing to family relationships—are framed by our relationship to paid labour, few of us question the dominance of work in our everyday lives or through our **life course.** In part, of course, this is because life without paid work, despite our enthusiasm for lotteries and gambling, seems a contradiction. Most of us simply know we must work for pay if we are to participate in our society and "time outs" from work (unemployment, even retirement) are seen as major upheavals in the normal course of events.

What is missed in this set of prevailing popular assumptions about social existence are a number of crucial social facts:

1. Work as we now know it was constructed in history. Its structure is neither inevitable nor unchanging.

2. Work is continuously socially constructed. Even today work in the so-called "**New Economy**" is in the midst of significant change.

3. Our assumptions about work reflect our society and our social positions in society.

4. The construction of work is a reflection of patterns of power in societies. To understand work at a particular time and social place, it is necessary to identify the major dimensions of power in a society and, increasingly, in the global context.

First, throughout the overwhelming majority of history human beings have not lived lives framed by paid employment. As we see even today in more traditional societies, work—in simple terms of efforts to provide food, shelter, and clothing—is typically interwoven with family and community relations, with the rhythms of day-to-day life, and with relationships with the physical environment. For example, the taken-for-granted lines between work and **non-work** often do not translate into the social realities of traditional societies. Productive activities, crafts, and **leisure** may seamlessly overlap with one another as group members may take time after a meal to combine storytelling, the making of clothing, and family banter. From this vantage point, it is clear that the modern social construction of work as an activity separate in time and space from non-work is a relatively recent historical phenomenon.

The last major historical re-orientation of work—industrialization—occurred in the 1700s in Europe. Through the course of the next several centuries, an economic path was laid in Europe and then internationally that led many workers away from fields, fishing grounds, and rural pasturelands into factories and urbanized centres. This process, which in many locations on the planet is far from complete, transformed the realities of workers and their families (Zaretsky, 1986). Lives that once centred on families, villages, traditions, and the local were eradicated and replaced by modern life rooted in urban centres, individuality, and cosmopolitanism. In this process, the "new" and social change became normative. Of course, numerous remnants of these former realities persist around the globe (and as tourist destinations) but they are typically seen as historic curiosities[2] more than commentaries on the paths we now pursue.

Not only are "work and employment" historically constructed realities that have emerged relatively recently in human experience, they are socially constructed. What is work for one individual or group may not be for others. The Inuit catching seal, the household worker "making dinner," the student "volunteering" for community service, and the auto worker welding car frames may not all be understood to be working. For example, until recently, work in the home, typically accomplished by women, was considered outside the realm of "real" work—in part because it was unpaid and in part because it was seen as constructed around gendered obligations (a "labour of love"). To a lesser degree, traditional occupations, such as hunting and fishing, occupy a murky marginality since they are "hobbies" for the well-to-do. The efforts of students, because they are conceptualized as a preparation for "real work," are also generally marginalized. In short, the activities that are construed as "real work" vary depending on prevailing beliefs and values in a particular social setting at a specific historical moment.

Similarly, the moral imperatives attached to work vary depending upon social location. The ancient Greek scholars argued that hard, physical work was to be avoided at all costs—such work soiled the spirit and was appropriate only for slaves, women, and the lower classes. The notion that hard work was redemptive and indicative of moral superiority emerges in other social contexts. As Max Weber argued in *The Spirit of Capitalism and Rise of Protestantism*, protestant religions that were popularized in the 18th century supported a link between morality, hard work, and economic success. Hard work was a reflection of one's moral goodness and was rewarded on earth by financial benefits.[3] Today the relationship between goodness and work is increasingly complex. Corporate malfeasance such as Enron and, in Canada, the $50-million Ponzi scheme concocted by Bertram Earl Jones along with the massive bonuses accrued by corporate and financial chieftains, have led some to associate financial success with corruption and greed. Similarly, the emergence of the modern celebrity class appears to associate consumption and freedom from work with high social status. In a related vein, the popularization of lotteries and gambling has suggested that there is a disconnection between hard work, economic success and moral worth. Regardless of the historical specifics, it is clear that the nature of work and its personal implications vary from one social setting to another.

Thirdly, the social and historical framing and reframing of work are ongoing processes. Work, even the narrow realm of paid work, continues to change dramatically and many commentators today talk about the "New Economy" in which new kinds of work—contract work, offshore work, marginal work, and guest work—are becoming increasingly prominent. Even the most superficial examination of the workplace will reveal tremendous transformations of working experiences as industrial robots, computerized production, cell phones, lap tops, and e-mails change the nature of work tasks as well as the physical location and time parameters of much modern work. Indeed, as discussed in detail throughout this book, in the last several decades paid work has been significantly reconfigured for many Canadians and it seems likely that further changes are imminent. Internationally, a variety of evidence suggests that the parameters of paid employment are shifting momentously. In this context, work for many Canadians is in turmoil and navigating the new world of employment requires an understanding of these fundamental changes.

Finally, comprehending the shifting realities of work requires recognition of the patterns of **power** and powerlessness in which it is deeply embedded. Paid work, as Karl Marx famously expounded more than a century ago, is a contested terrain in which many of the fundamental power struggles of our day are being played out. As discussed above, even the fundamental ability to define or differentiate between "work" and "non-work" is a reflection of the power dynamics in our society. For generations, labour in the home by women, children, and youth was dismissed or trivialized. The assumption was that real work was performed by men, and some women, in factories, mines, mills, and offices. Today, this narrow understanding of work has become steadily outmoded in a society that now routinely collects data on **unpaid work** in the home and in which the need to share domestic labour in the home is increasingly taken for granted (Sayer, 2005). Women's role in the household is even acknowledged in legal terms and in their right to access Canada Pension Plan benefits. A woman who devotes years of her life to unpaid domestic labour is now officially accepted as having rights to pension benefits that were previously only available to paid workers. These changes in the social legitimization of unpaid work, of course, reflect power struggles and the successful mobilization of women's groups over the course of the last several decades.

This mobilization of social power relations not only impacts on what is or is not considered to be "work," but also on the structure and outcomes of work. For example, how long workers are expected to work daily, weekly, and through their lives, how much risk they should reasonably run on the job, and how much they should be compensated for their efforts are at the core of struggles around work. As Marx so cogently pointed out, owner-employers have a vested interest in minimizing the costs of labour since such costs[4] (wages, pensions, even safety provisions) will cut into the rate of profit they will garner. Conversely, workers recognize that maximizing the pay-offs from their employment is central to their own well-being and that of their families. This relationship speaks to a power struggle that has lasted for several centuries and that is very much ongoing in Canada and globally (see also Dyer-Witheford, 1999).

Taken together, these social facts provide the foundation for what has been termed a political economy perspective. The contributors to this volume work within this framework—they are interested in the historical forces that frame modern issues and focus on the power relations that underlie many of the contemporary realities surrounding work. Finally, without exception, they work from the premises that change is possible, that work and the workplace can be made better, more humane, and more fulfilling, and that specific contemporary power relations are neither inevitable nor intractable.

ORGANIZATION OF THE BOOK

Today as students look forward to graduation, many will see an uncertain future with many roadblocks to navigate as they set themselves on a path with hopes of achieving some level of economic security. Clearly many will readily understand that the place of work in their lives is bounded by economic turmoil and new political realities. Most will confront some degree of economic insecurity, either directly or indirectly, in one of its various forms—continuing high levels of unemployment, marginalized work, contractually limited work, too few hours of work, unpaid caregiving, inadequate pensions, a fraying social safety net, inaccessible training or retraining programs, deindustrialization, and crumbling communities, to name a few. Global patterns of change, including crises of unemployment and economic recession, paint a very depressing picture. Some will take charge of their futures, by opting for self-employment. This decision may provide a level of autonomy and freedom from direct corporate control. At the same time, striking out on one's own requires hard work, long hours, fewer benefits, and perseverance. Those who eschew self-employment must be relentless in their pursuit of decent work and may find that they too may face a number of difficult choices and circumstances, such as relocating, retraining, upgrading, restructuring, and plant closures. Certainly the labour market profiles of young workers today will not include the degree of stability experienced by workers a generation ago. Despite Canada's relative wealth, over the past 30 years the economy has been marked by rising income inequality, growth in low-wage **precarious work,** the destruction of well-paid unionized manufacturing jobs, and lengthier transitions to work for young people. In short, the twin engines of **globalization** and **neoliberalism**[5] have transformed the Canadian labour market.

The book is divided into three parts: **Scanning the Horizon, Working the Margins,** and **The Emerging Landscape**. The chapters in Part 1, **Scanning the Horizon,** examine the major economic changes and resultant labour market shifts that have been occurring over the past few decades. They account for the transition from an industrial and resource base to a service-oriented economy and analyze consequences for workers confronting new forms of social and economic insecurity. In Part 2, **Working the Margins,** the chapters analyze the impact of growing precariousness within the labour market. In particular, they consider hidden dimensions of discrimination, inequality, and racialization. They also consider the movements or displacements of both work and workers and the impact on marginality within the labour market. Finally, in Part 3, **The Emerging Landscape**, the chapters discuss ways in which workers and their **unions** are seeking to negotiate the new landscape.

Starting with a review of the attacks on nation-building initiatives such as Petro Canada, the Canada Development Corporation, and the Free Trade Agreement begun by Brian Mulroney's conservative, neoliberal agenda, in Chapter 1 of Part 1, **Scanning the Horizon,** Dan Glenday re-examines Canada's position in the world economy. Data from Canadian, United Nations, and other government sources reveal Canada's shifting tasks in the world economy. Glenday argues that where once Canada's nation-building initiatives contributed to strengthening its position in the world economy by exports of manufactured and high technology products from companies such as Northern Telecom, it is now exporting ever larger proportions of its natural resources to the U.S. and other developed or developing countries such as China. In other words, the country's wealth is increasingly based on returning to our one-time colonial role as "hewers of wood and drawers of water." Glenday considers the consequences for present and future generations of the ballooning of the low-wage service sector and the demise of the high paying jobs in the manufacturing sector and in salaried employment and "good" careers within "new economy" sectors, such as information technology and cultural industries. A recent example is the pending demise of the Canadian Foundation for Climate and Atmospheric Sciences. Margaret Munro, a CanWest news reporter, stated, "and young scientists, trained at substantial cost to Canadian taxpayers, have begun leaving the country in search of work."[6] The chapter concludes with two options for the future. Canada can both stay the course and continue to provide the world economy with our depleting natural resources or Canadians can be galvanized politically into pressing for a development state under the slogan of a "Just Society for the 21st Century."

Taking into account these transformations within the economy, in Chapter 2, Angelo DiCaro, Chad Johnston, and Jim Stanford examine the historical relevance of unions within the Canadian economy and raise questions about their struggle and survival within what appears to be an increasingly hostile environment. The authors provide strong evidence that a vigorous labour movement is key if the working class is to fight against the loss of jobs, the deterioration of working conditions, and the growing precariousness within the labour market, even within sectors previously thought to be secure, providing workers with excellent benefits and opportunities. Perhaps most significantly, the labour movement has challenged the neoliberal agenda head on, questioning the notion of individualism[7] and raising the banner of collectivism in an attempt to restore decent standards of living and social justice within our communities.

Focusing in particular on the massive shift to a service-dominated economy, Norene Pupo examines the process of **Walmartization** and how manufacturing has changed over the past decades. She considers the consequences for workers in both manufacturing and retail sectors of the shift in which big box retailers, and Walmart in particular, now dictate production needs to manufacturers, replacing earlier historical processes in which manufacturers took the lead in identifying and creating consumer demands. This shift has impacted heavily upon low-wage service sector workers who pay a high price for an economy driven by the marketing of low-cost largely imported goods through their poorly compensated insecure jobs in predominantly non-union or anti-union workplaces.

As Kate Bezanson explains in "Neoliberalism, Families, and Work–Life Balance," low-wage workers and their families will receive very little in the way of help from the contemporary neoliberal state. Focusing on the recession of 2008, this chapter examines the ways in which the neoliberal theory of the state and economy allowed the economic crisis to occur while doing very little to assist its primary victims. Drawing on one worker's personal account of the struggle to manage paid work along with caregiving responsibilities, Bezanson reveals the harsh lived realities of economic insecurity in the midst of a disintegrating social support system. With little in the way of an effective political challenge to neoliberalism, the future appears bleak for the many Canadian families seeking to find some balance between paid work and family life.

In Part 2, **Working the Margins**, the chapters examine various aspects of the growing precariousness faced by larger numbers of workers both within Canada and abroad. Changing conditions of work have affected the experience of work for individual workers and have impacted families, communities, and households as many workers face deteriorating conditions—longer hours, fewer benefits, less job security, and hidden forms of inequality and discrimination. Gerald Hunt examines the "trap" of invisibility of differences in the workplace. Being gay or coping with a long-term medical condition are two obvious **invisible** minority characteristics some individuals must address in the workplace. Legislation may forbid discrimination, but the *experience* of discrimination is another matter. While there are workplaces that welcome **diversity,** for those trapped in the shadows of the workplace "outing" oneself or being "outed" by a colleague, the fear of being judged negatively and suffering adverse career consequences is real. Hunt analyzes ways in which negative and pejorative **stigmas** function in organizations and how people manage hidden identities. He then considers what influences some individuals to disclose their invisibility to others at work. The costs to individuals and organizations associated with invisibility precludes what organizations can do, such as creating an "**integration paradigm**" or allowing employees' differences to matter and thereby contribute to an open and fair working environment.

Authors Kiran Mirchandani, Roxana Ng, Nel Coloma-Moya, Srabani Maitra, Trudy Rawlings, Hongxia Shan, Khaleda Siddiqui, and Bonnie L. Slade focus on visible minorities and discrimination by considering the insidious forms of racism within insecure employment at both macro and micro levels. Starting with the understanding that precarious forms of work are racialized, that immigrants and people of colour dominate short-term, contract, and various other forms of precarious work, these authors carry the analysis further to focus on the invisibility of power and politics at the micro level within the workplace and the social construction of race to expose how racialization is embedded within workplace relations and dynamics. Drawing on their interviews with women in three labour markets—sewing, telemarketing, and cashiering—the authors provide a detailed analysis of the processes through which racialized women are constructed as different and inferior and thereby marginalized.

Guest and migrant workers compromise one key component of Canada's racialized labour force. Canada shares with the U.S. and most western European countries the mushrooming of guest and migrant work programs not only in agriculture and domestic labour but expanding into construction and other occupations. Peter Sawchuk and Arlo Kempf examine the lived experience of Canadian agricultural guest workers who remain trapped in the margins. In a rapidly globalizing and polarized world, what happens to these workers is central to understanding global labour markets. Relying on interviews with Mexican farm workers, Sawchuk and Kempf speak to the forms of cultural and racial exploitation that can spawn organized and spontaneous resistance. The chapter seeks to develop a preliminary framework to understand not simply the historical roots of the **guest worker programs** in Canada but to situate the complexity of contemporary guest workers' cultural, political, and economic experiences within what the authors refer to as a broad "curriculum of experience."

In Part 3, **The Emerging Landscape**, the authors provide some insights into the future pathways for workers, their families, and their communities by examining agency, choices, and struggles of individual workers and their organizations to challenge the direction of change. Are there signs of resistance within the workplace? How are workers navigating difficult conditions within the workplace and balancing their work and lives? How are unions repositioning to confront new conditions within the globalized economy?

Ann Duffy starts this part with an examination of the ways in which the very basic parameters of work are being reframed in the "New Economy." In all aspects of workers' lives—from pre-work training and education to post-retirement employment—workers are spending more of their time devoted to work and work-related activities. In sharp contrast to concerns in the 1960s about how people would manage all their leisure, today women and men struggle to find enough time to manage their complex and demanding responsibilities in paid and unpaid work. The resultant pressures are then frequently reflected in the deterioration in emotional, physical, and relationship well-being. While challenges to the "time crisis" are emerging, it remains to be seen whether "downshifting," worktime reduction, anti-consumerism, and community involvement will provide long-term and widespread responses to time scarcity.

In this context, it is not surprising that some analysts would criticize the modern workplace as ever more controlling. After reviewing labour process theories and recent research employing the concept of "*Electronic Panopticon*," Dan Glenday confirms that most critical sociologists view managerial power in large organizations becoming ever more pervasive, even "totalizing." The recently employed concept of the "*Electronic Panopticon*" is made up of a cut down brandished version of Michel Foucault's notion of power combined with new managerial philosophies such as Total Quality Improvement and high technology monitoring equipment in the workplace. The question Glenday asks is in an age of large hierarchical organizations dominated by the ever watchful "Big Brother" managerial and surveillance strategies, is it possible for employees to exercise any freedom at work? Employing a truer version of Foucault's notion of power as constraining options for channelling behaviour and Deleuze and Guattari's views on power as creating spaces or gaps, Glenday advances the notion of "**loose time**" as captured labour time in which the employee can professionally develop or resist managerial constraints and even exercise individual creativity. Drawing on interviews he conducted with men and women scattered in a variety of occupations and work settings, Glenday identifies power limitations at virtually every level of the organization and offers new insights into the actual workings of large organizations, opening possibilities for exploring how employees can exercise freedom and creativity in the workplace.

In the final chapter, Alan Hall examines the concrete ways in which labour unions are seeking to wrest greater control in the workplace. In the past, most **collective bargaining** in Canada has been conducted in a decentralized, workplace by workplace fashion—a pattern that tended to be both inefficient and costly to organized workers. While through to the 1980s and 90s considerable progress was made towards more coordinated and **centralized bargaining** processes, economic globalization and neoliberalism put a halt to much of this progress. Not only was this achieved by explicitly opposing centralized bargaining but also by pushing for **privatization** of public sector work, **non-standard** work arrangements, and the contracting out of more and more work. Focusing specifically on the largest union in Canada, the Canadian Union of Public Employees (CUPE), Hall explores their efforts to create and implement a national strategy to coordinate and/or centralize bargaining while challenging privatization and the movement to temporary and **part-time** positions. Although progress has been uneven and unclear, there may be, as Hall suggests, cause for some cautious optimism. Indeed, the 2008 economic crisis and the perception that greedy banks and shady financiers triggered the economic insecurities imposed on hundreds of thousands of Canadians may help mobilize resistance to neoliberalism and corporate rule while encouraging support for a more worker-friendly public agenda and united union action.

LOOKING BEYOND

Working within a global economy under a neoliberal regime, workers face numerous and daunting challenges. Activists and trade unionists hold on to the notion that positive change is possible, although there is a diversity of views around what the road to positive change may be. For some the primary challenge is corporate power and decision-making, as evidenced by the popularity of Michael Moore and his "muckraking" films. Others focus on mending the fraying social safety net in hopes of establishing at least a modicum of social justice. Labour activists acknowledge that the movement has recently lost some ground in the shift from an industrial to a service sector economy, but remain steadfast in their support for the prospect that unions will still play a major role in levelling the playing field, in prioritizing equity and justice, and in improving the lives of working Canadians. Recent victories in organizing previously unorganized workers—rural mail carriers and part-time college instructors in Ontario, for example—are clear indications that the movement has not lost its will despite its losing some ground.

Finally, there are a growing number of workers both individually and collectively signalling "they just aren't going to take it any more!" A small but significant number of individuals have simply opted out, preferring to live an anti-consumptive, uncomplicated lifestyle. A growing number of workers are publicly drawing attention to various workplace injustices—marginalizing of racialized workers, firing of workers without cause, ignoring **labour standards**—thereby garnering momentum for social change. Others persist in their commitment to challenge corporate giants and expose their unfair practices and anti-union sentiments. Still others point to the possibility of rejuvenating national politics in this country through grassroots engagements. The promise to continue to confront workplace injustices and to raise awareness is critical as we look ahead to the future of work in Canada.

ENDNOTES

1. Students, of course, have their own work-related version of this theme in routinized inquiries about "what is your major?"

2. Of course, trips to rural Mexico or China may evoke memories of this pre-industrial past but they are inevitably contextualized by the modern realities of industrial societies. Whether workers remain in their rural settings or move into urban centres, their lives are circumscribed by the realities of a larger globalized and industrial context.

3. This religious connection between moral worth and economic well-being is, of course, a prominent discourse in Western religions.

4. This is not to ignore the complexity of the lived realities of this struggle. Owners must also consider the impact of negative publicity, law suits, the prospects for organized opposition from their workers, and so on.

5. Neoliberalism is discussed in considerable detail in the text. It refers to the conservative ideology popularized in the late 1970s and early 1980s and prominent to this day that encourages dramatic reductions in state-sponsored support for individuals in Canadian society (as reflected in reductions in budgets for education, social welfare, health care, and so on) and decries poverty, crime, and other social problems as the result of individual proclivities rather than social structures.

6. "Climate Scientists Fight for Renewed Research Funding," *The Gazette*, February 24, 2010, p. A11.

7. Neoliberalism has been directly related to various campaigns that urge individuals to solve their own problems (individualism)—by improving their education or retraining in a new field, by reducing their expectations and, in a very recent campaign, preparing for old age by saving much more than they currently do.

SCANNING THE HORIZON

Courtesy of Dan Glenday

Rich but Losing Ground: How Canada's Position in the World Economy Impacts Jobs, Social Choices, and Life Chances

Dan Glenday

DISCUSSION QUESTIONS

1. What are globalization and neoliberalism?

2. What neoliberal policies during the 1980s and 1990s weakened the Canadian state?

3. Where are the best paying and where are the worst paying jobs in the Canadian economy?

4. What makes Canada a semiperipheral country and why is this important to know?

INTRODUCTION

If asked on the street, nearly everyone in Canada could agree with the statement that Canada is a rich country when compared to most nations in the global economy. And yet, in a recent report by the Canadian Council on Social Development on the state of Canada's social programs, the authors state that "for young Canadians, the transition to work is taking longer and becoming more difficult [while] the dramatic increase in the labour force participation of women is unfortunately paired with the growing prevalence of low-wage work and precarious jobs" (2005, p. 2). To the extent that the authors point to "real progress" in reducing poverty among seniors, they also insist that "rising income inequality and the unequal distribution of wealth—helps to explain our failure to eradicate child poverty" (2005, p. 3). Add to these indicators, the large number of homeless in Canada's large and smaller cities, escalating unemployment resulting from the recent recession, and persisting regional disparities and the face of Canada as a rich country begins to show its blemishes.

Granted, Canada is not unique among the rich nations of the world when it comes to the shifting landscape of good and bad jobs and the retreating investments by government in social programs stemming from **neoliberalism** and **globalization.** Growing income inequality linked to the performance of national economies is disproportionately experienced in the world economy. The incidence and significance of the income gap in the U.S. and the United Kingdom, for example, is greater than in Japan or Germany. This is largely due to the continued role of the state in the redistribution of resources for education, health, and social programs in the two latter nations. However, Canada has not been immune from other social changes. Since the late 1970s, Canadian families now come in all "shapes and sizes" and the cultural and racial diversity continue to change the face of Canada's largest cities and towns. While difficult to point the finger at globalization to explain the diversity in Canadian families over the past several decades, the dramatic rise of international migration from the poorer regions to rich countries such as Canada can be traced to globalization.

Compared to today, the world of the late 1970s underwent significant transformations at virtually every level of the economy and society. The discovery and rapid dissemination of microchip technology in the realm of work, the advent and spread of the World Wide Web, and the widespread use of information and communications technologies from the portable laptop computer, to the Blackberry, to the iPod are all taken-for-granted by today's young people but were unknown to a generation earlier.

Taking the changed world of the first decade of the 21st century as my starting point, three decades have passed since I argued that Canada's position in the world economy had strengthened over the decades of the 1970s and early 1980s. Most agreed with this assessment. The differences rested on assigning the appropriate rank; for example, instead of a strengthened **semiperipheral** region of the world economy, at least one author called for Canada's entry into the "perimeter of the core"[1] (see Niosi, 1996; Resnick, 1989). At the conclusion of that essay, I questioned how Canada's status as a rich mature capitalist country could be maintained in the face of (1) the national state's embracing and extending neoliberal policies through its international trade and services deals otherwise known as the Free Trade Agreement (FTA), the North American Free Trade Agreement (NAFTA), the General Agreement on Trade in Services (GATS) and (2) other neoliberal actions aimed at the dismantling of nation-building projects such as the Canada Development Corporation (1989, pp. 254–56). I also pointed out that Canada's future role depended on the nation's changing *tasks* in the evolving world economy. What I neglected to mention were the advantages Canada's status in the world economy held for the **social choices**, **life chances**, **work**, and **career options** on present and future generations of Canadians. These are the consequences of Canada's present-day global positioning that I intend to explore in more detail in this chapter. Before I do, I address what has happened over the past three decades to Canada's rank in the world economy by beginning with a brief description of the changed political and economic climate of the world economy otherwise known as globalization and neoliberalism. I follow this discussion with an examination into Canada's recent international trade patterns. By asking did the country improve, lose ground, or remain a strengthened semiperiphery, I am establishing the foundation upon which not only our wealth as a nation is based but; as important, the consequences this holds for present and future generations of Canadians.

CANADA, GLOBALIZATION, AND NEOLIBERALISM OVER THE PAST 30 YEARS

Globalization is the latest stage in a process of the spread and intensification of capitalism across the globe. The primary agent of globalization is the transnational corporation. Today, globalization involves the interaction and integration of more and more people in the world through international trade and investment, travel and tourism, and information technology and the mass media. Globalization brings with it effects on national cultures and political systems, on economic development and prosperity and on human health and wellness.

What is neoliberalism? Neoliberalism is more than an economic point of view with a set number of policies; it is a worldview or philosophy. Its principle economic standpoint is the following; the freedom of the market—freedom for capital, goods, and services to move where it is most profitable resulting in the "trickle down" notion of wealth distribution. It also calls for the elimination of trade **unions** in the labour force[2] and the removal of any impediments to capital mobility, such as regulations passed by democratic governments. The freedom is from the state, or government through deregulation.

When it comes to the role of the government, public expenditure for social services, such as health and education, should be reduced as much as possible. Another essential feature of neoliberalism is the privatization of public enterprise. Governments should mainly function to provide the infrastructure to advance the rule of law with respect to property rights and contracts.

As a social philosophy, neoliberalism means changing people's perceptions about what is morally right and what is morally wrong. Neoliberalism requires citizens to abandon attitudes about the public and community good and substitute the centrality of individualism, especially entrepreneurial capitalism and individual responsibility (Robbins, 1999). For example, the hardline Thatcherites in Great Britain called themselves "Dries" to demonstrate their opposition to the "Wets," a British public school nickname for any boy who showed any sign of caring for his fellow human beings.

Margaret Thatcher herself coined the phrase "There Is No Alternative" (TINA), meaning those economic, political, and social policies that became associated with neoliberalism constituted the *only* way to create wealth and good jobs, reduce poverty, and increase the standard of living for all; including the less developed countries. And, to this day, her nickname, "TINA," has stuck. The era of Margaret Thatcher as Prime Minister of Great Britain was the high point for neoliberalism and coincided with Ronald Reagan as President of the USA and Brian Mulroney as Prime Minister of Canada.

CANADA'S POSITION IN THE WORLD ECONOMY: UP, DOWN, OR NO CHANGE?

Bi-polar explanations for global inequality such as core-periphery, or dependent-developed nations became inadequate in the face of globalized economic development in some of the once poorer countries in the world. Mostly spearheaded by transnational corporations, these nations belied the simple dichotomies in vogue among many social analysts. How could some countries develop and move slowly out of dependent or peripheral status? This was the nagging question that refused to disappear, and then there was Canada. A rich country to be sure but one that displayed features of both peripheral status—the export of natural resources from oil to gold—and core characteristics—a dynamic manufacturing sector mostly under foreign control. These were the principle theoretical and methodological issues addressed in the earlier essay.

Thirty years ago, I placed emphasis on A. Emmanuel's (1972) notion of the "unequal exchange of material goods and services on a world level" to help explain Canada's unique position in the world economy (1989, p. 242). A hierarchical structure of the earth's nations resulted from the transfer of surplus labour captured by the "international trade in material goods and services" (1989, p. 242). The nature of these "commodity chains," according to Wallerstein, generates a three-tiered world economic and political system he termed the core, semiperiphery, and periphery (Wallerstein, 1979).

Examining the pattern in merchandise trade imbalances between selected countries[3] over the 10-year period between1975 and 1985, the data indicated a strengthening of Canada's position as a semiperipheral country in the world economy. The principle reasons offered were theoretical and empirical and based on Wallerstein's notion of the role of the state in semiperipheral countries. The semiperipheral state exercises a pivotal role in its potential to maneuver either up or down in the world economy. Wallerstein argued that one mechanism of mobility for semiperipheral countries is the exploitation of peripheral markets. A country's rise in position, taking Japan as an example, can result from that country's expanded trade with the periphery (Glenday, 1989, p. 241; Wallerstein, 1979).

There was little, if any, support for Canada's trade expansion with less developed countries during this period. Instead, there was evidence of the broadening of Canada's manufacturing base over the previous 10 to 20 years. First, the national government's signing of the Auto Pact in 1965 with the United States contributed to making Canada the sixth largest automobile producer by the 1980s (Forsyth, 1999). The Auto Pact accounted for a significant portion of merchandise trade to and from the U.S. Naturally, the auto industry became the preferred location for many young, non-university-trained men and women seeking well-paid, unionized employment. These jobs helped sustain Canada's image as a middle-class nation.

Canada's telecommunications equipment giant of the 1970s, 1980s, and 1990s, Northern Telecom, later crowned Nortel, boasted a capital base half the size of Mexico's gross national product, employed approximately 90,000 men and women worldwide by the beginning of this millennium and was the largest spender of research and development (R&D) in Canada (Evans, 2008). By some estimates, Nortel equipment was carrying 75 percent of the Internet traffic in North America by the end of the 1990s (CBC, 2009).

Canada's cultural industries in film and popular music, for example, benefited from national government tax incentives and other subsidies. These incentives contributed to a budding television and movie industry in Vancouver, Toronto, and Montreal along with launching the careers of numerous Canadian pop, rock, and modern jazz musicians and artists. And, there was the Canadian state's struggle to build up other domestic industries through the establishment of the Canadian Development Corporation in 1971, the control of foreign investment by the 1974 creation of the Foreign Investment Review Agency, the creation of Petro Canada in 1975 as a Crown corporation to establish a strong Canadian presence in the oil industry and to identify new Canadian energy sources, and the 1981 National Energy Policy (NEP) to promote "Canadianization" of the natural gas and oil sectors. Together, these initiatives over the short period of their existence, I argued, worked to strengthen the nation's position in the world economy.

In the end, there was little doubt that Canada stood on the threshold of further possibilities. The essay ended, however, with these closing thoughts:

> My main argument has been that the pattern of merchandise trade confirms an upward movement during the period that corresponds to the last ten years of Pierre E. Trudeau's Prime Ministership. Canada has strengthened her position as a semiperipheral country and may have entered the perimeter of the core....
>
> The recent dismantling of Trudeau's "economic nationalist" policies by the present government [the Progressive Conservative government of Brian Mulroney] may *reverse* this trend. Organized labour sees the recent signing of the Free Trade initiative between Canada and the United States as "hemorrhaging" our economic and cultural identity. The fate of Canada awaits the outcome of the present restructuring of capital accumulation. (Emphasis mine)

How prescient were these remarks? On the surface and before the recent recession, many Canadians, if asked, might say they were better off now than 30 years ago. We are a rich country to be sure. However, the present appearance of relative affluence is not enough. We need to ask ourselves: What is our wealth based upon? And in the present era of globalization and the aftershocks of neoliberalism, this means focusing on our position in the world economy. Has Canada maintained, strengthened, or has her position weakened over the past 30 years? This assessment requires demonstrating macro developments in the broader social and economic universe. Delving deeper requires evidence. As before, the character of Canada's international trade will be examined and the evidence will derive from published materials and data sets from Statistics Canada, the United Nations, and other agency sources.

The remainder of the chapter proceeds with a description of Canada's ranking in terms of income per capita to establish that we are indeed a rich country. This will be followed by an examination of changes to the pattern of Canada's international trade in order to determine the sources for Canada's wealth as a nation. The discussion will move to a brief portrait of the life chances and social choices Canadians experience today. This will be followed by an overview of the work and career options available to Canadians over the 10-year period from 1996–2006 by looking at which economic sectors are expanding and which ones are contracting. The chapter concludes with a discussion of the recent global recession and where we go from here. This exchange will scrutinize the case for returning to an active developmentalist state.

WHAT HAS HAPPENED SINCE THE MID-1980S? CANADA'S WEALTH AND INTERNATIONAL TRADE PATTERN

The United Nations uses Gross Domestic Product per capita as one important measure to gauge a country's wealth. Countries can then be arranged in a hierarchical order with the wealthiest at the top and the poorest at the bottom of the list. Table 1.1 provides evidence for Canada's status as a rich nation. Throughout the 1990s until 2007, Canada ranked among the top five countries in the world based on income per capita (purchasing power parity US$). Note, however, Norway's higher ranking than Canada's throughout this period while since 1995 Ireland witnessed its meteoric jump. Both are much smaller geographical nations than Canada. Norway's oil exports have sustained its ranking while the recent global recession has hit Ireland particularly hard.

What is Canada's wealth based on? One way to scrutinize the sources of wealth is to examine the character of international trade. That is, what do we sell on the international market that others want? What are we well known for

TABLE 1.1

GROSS DOMESTIC PRODUCT BASED ON PURCHASING POWER-PARITY PER CAPITA (US$) (SELECTED DATES AND COUNTRIES)

	1990	1995	2000	2005	2007
AUSTRALIA	16,514.85	20,094.94	25,274.83	30,897.15	33,490.39
CANADA	**19,287.55**	**22,396.28**	**28,424.33**	**34,273.00**	**37,289.49**
FRANCE	17,472.87	20,461.45	24,961.26	29,316.42	31,595.12
GERMANY	18,353.60	22,316.80	26,499.24	30,579.40	32,683.52
IRELAND	**13,717.78**	**18,900.33**	**30,666.66**	**40,609.77**	**45,134.56**
JAPAN	18,982.75	22,719.37	22,719.37	30,615.21	32,980.41
NORWAY	**21,037.80**	**27,906.95**	**35,096.70**	**42,364.22**	**45,448.50**
UNITED KINGDOM	16,272.26	19,715.00	24,732.60	30,469.84	32,993.05
UNITED STATES	22,882.07	27,373.10	34,285.86	41,399.42	45,218.17

Source: International Monetary Fund, *World Economic Outlook Database*, April 2006.

by our trading partners? We understand that Japan, for example, is recognized for the cars and consumer electronics it sells. Table 1.2 displays Canada's merchandise trade over the past 15 years.

Covering the 10-year period from 1995 to 2007, the first item to note is the *doubling* of Canada's exports of crude materials from 10 to just over 20 percent. Not surprisingly, by 2007 petroleum and natural gas made up over three-quarters of these exports. Add to the above the jump from 5 percent to over 12 percent of semi-processed petroleum and coal products and it becomes easy to see where one of the strengths resides in the Canadian economy. On the other hand, the halving of the export of lumber, wood pulp, and newsprint probably reflects both the U.S. duties on Canadian lumber during this period and the weakening of the newspaper industry in the United States.

TABLE 1.2

CANADA'S MERCHANDISE TRADE EXPORTS ($000,000) (ANNUAL AVERAGE, 1995–2007)
MERCHANDISE IMPORTS AND EXPORTS, BY MAJOR GROUPS

EXPORTS	1995	2000	2007
Total Merchandise Trade	$22,111	$35,781	$38,588
Crude materials (inedible) Total	2,206 (10%)	4,450 (12.4%)	7,977 (20.7%)
Crude petroleum + natural gas	1,157 (52.6%)	3,309 (74.4%)	5,781 (72.5%)
Fabricated Materials (inedible) Total	7,000 (31.7%)	9,425 (26.4%)	11,151 (28.9%)
Lumber, Wood Pulp, Newsprint	2,624 (38%)	2,911 (31%)	1,979 (18%)
Petroleum & Coal Products	326 (5%)	684 (7%)	1,366 (12%)
Electricity	98.9 (1%)	338.2 (3.5%)	262 (2.3%)
End Products (inedible) Total	10,605 (48%)	18,595 (52%)	15,789 (40.9%)
Passenger Cars + Trucks	3,916 (36.9%)	5,806 (31.2%)	4,418 (28%)
Motor vehicle parts	1,327 (13%)	2,350 (13%)	2,024 (13%)
Aircraft, Aircraft Engines, & Parts	551 (5%)	1,217 (7%)	1,307 (8%)
Telecommunications	739 (7%)	2,072 (11%)	861 (6%)
Office Machines & Equipment	751 (7%)	901 (5%)	600 (4%)

Source: From the Statistics Canada *CANSIM* database http://cansim2.statcan.gc.ca, Table 228-0001, Merchandise Imports and Exports, by Major Groups. Statistics Canada information is used with the permission of Statistics Canada. Users are forbidden to copy this material and/or redisseminate the data, in an original or modified form, for commercial purposes, without the expressed permission of Statistics Canada. Information on the availability of the wide range of data from Statistics Canada can be obtained from Statistics Canada's Regional Offices, its World Wide Web site at http://www.statcan.ca, and its toll-free access number 1-800-263-1136.

However, even with the decline in the value of these exports, their share accounted for almost 20 percent of exports from this sector. Other semi-processed materials such as organic and inorganic chemicals, fertilizer, nickel and zinc alloys, and synthetic rubber and plastics posted double, triple, even greater proportional growth in export sales for this period. Taken together, the crude and semi-processed materials exports climbed from just under 42 percent in 1995 to almost 50 percent by 2007.

During the same period, the automobile sector (including trucks) posted a decline from almost 37 percent of export sales in 1995 to 28 percent in 2007 while motor vehicle parts maintained their proportion at 13 percent. Aircraft, aircraft engines, and parts showed a small increase from 5 to 8 percent of export sales. Other areas of expanded exports included industrial machinery, tools and other equipment, and other consumer goods. However, telecommunications and office machines and equipment, on the other hand, ended the period with declines in export sales. The spike in foreign trade for the telecommunications sector for the year 2000 is accounted for, most likely, by Nortel's growing influence in this significant segment of the new economy. Unfortunately, the demise of Nortel, to be discussed shortly, probably accounts for the remarkable decline in the telecommunications sector to 6 percent for 2007.

Over 60 percent of all imports over this time-period were in manufactured end products. The largest ticket items included passenger automobiles and trucks, motor vehicle parts, communications equipment, office machines and related equipment, and other equipment and tools. Canada's overall export trade surplus of oil, natural gas, and other natural resources over the past two decades has to a greater extent than before helped pay for the high-technology manufactured imports the country needs to support its established and nascent industries and services. Moreover, Canada has made up for its continued trade deficits with the European community and Japan by our large surpluses in natural resources, automobiles, and trucks with the United States.

It would appear Canada's wealth is increasingly dependent on the export of primary and semi-processed materials. The export data indicates a gradual shift in Canada's role within the world economy. That is to say, the abundance of natural resources in this vast country of 25 million square kilometres, geographically the second largest nation in the world, likely accounts for Canada's repositioning in the world economy.

THE WORLD AND CANADA: A CONFERENCE BOARD REPORT

According to a recent Conference Board of Canada Report entitled "The World and Canada: Trends Reshaping Our Future (2005), "while the Canada of

2005-06 is, in many respects, a better place than the Canada of 1996, our relative performance has slipped" (2005, p. 1). According to the authors of this report, Canada is not living up to its international reputation as "a wealthy, environmentally responsible, socially conscious, healthy society" (2005, p. 1). This would appear to be as much the result of other countries improving their performance in the world economy as it is of Canada losing ground. Take, for example, investment spent on research and development. The authors of this report point out that since 2001, "Canadian R&D expenditures as a proportion of gross domestic product (GDP) have been decreasing, albeit slightly, whereas those of several Western European countries have steadily increased" (2005, p. 4) When it comes to patents registered per million population, Canada "stood still" over the period from 1991 to 2001 relative to the other 24 countries tracked (2005, p. 67).

To be clear, the authors are not suggesting Canada's imminent demise. Far from it! Canada is a rich country. Their point is that Canada is slipping behind instead of progressing ahead. And, international trade data outlined above confirms our growing reliance on natural resources and second-generation manufacturing of automobiles and trucks. As the title of this chapter points out, we appear to be losing ground, albeit incrementally.

CANADA'S INFORMATION AND COMMUNICATIONS SECTOR OF THE ECONOMY: LOST DYNAMISM

Let us look more closely at the information and communications industries of the Canadian economy. The dynamism of an economic subdivision is demonstrated by the extent of direct foreign investment (DFI) it attracts and the degree of direct investment it exports. By contrast, a sector that is languishing attracts little direct foreign investment and neither exports direct investment to other nations. Table 1.3 depicts the sizeable decline in direct investment in the Canadian information and communications sector over the seven-year period from 2000 to 2007.

The export data indicates as well Canada's participation is faltering in the important information and communications technologies revolution and the products and services associated with the **New Economy.**

Neoliberalism, the Mulroney Years, and the Present

Take for example Canada's one-time beacon of the New Economy—Nortel. Recently Nortel filed for bankruptcy protection in Canada and the United States (CBC, 2009). If Nortel is sold or broken up, Canada's high-tech community of well-trained and experienced engineers, developers, and entrepreneurs will shrink dramatically in the short term while future members of

TABLE 1.3

FOREIGN AND CANADIAN DIRECT INVESTMENT IN INFORMATION AND COMMUNICATIONS TECHNOLOGIES IN MILLION $ (2000–07)

YEAR		2000	2001	2002	2003	2004	2005	2006	2007*
CANADIAN DIRECT INVESTMENT ABROAD	Total, all countries	50,545	39,347	26,623	25,015	25,444	19,105	19,855	18,416
	U.S.	36,609	23,233	12,583	12,319	12,372	10,499	10,402	9,695
	Asia & Oceania	1,644	2,477	2,471	2,142	1,902	1,954	2,251	1,933
	Europe	9,561	11,174	9,791	9,169	9,803	5,903	6,312	6,028
FOREIGN DIRECT INVESTMENT IN CANADA	Total, all countries	37,256	23,239	22,747	23,088	19,925	22,196	20,291	18,996
	U.S.	22,832	18,344	17,727	17,873	14,823	16,975	16,167	14,044
	Asia & Oceania	309	457	448	486	530	522	388	396
	Europe	14,017	4,102	4,355	4,649	4,501	4,645	3,523	4,359

* Preliminary data.

Source: From the Statistics Canada *CANSIM* database http://cansim2.statcan.gc.ca, Table 376-0052.

Canada's high-tech community may be forced to seek opportunities outside the country. Then there was the Auto Pact which for several decades had become a fundamental plank in Canada's industrial policy and enormously important for the Ontario economy. The Free Trade Agreement of the mid-1980s followed by the North American Free Trade Agreement and finally the World Trade Organization's decision of 2001 abolished the last vestiges of the Auto Pact (Anastakis, 2005).

Rounding out this brief historical review are attacks on other nation-building initiatives. Petro Canada began as a "window" unto the global oil industry. Moreover, government ownership and control of these industries was not unknown among oil producing nations. However, Petro Canada pursued an aggressive strategy by expanding its interests in 1981 with the acquisition of Petrofina Canada, a Belgian-owned company. This purchase gave Petro Canada a refining and marketing presence in Eastern and Central Canada. In 1982, Petro Canada discovered oil at Valhalla, Alberta; the largest new oil field of the 1980s in western Canada and one year later bought British-owned BP Canada. Then, in 1990, the federal Conservative government announced it would privatize Petro Canada. By 1995, the government's interest in the company had been reduced to 20 percent. The remaining shares were sold in 2004 ending Canada's very short-lived experiment in the country's oil industry.

Finally, the Canada Development Corporation (CDC) was created in 1971 as the result of the Royal Commission on Canada's Economic Prospects and the 1968 Watkins Report. The CDC's mandate aimed at developing Canadian-controlled companies in the private sector through joint ventures. The federal government could own no more than 10 percent of the company's holdings and is credited with purchasing the Polymer Corporation, the profitable rubber and petrochemical company founded in 1942 during World War II. In 1976, Polymer changed its name to Polysar. The CDC was dismantled in 1986 by the Conservative government of Brian Mulroney. Polysar was privatized in 1988 and sold to Nova Corporation and the rubber division sold to Bayer AG of Germany. Today, Lanxess AG, an offshoot of Bayer AG, operates a rubber-manufacturing site at Sarnia, Ontario.

What the international trade data and the examples of neoliberal attacks on nation-building projects highlight are Canada's changing tasks from the posted strengthening of its semiperipheral status in the mid-1980s to its weakened, semiperipheral status today. Canada's dynamic telecommunications, information, and communications industries, for example, have been hollowed out. In their place, we find oil, natural gas, and other natural resources. Can the private exploitation of our natural resources sustain our status as a rich nation over the long term? At the conclusion to this chapter, a second alternative will be advanced. Attention will now turn to the following questions. As citizens of a rich country, how have Canadians on average fared? What are the positive contributions this wealth has created for its citizens?

GLOBAL POSITIONING AND ITS CONSEQUENCES: LIFE CHANCES AND SOCIAL CHOICES

Life chances is widely accepted as a Weberian term that designates a person's likelihood of acquiring economic, cultural, and social goods. This definition conforms to Ralf Dahrendorf's notion of life chances as "options" (1980). For Dahrendorf, options are real choices available to people. Where there is universal suffrage, people can vote. Where incomes are high enough, people can vacation in Vancouver, Halifax, Montreal, Toronto, the Caribbean, and so on.

Life chances and social choices will be defined here as material life chances in areas such as health and well-being while social choices are dependent on income from paid employment for the Canadian population as a whole.

What can we say has happened over the past 30 years? What research can we point to that tells us how much have Canadians benefited materially in terms of health care and income?

In terms of health care, we seem to be performing well. Our life expectancy at birth has increased for both men and women since the early 1990s. For example, men born in 1991 could expect to live for 72.1 years while women born in the same year could live for 79.3 years. By 2004, the life expectancy for men rose to 77.4 years and 82.4 years for women (Canadian Social Trends, 2008, p. 55).

An important measure of human and social development is the United Nations (UN) Human Development Index (HDI). This composite number measures the average achievements in a country along three basic dimensions of human development: a long and healthy life; access to knowledge; and a decent standard of living. The closer a country comes to 1.0; the better off the population is as a whole. Currently, the HDI is calculated for 175 UN member states. While the concept of human development is much broader than any single number can measure, the HDI offers a useful summary measure of human well-being.

By examining longitudinal data of the HDI for every 10-year period from 1975 to 2005, one can see that Canada placed fourth in 1975 with a score of .873, and 30 years later, we remained in the same position with a score of .961. The trend since 1985 has Canada hovering in the top four positions: Canada ranked first in 1985, second in 1995, and fourth in 2005. Of course, we are more than holding our own, especially when compared to the United States. Put into international perspective, the U.S. has declined from second place in 1985 with a score of .904 to eleventh place in 2005 with a score of .951. On the other hand, over the 30-year period from 1975 until 2005 both Japan and France remained relatively stable at eighth place. For 2005, this meant a score of .953 for Japan and .952 for France. However, for the year 2005, placing in the top 12 countries means a cluster of nations falling within a small range between .949 and .968. The top countries in the world economy continue to do well. The remarkable rise of Ireland from twenty-fourth among the world's industrial nations to fifth place in 2005 seems to reflect the country's dramatic rise in the world economy over the previous 20 years. The case of Ireland indicates that a country's upward movement in the world economy can have profound positive effects on the health, social development, and career options for its citizens. One might want to add, given the severity of the global recession on Ireland that a measured decline in the world economy could erode earlier gains made in life chances and social choices for a nation's citizens. How far Ireland has fallen and whether she can re-gain its advantageous position in the HDI will become clearer over the next few years.

GLOBAL POSITIONING AND ITS CONSEQUENCES: WORK, CAREERS, INCOME, AND SOCIAL CHOICES

When it comes to paid employment and who gets what jobs, clearly, a family's social class background matters (Bourdieu, 1990). So do gender, age, sexual orientation, race/ethnicity, and region in Canada. Each has not only a separate but also a cumulative impact on the educational choices and career options a person makes in his or her lifetime (Berger et al., 2007; Porter, 1979). Having said this, what is offered is a recent snapshot of the employment and earnings levels of Canadians. That is, on the one hand, I wish to avoid undue complications to the picture of employment choices and income while recognizing their inherent complexity. The picture to be described below pinpoints those areas of employment where opportunities exist and those that are languishing or disappearing.

The Canadian economy has grown over the 20-year span since 1989. For example, between 2000 and 2008 the annual growth rate has hovered between a high of 4.2 in 2001 to a low 1.7 in 2004. However, what about the labour market and the average weekly earnings of Canadians? Have earnings kept pace with growth? Are some sectors more attractive than others when it comes to income? Which ones? And which sectors are targeted for growth and which are in decline?

For the purposes of this chapter, the simplest measure of social class used by Statistics Canada is the occupational divisions of the population into goods producing and services. Table 1.4 contains data over the 10-year period from 1996 to 2006. It provides information on weekly earnings including overtime adjusted to 2002 constant dollars. The table breaks these figures down for the five sub-categories within the goods-producing and the 14 divisions within the service sectors. In addition, the table contains employment figures for each of the goods-producing and service sectors of the Canadian economy and their associated sub-groupings.

Beginning with economic sectors reporting increases in average weekly earnings over the 10-year period from 1996 to 2006, not surprising the mining and oil and gas extraction category reported continuous earnings increases and the highest average weekly income pegged at $1,233.35! This was followed by employment in the forestry, logging, and support sector with $886.07. In other words, it was in the natural resource sector, an area well known for high concentrations of trade union membership and export driven, that the highest weekly wages/salaries are found in Canada.

The financial and insurance grouping within the service sector reported the third highest weekly earnings with $884.45 followed by those employed in professional, scientific, and technical occupations and information and

TABLE 1.4

AVERAGE WEEKLY EARNINGS AND EMPLOYMENT, BY INDUSTRY GROUP (1996–2006)

2002 CONSTANT $	1996	2001	2006
INDUSTRIAL AGGREGATE EXCLUDING UNCLASSIFIED ENTERPRISES **TOTAL EMPLOYMENT**	$687.58 11,254,543*	$680.27 12,693,636*	$684.77 14,098,545*
GOODS-PRODUCING INDUSTRIES **EMPLOYMENT**	**$859.36** **2,549,000**	**$852.36** **2,903,447**	**$860.63** **2,943,447**
FORESTRY, LOGGING, AND SUPPORT EMPLOYMENT	**$838.80** **83,598**	**$849.53** **75,829**	**$886.07** **58,409**
MINING AND OIL AND GAS EXTRACTION EMPLOYMENT	**$1,164.39** **128,240**	**$1,179.06** **138,705**	**$1,233.35** **191,514**
UTILITIES EMPLOYMENT	$1,055.04 109,805	$1,062.20 112,349	$997.09 122,966
CONSTRUCTION EMPLOYMENT	$863.40 447,987	$820.01 580,362	$820.54 785,836
MANUFACTURING EMPLOYMENT	**$825.44** **1,779,368**	**$827.53** **1,996,202**	**$830.05** **1,784,722**
SERVICES-PRODUCING INDUSTRIES **EMPLOYMENT**	$637.08 8,705,544	$629.02 9,790,189	$636.89 11,155,098
TRADE (WHOLESALE + RETAIL) EMPLOYMENT	$555.04 1,960,478	$554.85 2,216,984	$551.00 2,548,768
TRANSPORTATION AND WAREHOUSING EMPLOYMENT	$754.50 555,148	$759.22 613,930	$719.28 652,710
INFORMATION AND CULTURAL INDUSTRIES EMPLOYMENT	**$835.31** **283,051**	**$817.25** **328,509**	**$855.30** **354,263**
FINANCE AND INSURANCE EMPLOYMENT	**$865.57** **NA**	**$870.63** **558,384****	**$884.45** **624,222**
REAL ESTATE AND RENTAL AND LEASING EMPLOYMENT	**$606.66** **NA**	**$624.66** **223,058****	**$618.79** **251,084**
PROFESSIONAL, SCIENTIFIC, AND TECHNICAL EMPLOYMENT	**$868.50** **456,240**	**$906.37** **640,839**	**$882.73** **725,511**
MANAGEMENT OF COMPANIES AND ENTERPRISES EMPLOYMENT	$1,041.86 68,484	$858.55 83,802	$869.32 97,924
ADMINISTRATIVE AND SUPPORT EMPLOYMENT	**$535.34** **368,762**	**$544.92** **512,518**	**$551.02** **678,384**

(Continued)

TABLE 1.4 (CONTINUED)

2002 CONSTANT $	1996	2001	2006
EDUCATIONAL SERVICES	$751.68	$703.23	$745.21
EMPLOYMENT	935,277	952,307	1,078,856
HEALTH CARE AND SOCIAL ASSISTANCE	**$603.87**	**$593.72**	**$622.28**
EMPLOYMENT	**1,208,887**	**1,264,467**	**1,475,005**
ARTS, ENTERTAINMENT, AND RECREATION	$439.64	$448.49	$400.20
EMPLOYMENT	180,633	204,479	239,268
ACCOMMODATION AND FOOD SERVICES	$295.79	$272.91	$278.97
EMPLOYMENT	820,377	945,034	1,046,193
PUBLIC ADMINISTRATION	**$815.92**	**$805.59**	**$853.21**
EMPLOYMENT	**722,749**	**743,698**	**822,716**
OTHER SERVICES (INCLUDING MOTOR VEHICLE REPAIRS, FUNERALS, PET CARE, PROMOTING RELIGIOUS ACTIVITIES, ETC.)	**$528.20**	**$532.38**	**$534.85**
EMPLOYMENT	**128,007**	**144,317**	**149,460**

Notes: Based on the North American Industry Classification System (NAICS), 2002.

Data include overtime.

  * 2007 Labour Force Data.

** 2002 Labour Force Data

Source: From the Statistics Canada *CANSIM* database
http://cansim2.statcan.gc.ca, Tables 281-0027 and 326-0021. Table 281-0024.

cultural industries. When it comes to the public sector, occupations in educational services, health care and social assistance and public administration reported a low average weekly income of $622.28 for those employed in health care and social assistance to a high of $853.21 for those in public administration. Those employed in educational services collected somewhere in the middle with $745.21 a week.

Canadians holding the lowest average weekly earnings were confined to the service sector of the Canadian economy. Wholesale and retail trade, the arts, entertainment, and recreation, and the accommodation and food services groups reported weekly earnings of $551.00, $400.20, and $278.97 respectively. For the three largest metropolitan areas in Canada, individuals working in the last two categories would be classified as living at or below the poverty level.

The gross employment growth figures for all sectors except forestry and logging turned up expected increases. The highest growth occupations were in administrative and support (84 percent), professional, scientific, and technical (59 percent), retail trade (31 percent), accommodation and food services (28 percent), information and cultural industries (25 percent), and public administration (14 percent). The group within the service sector holding the largest number of employees was the wholesale and retail occupations with just over 2.5 million. However, the retail sector comprised over 70 percent of the group with almost 1,790,000 employees. Health care and social assistance, educational services, and accommodation and food services all reported over one million employees in 2007.

On closer examination of two important sectors of the "New Economy"—information and cultural industries and telecommunications an unsettling trend can be detected. While there has been growth in the information and cultural industries in Canada over the 10-year period in question, the growth has come at the expense of salaried employees who dropped in numbers from 166,038 in 1996 to 157,535 in 2007. Those paid by the hour saw a spectacular growth from 101,580 in 1996 to 177,882 in 2007. Telecommunications, another important group of occupations for the "New Economy" also witnessed a decline from a high of 83,480 in 1996 to 52,097 in 2007. Cheapening the value of well-educated information and knowledge workers is not likely to result in new innovative products or services. Neither does the loss of opportunities in the telecommunications industries bode well for present and future generations of Canadians looking for employment unless new initiatives can be generated soon. The squeeze is on to create new careers in the "New Economy."

Combined with impressive growth in administrative and support services and the professional, scientific, and technical occupations alongside those in the arts, entertainment, and recreation, accommodation and food services, and retail, the Canadian occupational structure is becoming more and more bifurcated. Unionized jobs and careers in the manufacturing sector of the economy are rapidly disappearing. What is taking their place? For many in community colleges and universities, policing and elementary and high school teaching have become the *secure* and financially rewarding occupations of which to aspire. However, the number of openings is limited due to their location within the public sector and their dependence on tax revenues. It would seem that instead of a burgeoning middle, Canada is looking more and more like an hourglass with a smaller and smaller group of well-educated and well-paid professionals and administrators and a burgeoning educated but low paid underclass working in call centres, retail, personal support workers and related fields in health and the hospitality industries (see Glenday et al., 1997; see also Dunn, 2002). Recent Statistics Canada data confirms the widening gap between Canada's wealthiest income earners and those of the poorest. Between 1999 and 2007, annual spending by the 20 percent of the poorest households rose $1,283 or 6.1 percent, while expenditures by the richest 20 percent increased $16,497 or 13 percent. The poor had the smallest improvement in dollar terms and the smallest percentage of any of the quintiles. The rich had the largest increases (Kerstetter, 2009).

This is not a pattern unique to Canada. The neoliberal policies of the U.S. and Great Britain, for example, which encourage the bifurcation of income and wealth report similar trends (for Great Britain, see Goodman and Shephard, 2002; for the U.S., see Domhoff, 2006 and Johnston, 2007).

Over the previous 30 years, Canada enjoyed a status among the top richest countries in the world. How does this translate into the experiences of an average Canadian family?

Global Positioning and Its Consequences: The Squeeze is On the Middle Class

In a telling story recently reported in *MoneySense* (2008), a magazine published by *Canadian Business*, Rob Gerlsbeck recounts how a middle-class family of two adults and two children aged 8 and 7 and living in a Calgary suburb are experiencing trouble "having any money left at the end of the month." He is a welder and she operates two Montessori schools. Gerlsbeck reports that the couple makes "slightly more than the average Canadian family." They own one vehicle, a 2001 GMC pickup truck, they pay off their credit cards every month, and four years ago bought a $240,000 home on a 20-year mortgage. But they feel "squeezed" because almost all the money that comes in for the month is spent on bills with virtually no room for savings, RRSPs for retirement, or RESPs for their children's education.

Gerlsbeck tells his readers that this family like so many other middle-class families in Canada has a paycheque that shows a decent income and when it comes to spending "are doing nothing wrong" but still has little or no money left over for a "rainy day." So, what is the matter?

Part of the problem Gerlsbeck says lies in the fact that "for more than a quarter century, middle-class incomes have flat-lined in terms of real purchasing power" while costs have risen dramatically. He quotes Statistics Canada sources when he points out that "in terms of inflation-adjusted dollars, the median annual salary of a full-time worker rose by $53 a year . . . the equivalent to a family night out at Swiss Chalet" . . . and concludes "the years between 1980 and 2005 turn out to be a dead zone for middle class prosperity."

Gerlsbeck's account of the stagnation in real incomes for middle-class families over the past 25 years makes a serious point. The thrust of the argument being this happened during a period of relative prosperity in recent Canadian history. Now that Canada and the entire world economy is experiencing a serious credit crunch and a long-term recession, the working and the middle class in Canada may become crushed under the weight of high unemployment and large government debt. To be sure, there will be those who may be more able than others to hold their own during these trying times while many more will slip even further behind.

WHERE TO GO FROM HERE?

Without a doubt, Canada has been and continues to be a semiperipheral nation and on average one of the world's richer countries. Semiperipheral status in the world economy has never meant we are poor. What has been argued in this chapter is the relative weakening of the economic base on which Canada's wealth is secured. The evidence presented included the neoliberal dismantling by Brian Mulroney's government of nation-building projects outlined above and the shift in Canada's international trade from potentially dynamic manufacturing in the telecommunications and information and communications technology industries to the present increasing reliance on the export of raw and semi-processed natural resources.

However, the recession has hit Canada hard. Over 300,000 jobs have been shed in the five months between October 2008 and February 2009 with Ontario accounting for just over half the country's employment losses. The federal and provincial governments are actively stimulating the economy with tax breaks, incentives for individuals, and infrastructure construction. By the end of 2009, talks about the appearance of recovery abounded in the media. Huge provincial and federal government debts need to be addressed soon while unemployment figures remain stubbornly high.

Option #1: Staying the Course

The first option: staying the course is in all likelihood what will happen in the foreseeable future. That is to say, over the past two decades, one of the main engines of economic growth and prosperity in Canada has been the export of our natural resources: "black" gold or oil and natural gas, and "green" gold or forest products. Soon the potential for exploiting Canada's abundant supply of "blue" gold or water may surface. Certainly, "blue" gold is plentiful in remote areas of Canada but the more conveniently located sources close to the U.S.

border help sustain Canada's major metropolitan centres and therefore, are a political powder keg as a trade issue.

When prices for these resources were high on the world market, Canada as a whole benefited through job creation not only in the natural resource sectors but also in other sectors as well, including an array of personal and business services. Increased tax revenues for all three government sectors meant gradual increases for services in health, education, and welfare.[4] Some provinces such as Alberta and Saskatchewan recorded booming economies. Today and for the foreseeable future, these commodity prices are close to or at record lows. There will be short-term fluctuations but a return to sustainable higher prices must wait for countries such as China and the U.S. to grow. What else does Canada have to fall back onto? Are there other sources of economic strength in these challenging times? Or, does Canada stay the course and wait it out until commodity prices rise and there is resurgence in automobile and truck sales in the U.S.?

Option #2: The Development State

The option to be advanced here is not necessarily new, nor likely to be introduced by any Canadian political party or social movement in the near future. It is put forward here to demonstrate that the course of action a national state pursues may be constrained by prior events and social forces but is not determined. Moreover, it is put on the table hopefully to spark discussion and debate among concerned citizens about the direction the country has taken over the past 20 or more years.

Simply stated, one important plank in the Canadian government's proposed development strategy is a "dollar for dollar" New Economy international trade initiative. This means that in the dynamic telecommunications and information and communications technologies sector of the Canadian economy, for instance, any international trade arrangement would require matching investments. That is, for every dollar we buy from country X for New Economy manufactured goods such as computers or office equipment, country X must buy or invest the equivalent amount in the same economic sector in this country. Working out the particulars of this form of inter-government managed trade agreements requires public debate and discussion among the many stakeholders. Inter-government trade agreements are not unknown to Canada's political and economic elite. Let us take just two examples—FTA and NAFTA. Both took years to iron-out. However, the political will was there to sustain the momentum.

As option #2, what will be required to advance a developmental option? First and foremost is the need to build the necessary consensus for a new national development project. This will be a daunting task. In a recent Environics poll (2006), Canadians were asked "In your opinion, is the Canadian economy getting stronger, weaker, or staying about the same?" Only 18.5 percent stated that Canada was getting weaker while almost 49 percent reported "staying the same." Only a little over 30 percent saw Canada getting stronger. This poll was taken before the world-wide recession. That is to say, before the advent of the global financial meltdown, over two-thirds of Canadians (67 percent) reported the Canadian economy had either stayed the same or had weakened. This was at the end of the era of neoliberalism. A political consensus could be worked out from this seedbed. All that is needed now is the political will to advance a vision for the future of Canada. One thought is refashioning Trudeau's "Just Society" for the 21st century.

Oddly enough, a new political and social project such as Trudeau's "Just Society" depends on going back to the future to refresh the more salient theoretical and practical features of welfare capitalism. That means supporting the positive impacts for social choices, life chances, and career opportunities resulting from a strong development state. It will certainly call for the liberal academic community to assist in reconstructing a national vision. Regardless of which option Canada follows, one thing is clear. Any new national agenda must shed the pernicious influence of neoliberalism.

ENDNOTES

1. Canada as a member of the "perimeter of the core" or strong semiperiphery.

2. The neoliberal attack on trade unions and their responses are detailed in Chapter 2.

3. The countries selected were: Canada, the U.S., Japan, F.R. Germany, France, the U.K., Italy, Australia, and Greece.

4. Notwithstanding the pressures on government revenues brought on by the recession of the mid 1990s.

2

Canada's Labour Movement in Challenging Times: Unions and their Role in a Changing Economy

Angelo DiCaro, Chad Johnston, and Jim Stanford

DISCUSSION QUESTIONS

1. Based on your own personal experience, what is your impression on the role of unions in Canada? If you are, or have been, a member of a union, what are some of the benefits you enjoyed? What were the challenges you faced?

2. With new jobs in the Canadian labour market increasingly typified by precarious and non-standard conditions, and with union density (unionization) in decline over the past three decades, what are the possible consequences of deunionization for working people, both in the workplace and in their communities? What are the consequences for society at large?

3. In addition to negotiating collective agreements with private and public employers, what other roles do unions play in the day-to-day lives of Canadians?

4. How are neoliberal economic and social policies challenging and changing the role of unions in Canada? How has the broader cultural shift in society towards a stronger emphasis on individualism (individual responsibility and individual success) rather than collective responsibility and entitlement impacted the work of unions? How can unions counteract this cultural shift?

INTRODUCTION

Unions: to many today, the term has highly negative connotations. Unions were invented to try to improve the economic lot of some of the exploited in society. Yet instead of being seen as a friend of the "underdog," unions are seen in many quarters today as self-serving, protected, and elitist. How is it that much of the population seems to hold such a negative view of **unions**—a sentiment that anti-union businesses and governments happily manipulate, in their efforts to weaken and even destroy unions? Almost everyone can tell a story about an unproductive, uncaring union worker that they encountered somewhere (as a colleague, a customer, or a neighbour). Even low-paid, vulnerable workers, who would benefit greatly from belonging to a union themselves, often express envy and bitterness toward other workers who do enjoy the benefits of union protection (as if taking away the benefits of unionization from other workers, would somehow make those low-wage workers better off). Are these anti-union perceptions backed by fact? Or do they reflect the consistent anti-union messages communicated in corporate culture, the failure of unions to get their message across, or even simple envy among those who wish they had a union but don't?

Of course, unionized workers do their jobs, too. They aren't lazy: in fact, their measured productivity on average is higher than that of non-union workers.[1] They face tremendous economic uncertainty and hardship, just like other workers—despite the protections that are afforded by their union contracts. Nevertheless, there is a knee-jerk storyline that blames unions, and union members, anytime the economy, an industry, or a particular company encounter problems. "When in doubt, blame the union," is the motto for the attempts by corporate executives and conservative politicians alike to scapegoat organized labour for whatever ails the economy.

Unions in Canada and elsewhere have much to be proud of. They have improved the lives of working people: enhancing their incomes, their job security, their health and safety, and the well-being of their entire communities. Moreover, it's not just union members who benefit from unionization; empirical evidence suggests that strong unions have a spillover effect on equality, social cohesion, and even environmental protection in broader society. So why then all the bad publicity?

This chapter will explain why unions were formed and what they do. It will also consider the host of challenges that face unions. Do unions still have a role? Are they still a progressive force? How will unions survive in an economic and political climate that is increasingly hostile to them? And how will they win back more confidence and support from the common working people that unions were invented to benefit?

BOX 2.1

TIMELINE OF CRITICAL EVENTS IN THE CANADIAN UNION MOVEMENT (20TH CENTURY)

1907—Introduction of the Industrial Disputes Investigations Act (IDIA)

1919—Winnipeg General Strike

1929—Stock market collapse, start of Great Depression

1935—Wagner Act (United States), part of U.S. economic "New Deal." First U.S. law to recognize and enshrine collective bargaining

1944—Order-in-Council PC 1003, Canada war-time legislation that recognized collective bargaining and union representation (similar to Wagner Act)

1945—Ford Strike in Windsor, Ontario; led to Rand Formula (compulsory union dues check-off)

1948—Introduction of the Industrial Relations and Dispute Investigation Act (IRDIA) (consolidation of the IDIA and PC 1003)

1956—Canadian Labour Congress formed (merger of the Trades and Labour Congress of Canada and the Canadian Congress of Labour)

1965—Establishment of the Canada/U.S. Auto Pact

1966—Introduction of the Medical Care Act (Medicare)

1967—Public Service Staff Relations Act passed (established collective bargaining regime for public sector workers)

1969—Royal Commission on Status of Women

Mid 1970s—Period of "stagflation"; postwar "golden age" comes to an end

1976—One-day general strike against Trudeau government wage and price control measures

1980s—Rise of neoliberal government policies (Thatcher, U.K.; Reagan, USA; Mulroney, Canada)

1986—Employment Equity Act established

1988—Canada-U.S. Free Trade Agreement is signed.

1992—Public Service Reform Act introduced.

1994—Implementation of the North American Free Trade Agreement (NAFTA)

1995—Formation of the World Trade Organization (WTO)

1995—Federal budget cuts lead to major public sector job losses

1996—Ontario Days of Action against Mike Harris government reform policies

2001—WTO strikes down Auto Pact

2003—Public Service Employment Act

2007—Supreme Court deems collective bargaining protected by Charter of Rights and Freedoms

UNIONS AND THEIR PURPOSE

Employment is a form of work in which employees perform tasks determined and supervised by their employer, in return for a wage or salary. Employees do not own the firm where they work, the tools they work with, nor the raw materials or goods in process that they work on. Within the formal (or "paid") economy,[2] about 85 percent of Canadians perform their work within the context of this employer-employee relationship.[3]

This employment relationship reflects a deep and fundamental asymmetry between employees and employers. Individual workers need a job to support themselves and their families. Their ability to find and keep paid work is always in question, limited by factors such as unemployment, labour market segmentation (which prevents certain groups of workers from access to certain types of jobs), or a shortage of potential employers (such as in smaller "one-industry" communities). An employer, on the other hand, can easily replace any individual worker (unless that individual possesses some very special skill). So at the individual level, workers need their employer more than their employer needs them. That gives the employer a disproportionate power over the employee.

At the same time, though, in aggregate employers clearly need their workers, too. Employers rely on their employees to perform all or most of the work required for private companies to operate and generate profits. Without that work, the company's ability to produce and generate a profit grinds to a halt. Workers can thus make gains by combining forces to utilize the bargaining power that comes with their *collective* indispensability to the employer.

Collective bargaining is the process whereby workers' representatives negotiate the terms and conditions of the employment relationship on behalf of most or all of the workers in a particular workplace, company, or industry.

By forming **business unions** and negotiating collectively (for better wages, pensions, and benefits, and safer and more comfortable working conditions), workers aim to offset the power imbalance between the employer and each individual worker. It is difficult (although not impossible) for an employer to replace their whole workforce at once. Therefore, workers have much more clout dealing with their employer as a united group, rather than one at a time—especially when the workers are collectively willing to impose some cost on an employer (through actions such as work stoppages, work-to-rule campaigns, or other collective actions) in order to back up their bargaining goals.

A union, therefore, is simply a workers' organization that aims to negotiate collectively with an employer (over wages, pensions and benefits, working conditions, and related issues) on behalf of all its members. It represents an attempt by workers to *regulate* the conditions of their employment, and to partly insulate themselves from the effects of market pressures and competition.[4]

Unions can be organized in many different ways.[5] Unions may represent workers with a particular skill or profession. Some of the earliest unions in Canada, for example, were organized around particular *crafts* or trades; this model of unionization still applies in the construction industry, and in specialized professions (such as medical associations). Beginning in the 1930s, *industrial* unions were organized, which covered most or all of the workers employed in a particular workplace (and thus uniting workers from different skills and job classifications). In North America (and most other English-speaking countries), the standard practice is to have a single union covering a particular group of workers (in a particular workplace, or a particular skill category). In other countries (especially in continental Europe), multiple unionism is possible, whereby workers can choose between different unions, all operating in the same workplace, depending on their political or religious affiliations. In some places (including Europe and Latin America), unions take on a broader function of political and/or community organizing, in addition to or instead of focusing on negotiations with specific employers. The goal of this broader, more politicized trade unionism is to unite workers from different employers and industries into campaigns for political and legislative change, economic and community development, and other broader goals.

The first step in trade unionism is for union activists to attempt to organize a union in a particular workplace. This involves speaking with workers, highlighting the economic gains and other benefits that can be gained through collective bargaining, and attempting to sign up a sufficient number of workers to give the union bargaining power with the employer.

Union security and *recognition* provisions then determine the extent to which a union is officially recognized and accepted as a core, permanent presence in the workplace. In North America, the traditional approach to **union security** has been for a quasi-governmental body to recognize (or "certify") a union as the official **bargaining agent** for a defined group of workers, following some legally specified organizing and **certification** process.[6] The employer is then generally compelled (with varying degrees of legal force) to bargain with that certified union. In recent years, given the increasing difficulty of winning union certification through these official channels (in the face of unfriendly labour boards and ruthless employer opposition), several unions in North America have experimented with strategies of *voluntary recognition*—whereby pressure is brought on an employer[7] to accept and recognize the union, without recourse to these increasingly unfriendly official certification procedures.

In Europe and other parts of the world, unions may be given official standing and bargaining status by direct law (such as requirements in several European countries that all employers of a certain size negotiate with a union or workers' council). In some cases workers in a workplace that has been officially unionized may be required to join the union (or at least to pay the equivalent of **union dues**) in order to prevent "free-riding" (whereby workers would be tempted to enjoy the wages and benefits that a union negotiates, but without contributing anything back into the union). Where union security provisions are curtailed or prevented (such as in the deep southern states of the U.S., where so-called "right-to-work" laws prohibit union security and compulsory dues arrangements), it is very difficult for unions to build the strength and staying power required to effectively bargain wages and working conditions over time.

The ability of unions to organize and bargain effectively depends on several factors:

Labour Laws and Regulations

Union organizing, bargaining, work stoppages, and other aspects of collective bargaining and labour relations are governed by a complex set of rules and laws. By making it easier or harder for unions to form and pursue their goals, those laws can alter union success in subtle but powerful ways. For example, even small changes in the mechanisms by which workers are allowed to form a union (such as whether unions can be formed simply by signing up a majority of workers in a workplace, or whether a secret-ballot vote is required to certify the union) can dramatically affect unions' organizing capacity. Political attitudes toward unions will therefore be important—since they will influence whether governments display a sympathetic and welcoming approach to unions (as was true, to some degree, in Canada in the 1960s and 1970s), or are hostile to unions and attempt to limit their growth and influence (as has been the case more recently).

Workers' Attitudes

Whether workers are willing to invest the energy, financial commitment, and possible employment risk required to join and form a union, clearly depends on whether they feel satisfied or dissatisfied with their employment circumstances—and that subjective attitude depends greatly on workers' prior attitudes and expectations. Workers who demand better treatment from their employers will be more prone to unionization than workers who have been conditioned to accept their lot in life. Importantly, workers must demonstrate a willingness and ability to stick together in order to win things collectively—otherwise, the collective strength that comes with unionization is foregone. (Trade unionists call that *solidarity*.)

Social and Economic Context

If workers are generally less secure in their overall economic and social condition, they may feel more intimidated about challenging their employers through unionization. Higher unemployment, reduced social programs, and sharper labour market *segmentation* (that is, systematic inequality between the quality of jobs available to workers of different genders, racialized identity, ethnic background, etc.) all tend to make workers feel more precarious, and hence undermine union activity—not least because union activists may fear being fired for their activities. On the other hand, when things get really bad, workers may conclude that they have nothing to lose by trying to unionize.

Profits, Productivity, and Competition

The general business environment facing employers will also influence workers' desire to unionize, the degree of employer opposition to those efforts, and the likelihood of union success (first in organizing, then in collective bargaining). If competition between companies is very intense, then it is difficult for a union to make gains with any individual employer—who may then experience higher costs, lower profits, and lower sales than competitors. There is no doubt that competitive pressures have become more intense in recent decades in most industries (thanks to deregulation, globalization, and other trends); this has certainly contributed to the erosion of union power in many sectors. The alternative for unions is to organize and bargain for all workers across an industry at once (using sectoral or **pattern bargaining** techniques); this is more effective, but requires unions to have a higher level of economic and political power in order to create these industry-wide structures. On the other hand, when competition is less intense, and business profits are strong, employers may be somewhat less resistant to unionization. Likewise, in capital-intensive industries, labour accounts for a smaller share of total cost—and hence unions may have more economic space to improve labour conditions and compensation, without increasing employers' total costs so significantly. Similarly, if total productivity is growing rapidly, then workers can win higher compensation without harming profits or threatening their company's future; hence unionization and collective bargaining may be more successful during times of vibrant economic expansion and productivity growth (such as typified the long postwar economic boom from 1945 through the late 1970s).

No society without strong and effective unions has ever achieved truly mass prosperity.[8] Unions are essential institutions to ensure that the benefits of economic growth and technological change are at least partially shared with working people. Even rich countries will demonstrate tremendous inequality and pockets of stark poverty, without unions to influence the distribution of income and give workers a better share of the pie they produce. (The U.S.

economy, one of the wealthiest in the world but demonstrating the highest poverty and inequality levels of any developed country, is a jarring example of the social consequences of deunionization.) In short, the degree of unionization is one of the most important factors determining wage levels, workplace safety conditions, the incidence of poverty, hours of work, and general social well-being. The ability of workers to protect and strengthen their unions will be essential for limiting and eventually reversing the many negative economic and social consequences of the pro-business direction that has dominated policy-making over the past quarter-century.

FEATURES OF COLLECTIVE BARGAINING

Many different issues are negotiated between unions and employers. The most common topic (and the one that generates the most headlines) is wages. In Canada in 2008, the average hourly wage for a unionized employee was about $4.50 higher than the average for non-union employees—an advantage of 23 percent. As indicated in Table 2.1, the size of this union "premium" has declined over time, and varies across different segments of the labour market.[9] In proportionate terms, the union premium has narrowed considerably over the past decade: in the late 1990s, union members made on average about one-third more than non-union members, whereas today they make about one-quarter more.

TABLE 2.1

THE CHANGING UNION WAGE PREMIUM (DIFFERENCE BETWEEN UNION AND NON-UNION WAGES)

	1997		2008	
	$ gap	% gap	$ gap	% gap
ALL WORKERS	4.43	31.4%	4.57	23.0%
PERMANENT WORKERS	4.10	28.1%	4.11	19.9%
TEMPORARY WORKERS	6.11	56.9%	7.25	49.6%
MEN	3.66	23.1%	3.04	13.7%
WOMEN	5.09	41.4%	6.17	35.3%

Source: Authors' calculations from Statistics Canada data, CANSIM Table 282-0073.

The lower paid is the job, the more important is the union wage premium. For example, women union members make 35 percent more than non-union women workers, while unionized males make only 14 percent more than non-union males. Similarly, unionization is especially important in lifting wages in temporary and part-time positions. When the goal is greater equality of wages, then it is natural that unions will have their most visible impact on wages in industries and jobs that are typically low paid.

Through collective bargaining, unions are also able to improve other elements of compensation (including pensions, health and dental benefits, insurance and security packages, and other supplementary benefits). Providing quality medical, vision and dental care for workers and their families, and a safety net of insurance programs, promotes well-being and social and economic stability for the union's members. Indeed, often the impact of unionization is more dramatic on these non-wage forms of compensation, than on wages per se.

For example, about four-fifths of unionized employees in Canada are members of a workplace pension plan, compared to only one-quarter of non-union workers.[10] Thus, winning workplace pension benefits is one of the most visible impacts of unionization, and unionization is the most important factor determining whether a worker receives a pension or not. Changing social conditions and social norms will impact the types of benefits demanded by unions—such as the emphasis in recent years by unions in negotiating employer-supported child care benefits, or new medical choices and procedures (such as naturopathy or massage therapy). Similarly, unions have always striven to regulate working hours, reducing both the length of the standard working day and providing for adequate vacation and holiday time away from work.[11] In recent years, this longstanding demand has evolved to reflect the increasingly difficult challenge of work–life balance—including negotiated provisions for family care leave, lifelong training opportunities, and other time-off provisions.

In sum, unionization clearly has had a historically positive effect on workers' compensation (including wages, non-wage benefits, and paid time off). And when unions are successful in raising compensation (including wages and non-wage benefits) for their members, there are often additional spill-over benefits (or "externalities") that flow from that improvement. Other non-unionized workers in the industry will see their wages improve too— since non-union employers must increase wages or run the risk of having their workers leave for a higher-paying union job, or else choose to organize a union in their workplace. Broader social conditions are improved by the provision of non-wage health benefits and social insurance provisions to unionized workers; moreover, the fiscal cost to governments of universal social programs is reduced when at least some of the population receive high-quality pension and benefits through negotiated workplace benefits.

Another crucial impact of unions is to reduce inequality, both within a unionized workplace and across society more broadly.[12] Contract provisions that limit wage gaps between different categories of workers, and address systemic wage differentials through initiatives such as pay equity and employment equity, serve to compress wage distribution in unionized workplaces (compared to non-union workplaces). And when unions are successful at unionizing most of an industry, this can serve to reduce wage inequality across the whole sector—by establishing sector-wide wage norms, in essence trying to take wages "out of competition" between firms (which must now compete on the basis of product attributes or fundamental efficiency, rather than wage-cutting).

In addition to compensation, unions also negotiate over non-monetary issues related to the workplace and working conditions. Union contracts often include provisions regulating health and safety conditions, establishing processes (such as joint health and safety committees) to enhance workplace safety, and taking other steps to enhance the safety and quality of the work environment. Clauses that set out the scope of the work covered by a **collective agreement** are also essential to protecting the union's role within the workplace. Dispute resolution language establishes the process through which the collective agreement is interpreted and enforced. These provisions will generally lay out the right for workers to have access to union representation and a **grievance** process. Unresolved issues must be settled through a grievance and **arbitration** process, which is vital to the overall effectiveness of labour relations. In Canada, **strikes** and other work stoppages are generally illegal during the term of a collective agreement, which means that workers must have confidence in the effectiveness of a dispute settlement system to enforce contract terms during the time an agreement is in effect. Indeed, the PC 1003 model of certified majority unionism effectively traded labour peace during the term of a collective agreement (since work stoppages during the term of the agreement are now prohibited) for the union's recognized security (including union recognition and some form of dues check-off system). The outcome was labour peace during the life of the collective agreement, in exchange for workers having the right to strike (and employers having the right to lock out) whenever the contract was renegotiated.

If the parties cannot reach agreement on a new contract, labour peace comes to an end. The most common forms of work stoppage are strikes and **lockouts.** In a strike, the members of a union collectively refuse to come to work until a satisfactory contract resolution is attained; in a lockout, the employer bars workers from coming to work until a satisfactory resolution (from the employer's perspective) is attained. Depending on the jurisdiction there may be a set of conditions and procedures that must be followed prior to any work stoppage (whether initiated by the union or by the employer). This may include conciliation or mediation, in which government-appointed professionals moderate discussions between the parties in the hopes of getting the two sides closer together. There may also be a cooling off period: a compulsory time delay before any work stoppage can be initiated, in hopes of allowing more time for the parties to reach a settlement.

In the end, if no agreement is reached, a work stoppage or some other form of collective action will occur, through which the workers collectively try to impose a cost on the employer in order to push the employer to recognize and accept their demands. Examples of collective action include strikes (possibly targeted at specific parts of the operation, or across an entire company or workplace), work-to-rule campaigns (in which workers strictly follow all workplace procedures, showing none of the usual flexibility that allows workplaces to operate effectively), overtime refusals, and other actions. The idea is to use the workers' collective strength to increase the cost to the employer of refusing the union's bargaining demands—although the workers, too, bear a cost (of foregone wages) from these actions. In a lockout, in contrast, it is the employer who takes the offensive: refusing to employ the workers unless and until the union accepts the company's demands.

The conduct of these work stoppages is governed by a whole set of rules and laws regarding picketing (through which striking workers try to discourage other workers from attending their jobs), secondary picketing and boycotts, the use of replacement workers (called "scabs" by union members), and other issues. Obviously, the more economic pain the union and its members are able to inflict on the employer (by stopping production and otherwise interfering with business), the greater the chances of winning their bargaining demands. Laws that limit the impact of work stoppages (by limiting or prohibiting picketing, allowing replacement workers, and/or prohibiting secondary actions against the employer) will therefore tend to undermine the bargaining position of the union.

UNIONIZATION IN CANADA

In Canada, over 4.4 million workers belong to a union. Despite operating in a more harsh economic and political climate in recent decades (discussed further below), Canadian unions have continued to grow in absolute numbers. Since 1997, the number of unionized workers in Canada grew by nearly

10 percent, or by some 400,000 new members.[13] In terms of absolute numbers, organized labour is probably the largest and most influential membership-based movement in the country.

However, to better understand organized labour's significance within the broader economy, it is important to look at union membership as a proportion of the entire Canadian labour force (including all wage and salaried workers). This measure is called *union density* (or *unionization*).

Union density figures are often used as a metric to determine the relative size and strength of the labour movement across the workforce and various economic sectors. Higher union density in any sector of the economy allows unions to establish and protect better compensation and working standards, by moderating the extent to which any particular unionized employer can be undercut by non-unionized competition. Indeed, when union density is sufficiently high, the benefits of unionization actually spill over to workers in non-unionized workplaces. In order to attract new workers, even non-union companies may benchmark wages against the union standard. (Consider, for example, the wage and benefit structures at non-union Toyota in Cambridge, Ontario, or non-union Dofasco in Hamilton, Ontario, which closely mirror those set in unionized auto and steel plants, respectively.)

Economic and political forces crucially affect union growth or union decline. Particularly, the rise of a more aggressive, business-friendly political and economic agenda since the early 1980s has had a markedly negative effect on unions' ability to organize new members, as is discussed further below. Similarly, free trade agreements have undermined employment in manufacturing (a traditional pillar of unionization); Canadian manufacturing lost over one-half-million jobs (or close to one-quarter of its initial workforce) between 2002 and 2009. This makes it increasingly difficult for unions to negotiate and protect wage and benefit standards, as employers can meaningfully threaten to relocate work to lower-cost jurisdictions. The same logic can even apply to tradable service industries (such as call centres), which also migrate in search of lower labour costs. Meanwhile, trends toward deregulation and privatization have increased the intensity of domestic competition, which as noted above generally undermines union success.

The combination of these factors has contributed to a notable reduction in union density levels in Canada over the last three decades. Union density for the non-agricultural paid workforce dropped by over one-sixth: from 37.6 percent in 1981 to under 30 percent today.[14]

One of the most noteworthy shifts in the composition of union membership during recent decades has been the growing participation of women in organized labour. In fact, by 2008 the union density rate for women was higher than the rate for men—a significant departure from the membership pattern even a decade ago. Table 2.2 provides a complete breakdown of union density in Canada by gender, age, sector, skill, and province. The new majority status of women with the labour movement reflects the relatively stable rate of unionization in female-dominated occupations in the public service (such as health care, education, and public administration), combined

TABLE 2.2

UNION DENSITY IN CANADA
(PERCENT OF TOTAL EMPLOYMENT, 1997–2008)

	1997	2008
TOTAL	33.7	31.2
GENDER		
MEN	35.2	30.8
WOMEN	32.1	31.6
AGE		
15–24	13.0	15.7
25–54	37.8	34.1
55+	37.8	36.3
PROVINCE		
NEWFOUNDLAND/LABRADOR	40.7	38.4
PRINCE EDWARD ISLAND	29.1	30.9
NOVA SCOTIA	30.2	28.7
NEW BRUNSWICK	29.9	29.2
QUEBEC	41.5	39.4
ONTARIO	29.8	27.9
MANITOBA	37.6	36.7
SASKATCHEWAN	36.0	35.1
ALBERTA	25.8	24.0
BRITISH COLUMBIA	36.6	31.0

(Continued)

TABLE 2.2 (CONTINUED)

	1997	2008
SECTOR		
PUBLIC SECTOR	74.6	74.2
PRIVATE SECTOR	21.3	17.9
INDUSTRY		
NATURAL RESOURCE INDUSTRIES	30.9	24.4
CONSTRUCTION	32.4	31.5
MANUFACTURING	36.3	28.6
RETAIL WHOLESALE TRADE	14.8	14.0
TRANSPORTATION & WAREHOUSING	45.2	42.0
PROFESSIONAL SERVICES	5.8	5.4
EDUCATION	73.5	71.3
HEALTH CARE	55.7	54.7
HOSPITALITY	8.6	7.3
PUBLIC ADMINISTRATION	71.4	72.5

Source: From the Statistics Canada *CANSIM* database http://cansim2.statcan.gc.ca, Tables 282-0074 and 282-0078.

with a drop in union levels in traditionally male-dominated manufacturing and resource industries.

In 2008, Quebec maintained the highest level of unionization in Canada with nearly 40 percent of the workforce belonging to a union. This reflects the impact of more union-friendly labour laws (including a majority sign-up or "card-check" certification system, and a ban on the use of replacement workers during strikes). Alberta, with the most anti-union legal framework, has the lowest unionization rate (24 percent).

Another historic change since the 1960s has been the growing importance of the public sector in the overall labour movement. Unionization has stayed constant in the public sector (with unions representing about three-quarters of all public sector employees), in contrast to the steady decline in unionization evident in the private sector. In this regard, the decline in overall union density in Canada (to 30 percent or lower) can be seen as the result of two distinct trends, both of which reflect the pro-business shift in economic and social policy in recent years: the decline in union density in the private sector (in the face of heightened employer resistance and anti-union shifts in labour law), and the downsizing of public sector employment (which is much more heavily unionized) relative to the overall labour force. Unions in the public sector have been relatively more insulated from the fierce employer opposition and do-or-die competitive pressure that have constrained union organizing in the private sector. (This is not to imply that governments have been "friendly" to unions in the public sector, only that the intensity of employer opposition, and the additional constraints imposed by private competition, have not been as severe as in the private sector.)

One interesting and perhaps counter-intuitive aspect of the unionization data is the relationship between union density and education level (see Table 2.3). In general, the more educated are the workers, the more likely are they to be unionized. University graduates are the most heavily unionized skill category in the whole labour market (with over 34 percent belonging to a union in 2008). Those with less than high school education, in contrast, are the least unionized. This runs counter to the stereotypical notion that unions are only needed by those whose skills do not command a high value in the "marketplace." To the contrary, more highly educated workers are in fact the most likely to have sought out, and then achieved, the protection that comes with a union contract. Given that average education levels in the economy are growing, this is one factor that may help to boost overall unionization (or at least to limit its decline) in the years ahead.

TABLE 2.3
UNIONIZATION AND SKILL LEVEL
(PERCENT OF ALL WAGE AND SALARY EARNERS)

	1998	2008
LESS THAN HIGH-SCHOOL GRADUATE	26.8	20.7
HIGH-SCHOOL GRADUATE	27.9	25.9
SOME POST-SECONDARY	23.3	22.1
POSTSECONDARY CERTIFICATE OR DIPLOMA	34.1	33.0
UNIVERSITY DEGREE	35.3	36.9

Source: Authors' calculations from Akyeampong (1999), Statistics Canada (2008).

In terms of the sectoral composition of union membership, a range of trends is visible in the data presented in Table 2.2. The steady decline of Canadian manufacturing employment, and the deunionization of that sector (which declined by 8 percentage points between 1997 and 2008—a faster decline than any other sector) both clearly reflect the impact of globalization and free trade. By weakening labour standards and producing a more intensely competitive economic environment, globalization has hindered unionization and depressed wages and workplace standards. Canada's resource industries, in contrast, have grown under free trade; global market forces are increasingly pushing Canada to focus on resource extraction and export to "pay our way" in world trade.[15] But paradoxically, unionization in the resource sector has also declined—due in part to the rapid expansion of the relatively union-free petroleum sector. Construction has been a bright spot for unions in recent years, thanks to both a relatively stable unionization rate (the result of successful sector-wide certification[16] and bargaining structures that have been established in the building trades) and strong job creation in the construction industry.

Three-quarters of total jobs in Canada's economy today are now located in the broader service sector. Many market advocates argue that this shifting sectoral composition of work simply reflects a natural evolution towards a more technologically advanced, innovative, and productive economy—the so-called "knowledge-based" economy. However, the growth of service industries has generally accentuated downward pressure on workers, wages, and unions, and it's not at all apparent how much "knowledge" this new services economy actually entails. Apart from a few relatively high-skill service sectors—like health care, education, finance, and business services—most services jobs are typified by lower-wage and precarious positions, in retail, food service, and personal and consumer service industries. These high-growth industries have below-average rates of union density (such as retail, with 14 percent unionization, and hospitality, with unionization of only 9 percent). Hence the service-oriented restructuring of the labour market has clearly contributed to the decline of unionization, and consequently of wages and labour standards. Moreover, the rapid growth of service sector employment is intrinsically tied to the expansion of **precarious work** in Canada's labour market—such as the greater use of part-time, temporary, contract, agency, and other forms of non-standard employment.[17]

Some commentators argue that the decline in union density is partly due to the inability of unions themselves to organize new members, and not solely to the effects of a more hostile economic, political, and legal climate.[18] Whether it has been the reluctance of unions to prioritize union organizing efforts in traditionally non-organized sectors of the economy (like retail stores, fast-food restaurants, and other service-sector workplaces), or the belief that more attention should be paid to servicing the needs of existing members (rather than devoting more resources to new organizing), few unions have succeeded in implementing the coordinated, well-resourced strategies that are clearly necessary to preserve unionization in the face of changing economic and labour market conditions.

CANADIAN UNIONS IN INTERNATIONAL PERSPECTIVE

Union density in Canada has declined steadily in the past decade, despite an overall increase in the number of unionized workers. Yet close to 1 in 3 workers in Canada are still union members. And a larger number is covered by union contracts (about 2 percent of paid workers in Canada are covered by a union arrangement, even though they don't personally belong to a union). How have Canadian unions performed, relative to those in other countries?

As indicated in Table 2.3, Canada's unionization rate is relatively low compared to union density rates in some European countries (especially the Nordic countries, where union density can reach 80 percent of the workforce). On the other hand, union density in Canada is higher (and has remained more stable) than in several other Anglo-Saxon economies, including the U.S., the U.K., and Australia. Canada's economic and social policies have been typified by the same emphasis on market forces and business-led economic development as has been visible in the other major Anglo-Saxon economies; yet Canadian unions have been more successful at retaining their organizational and economic influence. In fact, of the countries listed in Table 2.4, Canada has experienced one of the smallest declines in national union density over the past quarter-century, suggesting that Canadian unions have responded relatively well to the unfavourable shift in the economic and legal environment in which they operate. Clearly, the challenges facing Canadian unions are similar to those facing unions around most of the rest of the world, in light of the increasingly hostile political and economic environment constructed under neoliberalism.

Canadian union density levels are most often compared to those in the United States primarily because of history, geography, and the strong economic connections between the two countries. At the end of World War II, Canadian and U.S. unionization rates were roughly equal (at less than 30 percent). However, the steady development of two very different labour law regimes—reflecting two very different political environments—led the industrial relations systems of the two countries down divergent paths. A series of important legislative decisions (including the 1947 Taft-Hartley Act, which allowed individual states to prohibit union security provisions and imposed strict rules on the collective action of workers through their unions), and the

TABLE 2.4

CANADA'S UNIONIZATION IN INTERNATIONAL CONTEXT
(PERCENT OF EMPLOYED WAGE AND SALARY EARNERS)

	2003	CHANGE SINCE 1980
CANADA	28.4	–6.3
U.S.	12.4	–7.1
AUSTRALIA	22.9	–26.6
NEW ZEALAND	22.1*	–47.0
JAPAN	19.7	–11.4
SOUTH KOREA	11.2	–3.5
GERMANY	22.6	–12.3
FRANCE	8.3**	–10.0
ITALY	33.7	–15.9
U.K.	29.3	–21.4
IRELAND	35.3	–21.8
FINLAND	74.1	+4.7
SWEDEN	78.0	—
NORWAY	53.3	–5.0
DENMARK	70.4	–8.2
NETHERLANDS	22.3	–12.5
BELGIUM	55.4*	+1.3
SPAIN	16.3	+3.4
SWITZERLAND	17.8†	–12.3
AUSTRIA	35.4*	–21.3

* 2002 data.

** Official French union membership is low, but most French workers are covered by compulsory collective bargaining arrangements and so French unions are much stronger than this figure implies.

† 2001 data.

Source: Visser (2006).

ongoing erosion of labour rights in the so-called "Right to Work" states of the U.S. south, has clearly undermined U.S. workers' effective ability to join unions. Unlike the U.S. structure, Canadian labour law has traditionally (though unevenly) promoted more conciliatory dispute settlement measures and provided for stronger union security provisions.[19] In the U.S. today, approximately 1 in 8 workers belong to a union (or 12.4 percent of the overall non-agricultural workforce in 2008).[20] U.S. unionization has fallen by almost half over the past 25 years—although it has increased marginally since 2006, and may be poised for a more significant rebound if the Obama Administration follows through on its promise to reinstate more union-friendly laws regarding union certification and first-contract arbitration.

Despite these differences, many union members in Canada have been (and still are) represented by U.S.-based **"international unions,"** which maintain a considerable degree of control over the operations of their Canadian branches. The influence of U.S. unions in Canadian industrial relations, almost entirely in the private sector, is a product of Canada's historic role as a "branch plant" economy to the U.S.—reflected in major foreign investments in Canada by U.S. companies in manufacturing and other sectors.

Since the 1970s, the influence of U.S. international unions in Canada has declined somewhat. This Canadianization reflects the rise of public sector unionization (which is almost exclusively based in Canadian-based unions), and also a trend among private-sector unions toward national independence (including the creation of the Canadian Auto Workers Union in 1985, and the formation of the Communications Energy and Paperworkers Union in 1992). Despite these trends toward more national autonomy, about one quarter of Canadian union members today (and over half of union members in the private sector) still belong to U.S.-based international unions. Canada is possibly the only country in the world in which foreign-based trade unions play such an important role in labour relations. At times the power of U.S.-based unions in Canada still causes controversy in labour relations,[21] although the issue of Canadian independence in the labour movement is less contentious than in past decades (perhaps because all unions, Canadian or international, share a common, overarching realization that the labour movement as a whole is threatened by the broader anti-union shift in Canadian politics, policies, and culture).

UNIONS AND NEOLIBERALISM

Early efforts to organize unions encountered ruthless, often violent opposition from employers, backed up in many cases by government and police efforts to crush organizing campaigns or outlaw unions altogether. In the 20th century, unions won more acceptance for both economic and political reasons. Labour-friendly political parties gained influence, and sometimes power. And after World War II, business leaders felt more pressure (both political and economic) to accommodate workers' demands (for better pay and labour rights).[22] Initially rapid productivity growth allowed companies to pay union-level wages while still generating strong profits. The postwar era (from 1945 through the mid-1970s) was thus a "golden age" for union expansion in Canada: membership grew rapidly (in both absolute numbers and as a proportion of the workforce), and the living standards of union members (and non-union workers, too, pulled up by the tide) improved dramatically. Unionization in Canada reached a peak of around 40 percent of the non-agricultural labour force by the late 1970s.

About the same time, however, the underlying economic dynamism that powered the long postwar expansion in the leading capitalist economies began to lose steam. By the 1970s, the economy encountered numerous challenges including inflation, growing unemployment, disruptions in the world supply of petroleum and other key input commodities, a relatively high incidence of strikes and labour disruption, and global political conflict (arising from the Cold War and the success of radical national liberation movements in the Third World). Most importantly, profit rates for private employers were squeezed by stagnant macroeconomic conditions on one hand, and the continuing demands of a historically empowered working class (represented by strong and confident unions) on the other.

After a period in which ruling elites in the leading capitalist economies grappled with the dimensions of this emerging crisis, they eventually settled on an aggressive new policy direction which has come to be known as **neoliberalism.** This name reflects the general orientation of this approach toward a "liberal" economic order, that is, one in which private businesses are given more leeway to pursue their profits free from government interference, regulation, or constraint.[23] The neoliberal approach to economic and social policy was first evident in the programs of Margaret Thatcher in the U.K. and Ronald Reagan in the U.S.—both of whom were elected at the end of the turbulent 1970s. But the key pillars of that vision have since been implemented in most developed economies and through most of the developing world as well. These key elements include:

- An emphasis in macroeconomic policy on inflation control rather than full-employment.

- The deregulation and privatization of industries, creating more terrain for profit-seeking private economic activity.

- The downsizing of public sector activities and regulation, and the consequent reduction in taxes.

- The international integration of market-friendly economies through globalization and free trade agreements.

- A multifaceted effort to shift the balance of power in employment relations and collective bargaining in favour of employers, through changes in social policies, labour laws, and collective bargaining systems.

The general goal of this last item on the list is to make it easier for employers to recruit, retain, and motivate workers, and to attain higher productivity for less cost (in wages and benefits). Many policy levers were brought to bear in this effort, including the deliberate effort to recreate and maintain a "sufficient" minimum level of unemployment in the economy (as a cushion against wage inflation and labour empowerment),[24] and cutbacks to social programs and income security systems (like employment insurance), with the result that workers are more economically desperate and hence compliant. Regarding unions and collective bargaining, governments and businesses alike returned to a more confrontational attitude under neoliberalism (compared to the relatively more tolerant attitude of the postwar decades), and have been working hard to undermine the power of unions ever since. As a result, the legal, economic, and cultural environment facing unions has become considerably more hostile in most capitalist countries, including Canada.

For example, the legal hurdles facing union organizers have become more daunting. One key dimension of this shift is the elimination of majority sign-up or card-based certification procedures in most jurisdictions, and their replacement with compulsory secret ballot votes to attain union certification. These ballots, while sounding "democratic," provide employers with ample opportunity to intimidate and coerce workers against joining a union (all the more so since the votes occur in the non-neutral environment of the workplace). Employers usually back up their anti-union campaign with the implicit (and sometime explicit) threat to close the workplace altogether if a union is formed. Similarly, rules against the dismissal of union organizers have become weaker, but limits on picketing and other strike-related activity have become stronger. Combined with the broader neoliberal cultural shift in society (whereby former attitudes of "entitlement" on the part of workers have been replaced by a cultivated emphasis on individual responsibility for individual success), these changes definitely explain much of the slippage in unionization during the neoliberal era.

WHAT LIES AHEAD FOR UNIONS?

Responding to the challenges of operating in a more hostile economic and political environment, Canadian unions have experimented with new strategies for organizing unorganized workers, responding to new demands and concerns of Canadian workers (such as the increasing urgency of work–life balance issues, or concern for the environment), and reaching out to groups of workers who have not traditionally identified with unions (such as new Canadians and racialized minorities, and the growing number of workers employed in precarious and non-standard jobs). However, the decline in union density, and the broader erosion of unions' economic and political influence, indicates that these efforts, while they have helped prevent the more dramatic fall in unionization that has occurred in some other countries, are not sufficient to preserve Canadian unions' role in our evolving economy.

Regardless of ongoing technological and sectoral changes in the economy, working people need unions as much or more than ever: to win a fair share of the wealth they produce, and to protect themselves against the worst risks and insecurities associated with modern-day employment. This is as true of workers designing video games in the 21st century, as it was of workers operating typesetting equipment in the 19th century. Only through a union can workers hope to collectively negotiate with their employers, and thus offset the power imbalance inherent in the paid employment relationship, and win more influence over their compensation and their working conditions. Income inequalities are widening in Canada, and labour's overall share of national income has declined fairly steadily since the late 1970s. Both of these outcomes are clearly linked to the decline of unionization.

For unions to meet the economic, political, and social challenges brought on by a changing economic and political landscape, they must be willing and able to reassess and re-evaluate the way they connect and identify with working people, the way they mobilize their members, and the way they communicate with the broader public. In this regard, we conclude with several suggestions for ways in which unions can revitalize their effectiveness in working for change (both through collective bargaining, and in the broader political and social arenas), and their credibility as a voice for *all* working people (rather than being seen as a vested interest for a lucky unionized minority).

Match Words with Deeds, with a Multifaceted, Sustained Commitment to Organizing

For years Canadian unions have recognized the long-term threat posed by falling union density, and the importance of halting and reversing that decline through more organizing of new members. But the heady rhetoric on this point has neither been matched by a corresponding commitment of resources, nor by a genuine willingness to experiment with new organizing methods. The only two sectors that have avoided falling unionization over the past two decades have been the public sector (which remains relatively insulated, so far, from the more intense threats of competition and aggressive union avoidance typical of the private sector) and construction (where non-traditional sector-wide certification and bargaining arrangements have proven effective in maintaining union density). Other experiments with non-traditional organizing initiatives (including community-rooted campaigns, such as the Justice for Janitors initiative of the Service Employees International Union, or voluntary recognition strategies attempted in various sectors ranging from auto parts to hospitality) have yet to pay measurable dividends in terms of new members. There is no single priority more important for the future of unions than new organizing—and no task that has proven more difficult, in practice. Unions must recognize that existing approaches have been inadequate, and do whatever it takes to get better organizing results. Perhaps the most important, if subtle, task for unions in this regard is to change the expectations of Canadian working people. As noted above, whether workers choose to unionize depends greatly on whether they accept the neoliberal vision of "everyone for themselves"—or whether they hope for, and demand, something better. If workers learn, in part by seeing unions winning things in action, that they can expect more from employment than what they are getting, then they will quickly find ways to organize *themselves* into unions (without relying on paid union organizers to do the job for them).

Find Ways to Fight For, and Eventually Organize, Precarious and Excluded Workers

Some of the most exploited workers in today's labour market are employed in a wide range of precarious and non-standard jobs—from workers on short-term contracts (which often roll over for years at a time), to those placed through employment agencies, to those who come to Canada on temporary work permits with few workplace protections and little opportunity to unionize. The logistical and legal barriers to unionizing these workers are daunting. But there are surely ways in which collective action can be brought to bear, to improve the lives of these workers in incremental but significant ways. Active union leadership in broader campaigns to win more legislative protection for precarious workers, as well as efforts to win improvements in their specific contractual arrangements (by bargaining or pressuring particular employers), is crucial. Community-led worker support organizations and agencies (for example, Justice for Migrant Workers and the Workers Action

Centre in Toronto) are alternative forums for worker engagement and organization that unions must continue to work with and support. On both national and local levels, unions must work to close off this especially exploitive dimension of the modern labour market, thus reinforcing the labour movement's credibility as a force that fights for all workers.

Recommit to the Principles of Social Unionism

Unions must connect their work at the bargaining table to community development, environmental sustainability and social justice initiatives across society. Unions' credibility as a voice for social justice and progress depends on them being seen as fighting for the interests of all workers, not just their own dues-paying members. In this context, unions must be integrally engaged in the full spectrum of broader social movements, campaigns, and coalitions—including the environmental movement; the anti-racist, women's, and LGBT movements; anti-globalization struggles; anti-poverty and housing campaigns; and student, cultural, and youth movements. Whether or not unions are seen by the masses of working Canadians as a progressive, egalitarian force, or as a narrow and defensive vested interest, will depend very much on the extent to which the labour movement leads and supports these varied social movements and struggles. Moreover, the success of those broader social justice struggles is itself critical to the ability of unions to win concrete improvements in the lives of their own members.

Develop More Consistent and Effective Strategies of Political Engagement

Social unionism is built on the assumption that workers' problems cannot be solved solely at the bargaining table. They require multidimensional campaigns in the broader social and political arenas, to win legislative reform and change popular attitudes. But in this regard, the political strategies of Canadian unions have been uncertain and inconsistent in recent years. The labour movement's traditional approach to political activism (rooted most strongly in the policies of the private-sector Canadian affiliates of U.S.-based international unions) was to equate labour's political agenda with the electoral campaigns of a designated labour-friendly political party (namely the New Democratic Party in English Canada, and the Parti Québecois and Bloc Québecois in Quebec). That approach has waned in recent years, reflecting both the growing importance of public-sector unions (which were always more reluctant to formally affiliate to a political party), and disenchantment among many activists with the political record of the NDP (including not least when it was in power).[25] Today the Canadian labour movement incorporates a diversity of political approaches. There are still a few unions that follow the traditional model of formal affiliation to a party (most important in this camp is the United Steelworkers). There are others (including many public sector unions) that limit their interventions strictly to non-partisan issue-oriented campaigns. And there are still others that combine issue-oriented and community campaigns, with more flexible and strategic interventions in election campaigns (including the Canadian Auto Workers union). Whatever strategy is ultimately adopted, it is clear that labour needs to focus and amplify its political voice. Unions must become more visible, consistent, and effective players in broader political debates and conflicts—which will, after all, affect the well-being of all workers, unionized or not.

Become More Inclusive and Diverse

Unions must encourage participation by marginalized groups (including workers of colour, indigenous peoples, young people, and workers in the lesbian, gay, bisexual, and transgendered communities). Most unions have supported a range of affirmative action, employment equity, and other organizing efforts to enhance participation from these constituencies, but there is still much more that needs to be done.

Draw the Line, and Fight Back

The present economic environment confronts unions with enormous challenges and threats. Competition, globalization, and anti-union political and legislative changes have made it extremely difficult for unions in some parts of the economy just to hang onto their past gains—let alone to make further progress for their members. And the onset of the global financial crisis and resulting recession in 2008 and 2009 will likely accentuate those pressures. But whether they are fighting to defend the provisions of their current contracts, or fighting to make breakthroughs and win new benefits for their members, unions must be aggressive, pro-active, and committed to mobilizing their members and supporters to the highest degree possible. The mere act of fighting back makes a difference—whether any particular fightback is successful or not. That's because every fightback shifts the expectations of all sides for future struggles, and shows union members (and others) that they are better off with a union fighting for them, than trying to negotiate the perils of the modern economy on their own.

The financial crisis and economic recession that struck Canada (and the rest of the world) in 2008 and 2009 may turn out to be a historical turning point for Canada's labour movement. The crisis provides an immense opportunity for labour activists to critique the market-oriented economic model that has governed Canada for a quarter-century—and that has failed so obviously to improve the working and living standards of the vast majority of Canadians. On the other hand, the crisis will also unleash additional attacks on workers and their organizations, as employers and governments attempt to shift the costs onto the backs of workers—taking advantage of the fear and insecurity that so many feel to push through radical, painful changes that would not be tolerated during "normal" times.[26] It became quickly apparent that employers and business-friendly governments would use the recession as an opportunity to step up their attacks on unions, attempting even to portray unions as the *source* of an economic downturn (that was actually caused by the failure of deregulated private financial markets!). Unions soon found themselves engaged in important defensive battles—such as the efforts by autoworkers and steelworkers to defend their pension plans (through the bankruptcy restructuring of General Motors and Chrysler, and through a historic strike at the former Inco operations in Sudbury), and highly controversial strikes involving municipal workers in Toronto, Windsor, and elsewhere.

If unions can respond effectively and creatively to the global financial crisis (and to the general deterioration in working and living conditions that so many working people experienced before the financial crisis arrived), finding new ways to motivate and mobilize workers to stand up for their interests, then the labour movement will reconfirm its historic economic and political importance.[27] If unions fail in this challenge, and end up trapped only in rearguard actions to defend past victories and their existing members, without rising to the necessity of a broader and more inclusive fightback, then the movement will likely continue to be pushed to the sidelines.

Despite the daunting challenges facing unions in Canada (like elsewhere), we remain fundamentally optimistic. For hundreds of years, unions have been a constant and essential mechanism by which workers band together to confront the fundamental imbalance of the employment relationship, and win themselves a better position in life. At their best, unions have also been a principled and powerful voice for wider social and political progress. Clearly, workers still need unions to play both of these roles. And we are hopeful that unions will live up to that responsibility, in part by reinventing and renewing their practices and strategies to reflect the evolving needs of modern workers.

Let's conclude by coming back to the question with which we opened this chapter: Why do unions, which were organized to protect the interests of vulnerable and exploited workers, encounter such criticism and opposition in so much of broader Canadian society? In light of our review of the evolution of unionism in Canada, and the full frontal assault on unions and collective bargaining, which is a centrepiece of neoliberalism, perhaps this problem is not so surprising. Employers and their allies (in think tanks, in the privately owned media, and in business-friendly political parties) have targeted unions with hostile business strategies, hostile laws and policies, and hostile media and cultural coverage, in an effort to restore a more amenable labour market— one in which workers can be compelled (through chronic economic insecurity) to work as hard as possible, for minimum compensation. More fundamentally, neoliberalism has also challenged the very idea that human beings can work together to better themselves; instead, life success is being redefined as a purely individualistic pursuit. In that context, it is not surprising at all that an anti-union mentality has been successfully cultivated among many segments of Canadian society. Canadian trade unionists need to understand the nature of this multidimensional attack, its tactics, motivations, and consequences. And then we must develop an organizational and political response that rises to the challenge. If we succeed in that, then unions can live up to their historical mission, which is to fight for the rights and interests of working people, and for a more equal and inclusive society for all.

ENDNOTES

1. That is partly because the higher wages that accompany unionization make it unfeasible for employers to hire union workers for the most menial, unproductive jobs.

2. Of course, a great deal of the total work performed in society is unpaid, and hence not measured within formal economic statistics such as GDP.

3. See Stanford (2008a), Chapter 8. Over 10 percent of workers in the formal (paid) economy in Canada are self-employed (although many of these nominally independent workers are in fact tied very directly to a particular employer-like entity). And a very small proportion of workers own and/or direct the operations of large firms in which the bulk of work is performed by paid employees. The rest—at least 85 percent of those participating in the formal, paid economy—perform their labour through the employment relationship.

4. See Stanford and Vosko (2004), Chapter 1, for an overview of recent trends in labour market regulation in the advanced capitalist economies, and how unionization interacts with other features and structures of regulation.

5. For more details on the history and practice of trade unions in Canada, see Godard (2005); Hebdon (2008); Heron (1996); Kumar and Schenk (2006).

6. This practice began with the U.S. National Labor Relations Act (known commonly as the Wagner Act) in 1935, largely replicated in its Canadian equivalent, Order-in-Council PC 1003 (a federal cabinet order) passed to stabilize and regularize labour relations during World War II. See Gonick, Phillips, and Vorst (1996) for an overview of the history of this approach, and analysis of its current relevance in Canada.

7. This pressure could consist of leveraging the union's strength at other unionized facilities of the same company; utilizing boycotts, community campaigns, and other public pressure tactics to indirectly compel a company to recognize the union; and/or wielding pressure through a company's suppliers or customers to accept the union.

8. A compilation of scholarly research regarding the economic and social consequences of unionization in Canada is provided in Pupo (2009).

9. For more discussion of the union premium, see Jackson (2009); Statistics Canada (2006); Verma and Fang (2002).

10. Akyeampong (2002).

11. Although in some circumstances in which employers misuse part-time workers, the union's goal may be to increase the number and stability of working hours.

12. Jackson (2009), Chapters 9 and 11, discusses these broader social effects of strong unions, especially visible in the Nordic countries.

13. Human Resources and Social Development Canada (2007).

14. See Morissette et al. (2005).

15. See Stanford (2008b) for a discussion of Canada's increasingly resource-dominated economic trajectory, and its various economic, social, and environmental implications.

16. For example, Ontario's labour laws were changed in 2004 to re-instate card-check certification in the construction industry.

17. For a detailed overview of precarious work in Canada, its dimensions, and effects, see Vosko (2006).

18. See Kumar (2008).

19. The Rand Formula, for example, requires all workers in a unionized workplace—who share in the benefits of a collective agreement—to join the union or, at the very least, pay an equivalent amount of union dues to a charity; it was devised by Judge Ivan Rand following a famous strike of autoworkers in Windsor in 1945, and set the stage for the postwar labour relations environment. In U.S. right-to-work states, this type of union security arrangement is prohibited. Card and Freeman (1993) document the specific historical causes of the divergent labour market outcomes of Canada and the U.S.

20. Bureau of Labor Statistics (2009).

21. Two recent examples of this controversy included the decision in 2006 by the U.S. leaders of the Labourers' International Union of North America to expel the leaders of its large Toronto local and place the local under direct trusteeship, and the actions the same year by the U.S.-based leaders of the United Transportation Union to remove from office the union's entire elected (Canadian) bargaining committee at CN Rail.

22. That pressure to tolerate unions reflected both the domestic influence of labour-friendly political parties, and the international competition between capitalism and communism (thanks to which elites in the West felt more pressure to justify the virtues of capitalism to their workers).

23. This reference to classical market-oriented "liberalism" is a bit misplaced, since even under neoliberalism the state continues to play a powerful and central role in enforcing property rights, establishing a business-friendly legal and economic climate, bailing out failed banks, etc. For a broader discussion of the rise and significance of neoliberalism, see Harvey (2005).

24. The curious belief that higher unemployment is thus "good" for the economy is reflected in the economic doctrine of the "natural rate of unemployment," due to Friedman (1968).

25. The assumption that the election of a labour-friendly social-democratic party would usher in a new era of egalitarian policies for workers has been bitterly disproven in many times and many countries—including Canada. Thus the partnership between labour and its chosen party has been fractured, and most unionists have realized they need an independent political platform regardless of which party is in power.

26. The consistent pattern of elites deliberately manipulating moments of crisis to force through painful, long-lasting structural changes in the economy and society is chillingly documented in Klein (2007).

27. For concrete examples of how Canadian unions could respond more effectively to the economic crisis, see the "Forum on Labour and the Economic Crisis: Can the Union Movement Rise to the Occasion?" published in the Autumn 2009 edition of *Labour/Le Travail*.

3

Walmartization and the McJob: The Jobs that Boomed in the New Economy

Norene Pupo

DISCUSSION QUESTIONS

1. What is the Walmartization effect and why should we as workers and as consumers be concerned about it?

2. What are some of the factors that have influenced the growth of the Walmartization effect?

3. What is the significance of the move from "push production" to "pull production" for workers in Canada and for workers in the Global South?

4. Given the power of Walmart and other giant corporations, how can workers fight back to improve conditions for themselves and for their communities?

Over the past few years, a new corporate-derived term has emerged, slipping into our descriptions of organizational processes, the structure of work, and globalization. **Walmartization** now joins **McDonaldization**, referring to processes shaping standards of living. While McDonaldization mainly pertains to the rationalization of the labour process, organization of work, and the effects of corporatization on aspects of culture and everyday life (Ritzer, 1996), the term Walmartization concerns the profound and insidious transformations in regional and global economies through sheer size, influence, and **power**. For some critics, Walmartization is a buzzword for the **New Economy**. In the marketplace, in the courts and political arenas, overseas, at home, and in our local communities, Walmart's activities, including marketing practices, strikebreaking, store openings, profits, fines, importing, and riches, are in the limelight. It is important not only to keep track of this retail giant's moves, but also to consider the ways it has transformed manufacturing, retail service, and the movement of goods around the globe. This paper examines the Walmartization phenomenon, the re-shaping of the Canadian retail sector, and the impact on service work and **McJobs** in the new economy.

WORKING 24/7: NEW REALITIES IN THE SERVICE ECONOMY

Key to the service economy is the **flexibility of employment** and the availability of a large, low-paid and vulnerable workforce. Out of necessity, particularly when adequate full-time work is not available, workers move from job to job, often balancing two or even three part-time jobs to make ends meet. A large percentage of these jobs are peripheral and **precarious**, offering little or no security and few opportunities to advance. Not only are these arrangements taxing for the workers, but also their families are affected by the need to juggle multiple schedules of work and **non-work** activities simultaneously. Accommodating a number of short-hour jobs often lengthens the working day as eight hours of work at multiple sites may span over a period of 12 or more hours in a day. Such busy schedules may be especially difficult for older workers or for those trying to balance family, **unpaid work**, caregiving, school, or any number of activities. As the reality or perception of job security becomes increasingly elusive, Rubin and Brody (2005) have found that feelings of attachment to the workplace may decline, especially among older workers who have experienced "a change in the social contract."

For many workers and particularly for those in lower-end service positions, insecurity and precariousness are the order of the day. No longer are workers concerned with temporary slow-downs and periodic lay-offs, but rather work insecurity has become a feature of the new economy and as such has profound implications for health and well-being at both individual and societal levels (Scott, 2004). As in the past, workers in the service economy lack control over decisions regarding their employment security. However, in the context of globalization and the permanent net loss of jobs, especially good jobs, the new insecurity results from an even greater imbalance in the shift of power to employers. As Adkins (2005) suggests, in the new economy the relationship with property, power, and people is restructured and new forms of property and commodity exchange emerge. The requirement for flexibility is coupled with an increasing demand for **emotional labour** as work is structured to focus on customer relations in the employment relationship, and as a result, such requirements are taking a toll on workers.

The growing insecurity, polarization, precariousness, and unrelenting time pressures within the new economy are exacerbated by the shift in labour market policies and practices embracing principles of **neoliberalism**. As Thomas (2009, p. 136) points out, the new models of labour market regulation promote "market-based, privatized, and individualized relations between employers and employees." Essentially, in what appears to be doublespeak, the requirements for flexibility have redefined the **non-standard employment** relationship as standard, thereby "putting the ball in the employer's court," and tipping the balance of power even further in favour of the employer, while leaving the employee vulnerable, powerless and without recourse. In an economy characterized by declining rates of unionization and a fraying social safety net, workers are left to rely on their own devices as the state adopts a neoliberal agenda promoting individual responsibilities, privatization, and a deregulated economy while moving further from ideals and practices of social welfare and social rights upheld in the previous Keynesian era (Broad & Antony, 2006, p. 35).

WHY WATCH WALMART: RANGE AND INFLUENCE

Worldwide Walmart is the largest retailer with billions in sales ($405 billion in 2008), an enormous and burgeoning labour force (more than 2.1 million workers in 2008), and by 2006 more than 176 million customers weekly worldwide (Fortune 500, 2009; Global 500, 2009, Pier, 2006). It is also the largest private employer in the U.S. In terms of its business transactions, Walmart does more business and imports more goods than most countries. Its income is four times that of its largest competitor. In sales it outpaces by far its closest competitors. It is bigger than U.S. icons, General Motors and General Electric. Together Target, Sears, Kmart, J.C. Penney, Safeway, and Kroger combined do not match Walmart's business. After two consecutive years in the top spot (2007 and 2008), Walmart is now ranked #3 behind Royal Dutch Shell (#1) and Exxon Mobil (#2) on *Fortune Magazine*'s list of the 500 biggest publicly traded corporations (2009). Walmart's presence, however, has not diminished. Driving from Buffalo to Boston on the interstate, the number of Walmart trucks—single and double trailers—passing every few minutes, presumably from a central dispatch is overwhelming.

Not surprisingly, the Waltons—billionaires Christy, Jim, S. Robson, Alice, and Helen—family members of founder Sam Walton, each hold positions in the top 20 on Forbes' list of the richest people in the world with each of these family members worth between $15.9 and $15.6 billion (Forbes, 2009). If all five of these family members were ranked together, the Waltons would dominate this list of the world's richest. Some argue that if Sam Walton were still alive, he would be twice as rich as the number one ranked Bill Gates who is worth over $50 billion.

Tracking Walmart's activities has become a major preoccupation for many analysts. But why is the Walmart watch so important? Walmart is not a gentle giant. Rather, Walmart is a bully—in our local communities, overseas, in its stores and warehouses, and in labour relations. When Walmart moves into a community, many smaller businesses, unable to compete, go bankrupt and invariably close their doors.[1] The lower prices mantra means lower standards and job losses. Walmart first entered Canada in 1994 when it purchased the 122 stores in the struggling Woolco chain. As a result of this move, over the next decade at least six major chains disappeared (Flavelle, 2006). Its current move to open superstores with massive floor space, carrying both general merchandise and groceries, has prompted Canadian icon, Canadian Tire, to experiment with a limited number of fresh and frozen food products in a couple of its stores (Flavelle, 2009, p. B1). As the market for growth in the number of U.S. stores wanes, Walmart has targeted markets in both developed and developing countries. By 2008 Walmart was operating in 13 countries but 80 percent of planned new stores that year were opened in Canada, Mexico, and China (Kabel, 2007a). By 2006 Walmart had over 50 percent of the market in Canada for general merchandise and had become Canada's largest non-food retailer with about $13 million in sales annually (Flavelle, 2006). Recently Walmart announced the decision to close its six Sam's Club stores in southern Ontario—a move that will affect 1,200 workers. This move will further streamline Walmart's operations, meeting its objective of offering one-stop shopping while maintaining market share and expanding. Walmart has, in fact, pushed the concept of one-stop shopping to the limit by its recent move to sell caskets and other funeral wares including floral arrangements on its U.S. website (Fredrix, 2009, p. A15). By the end of 2009 Walmart's presence in Canada will number 316 stores and 82 supercentres with over 80,000 employees overall (Owram, 2009, p. A18).

Wal-Mart Watch, an organization of citizens affected by Walmart's policies, found that three jobs are lost for every two that are created when Walmart moves into a community (Fishman, 2007; Ribeiro, 2005). Its tactics sometimes skirt the law. For example, in order to bypass an ordinance limiting the size of stores in a Maryland town, Walmart planned to build two separate stores adjacent to one another (New Rules Staff, 2005). However, communities, including Guelph and Burlington in Ontario, and Vancouver, British

Columbia, have fought back. Some have successfully kept Walmarts out of their backyards, while others have merely delayed the plans, but in the process, raised awareness of the transformations that occur when Walmart moves in. With regard to its workforce, Walmart's cost-saving strategies have included converting a greater percentage of its labour force to part-time, forcing workers to make themselves available to work any time, day or night, weekdays or weekends, and capping wages so that workers who earn above the cap will be denied annual raises (Greenhouse & Barbaro, 2006). Because of its size and power, the concern is that Walmart's practices will be adopted by competitors and will influence labour relations, standards, and policies generally.

As the company's executives admit, Walmart will stage fierce bidding wars between manufacturers in order to shake down prices to minimize costs and maximize profits (Banach, 2005). This has driven companies vying for Walmart's business to produce cheaper products usually by moving their operations overseas. This fierce competition drives the production process, affecting working conditions and the pace of work for thousands of workers. In 2006, for example, 40 percent of the foreign factories with which Walmart conducts business committed "high risk" violations such as failure to pay overtime while 52 percent committed moderate infractions such as failing to document workers' pay (Kabel, 2007, p. A16). Worldwide, its policy of low prices is maintained by paying workers substandard wages and few, if any, benefits. Moreover, it maintains the view that workers are expendable, relying on a largely part-time, low-skilled labour force.

Walmart is vehemently anti-**union** and has engaged in several different campaigns to thwart union drives in its stores. Recently, Walmart has even filed an injunction against a website, Walmart Workers Canada, operated by the United Food and Commercial Workers Union in Canada (UFCW Canada). In this case, Walmart is attempting to employ trademark law prohibiting the use of its name, colour scheme, slogan, employees' blue vests, and even "'oval, circular or semi-circular' designs" on this website that teaches workers about unions (Hanley, 2009, p. A11). Over the years, managers have pressured employees, dissuaded them from embracing unionism, disallowed employees from fraternizing with one another if management suspected "union talk," bought off workers with a few extra dollars in their paycheques, promoted a culture of **paternalism**, artificially promoted workers by naming them "associates," and closed stores that won union **certification** (Adams, 2005; Dicker, 2005; Ehrenreich, 2001; Featherstone, 2004; Lichtenstein, 2006). Walmart's aggressive tactics, including intimidation, have been cause for investigation (Marotte, 2005; Pier, 2007).[2] Recently, it has closed stores in Jonquiere,

Quebec[3] and a Walmart Tire and Lube Express in Gatineau, Quebec (CBC News, December 19, 2008); or threatened to close, as in Saint-Hyacinthe, Quebec (CBC News, February 14, 2005), at any mention of unionization.[4] Moreover, once a store has successfully unionized it has tied up the union's resources and eroded its support with countless appeals, leave to appeal applications, judicial reviews, and labour board proceedings (Murray & Cuillerier, 2009; Peritz, 2005). Even the large and resourceful United Food and Commercial Workers (UFCW) has had to back away at times from its unionizing efforts, as in Windsor, Ontario, and in Weyburn, Saskatchewan, a store that has now been granted union certification by the Saskatchewan Labour Board, despite Walmart's tactics (CBC News, December 9, 2008). After a four-year struggle, in a case that went to **arbitration**, the Walmart workers at the store in Saint-Hyacinthe, Quebec, became the first in North America to have a collective agreement (CBC News, April 9, 2009).

Juxtaposed to its anti-union tactics are Walmart's message of interest in families, workers, and communities (Featherstone, 2004). That Canadian market research found that Walmart was the "favourite company" of Canadian women (cited in Featherstone, 2004, p. 212) is fair warning that one of Walmart's greatest successes has indeed been in its construction of its own image as a community-oriented (smiley-faced) business and a family-centred, fair-minded employer. Capitalizing on the importance of a positive community representation and hoping to erase its image as a ruthless community "bully," Walmart has adopted a strategy to help small local establishments stay in business by providing businesses with small grants or producing free radio spots to run on the store's radio network (D'Innocenzio, 2006, p. A12).

WALMARTIZATION: SHIFTS AND DECLINES

> Every time you see the Walmart smiley face, whistling and knocking down the prices, somewhere there's a factory worker being kicked in the stomach. (Sherrie Ford, cited in Fishman, 2006, p. 79)

Structure and Process of Manufacturing: From "Push" to "Pull" Production

When Walmart flexes its muscles, manufacturers are attentive, vying with one another, shaving fractions of a cent off their commodities, in the hope of getting a Walmart contract. According to analysts (Fishman, 2006, 2007;

Freeman, 2003; Pier, 2007), Walmart has single-handedly contributed to the decline or demise of a number of companies ranging from smaller establishments employing hundreds of workers to brand names employing thousands, including Hoover Vacuums, Kids 'R' Us, Toys 'R' Us, Carolina Mills, Lovable Garments, Rubbermaid, and Vlasic Pickles (Fishman, 2006, 2007; PBS Video, 2004). For example, Vlasic Pickles signed an agreement allowing Walmart to sell 3-gallon [7.5 litre] jars of whole pickles for $2.97 in the U.S., a price that afforded Vlasic only a few cents profit and undercut its sales of fancier cut pickles. When the company appealed to Walmart to raise the price to $3.49, Walmart refused, threatening to cancel its contract altogether with the company and vowing not to carry any other Vlasic products. Eventually, Vlasic filed for bankruptcy (Freeman, 2003). When company officials at the headquarters of Rubbermaid in Wooster, Ohio, steadfastly refused to lower the quality of their products or their price to the retailers following a major increase in the price of resin, Walmart disciplined the company by dropping a number of its products and placing others in less conspicuous locations within the stores. As Rubbermaid's largest customer, Walmart's actions fuelled the company's demise, contributing to the loss of 1,000 jobs and to major economic decline in what was essentially a one-industry community. By 1999 Rubbermaid was bankrupt and began to sell off its machinery and equipment through public auction. As one commentator noted, Rubbermaid had been named the most admired company in the U.S. in 1994 for the quality of its products, but by 1999 Walmart had captured this coveted title for its low prices. This represented a significant shift in corporate values and standards (PBS Video, 2004).

Fifty years ago a number of multinational corporations engaged in manufacturing propelled the global economy in trade and commerce. Today, however, under **globalization** "retail-dominated **supply chains**" lead the way, setting the parameters for manufacturers and maintaining the upper hand in global transactions (Appelbaum & Lichtenstein, 2007). According to Edna Bonacich, this represented a change from "push production to pull production" (Bonacich, quoted in PBS Video, 2004; Bonacich & Wilson, 2008). In "push production" manufacturers produce goods and sell them to retailers who in turn market them. In "pull production" the retailers have the upper hand; they decide what they will sell and then dictate their orders to manufacturers who will produce the goods. In this process the manufacturers engage in price bargaining with the retailers. But in a company as expansive and powerful as Walmart, the buyer dictates the price with an eye to undercutting the producer. The buyer typically "calls the shots" (PBS Video, 2004) and basing the price on an understanding of the production process, the technology available and the cost of labour, calculates the lowest price possible.

As the world's largest retailer, Walmart stands in the forefront of this shift from the primacy of the manufacturer to the primacy of retailing and commerce. As a result as retailers search the globe for cheap manufactured goods, increasingly we witness a massive growth in manufacturing within the Global South and a corresponding expansion of low-wage retail workforces within the north. Tying production to consumption is not a new strategy and certainly Walmart should not be credited with this innovation. Today, however, the concern is with the scale and extent of this practice that not only affects marketing and consumption patterns, but more significantly, impacts on labour processes in both production and service sectors. In the 1980s, Benetton developed a method of tying inventories in the retail sector directly to its manufacturing sites, so that production was based on dwindling supplies at the retail sites and on consumers' interests in colours, fabrics, textures, and styles.[5] The system was well integrated. With its enormous size, Walmart commands the attention of millions in production revenue and its policies affect thousands of manufacturing sites and hundreds of thousands of workers. Walmartization refers as much to the power and influence as to the structure and process of manufacturing today. Declines in heavy industry, where jobs have traditionally been unionized and relatively well paid with good benefits, together with the **outsourcing** of production jobs, have facilitated the Walmartization effect. As a result there is general economic decline in the Global North as manufacturing is shifted out of high wage areas. In Canada, as a consequence of this process, the traditional pillars of the economy—steel, auto, auto parts, heavy equipment—industries that are traditionally unionized and male-dominated—are lost. Production has declined overall and outsourcing has increased. Companies at home in lower-end manufacturing including garments, textiles, and widgets of various sorts, are forced to compete directly with establishments within the Global South, particularly in China, which has been established as the primary source of Walmart's goods. According to Appelbaum and Lichtenstein (2007) this transformation in the relationship between manufacturers and retailers was facilitated by two primary factors: the revolution in information, communication, and transportation technologies including data storage, bar codes, containerization, and global communication links; and the shift to neoliberal practices.

Major concerns with the movement of manufacturing overseas include lowering **labour standards**, unfair labour practices, health and safety concerns, intense working conditions, and very poor wages with no benefits. The Walmart approach is to undercut manufacturers, many of which are dependent on contracts with this mighty retail giant to remain afloat. The mark-up on items imported from low-wage countries is higher—between 60 to 80 percent—and this means higher profits (PBS Video, 2004). In 2006 Walmart acquired about $9 billion worth of goods from China and many of the factories where these goods were produced were cited with violations including abuse and the use of child labour (Barboza, 2008). Walmart's influence is now extending beyond manufacturing. In its most recent move to penetrate markets, Walmart is turning to agriculture, contracting with small farmers in rural areas in places such as Guatemala. As Walmart increasingly moves into the "fresh" grocery business through its superstores, farmland is now the key to expansion. The usurping of small farmers, even those in very remote areas, affects local markets and consumption patterns and according to critics may push small farmers out of business forcing them to abandon their plots of land and move among the very poorest in the urban slums (Dickerson, 2008).

While Walmartization, or as Lichtenstein (2007) suggests, "the new world of retail supremacy" explains shifts in production, the dramatic expansion of production capacities and the burgeoning manufacturing workforce in China, this process has weakened labour standards on a global scale by way of inadequate and consistent monitoring practices and insufficient pressures from governments, consumers, labour, and activists including the anti-sweatshop movement, resulting in policies or "soft laws" that are "too weak for the job" (Wells, 2007). As a result, Walmartization has meant declining working conditions not only for production workers, but also for workers in logistics, transportation, and warehousing in many countries (Bonacich & Wilson, 2005, 2008). This chain of "weak links" in labour results from Walmart's unrelenting quest for the lowest prices for goods and impacts on the quality of all jobs within the chain. The process leaves all workers vulnerable, due to the increased use of part-time and temporary workers, the pressure on unions, the anti-union tactics employed and intense and otherwise poor working conditions. As consumers, Walmart workers, along with others in low-wage jobs, may be compelled by the "lowest prices" advertising campaigns and the "Save Money—Live Better" slogan to rely on Walmart. While exploited by their employers, in turn as consumers these workers may benefit directly from Walmart's exploitation of sweatshop labour in the Global South.

Manufacturing Decline

Historically, manufacturing was regarded as the primary driver within the Canadian economy, accounting for 26 percent of total employment in 1946. By 2007, manufacturing plummeted to 12 percent of total employment, less than half of the postwar share (Lin, 2008, p. 5). Between 2004 and 2008 more than 1 in 7 manufacturing jobs were lost (Bernard, 2009, p. 5). In 2007 129,000 workers lost their manufacturing jobs and 35,000 more joined them in 2008 (Usalcas, 2009, p. 23). Canada is not alone in experiencing this decline. Most member countries in the Organization for Economic Cooperation and Development (OECD) have experienced deep losses, a trend that dates back to the 1970s with particularly significant losses since 2004 (Bernard, 2009, p. 5), resulting in service-dominated economies throughout the OECD. A number of structural factors, including improved transportation and communication techniques, adaptable labour markets, an available labour force, and state support, have contributed to the movement of manufacturing from more developed locations in the north to areas of the Global South. This movement has placed China as the world's manufacturing centre and low-wage workers, primary women, from China and other areas within the Global South, now dominate the global labour force. Analysts note that by 2002 there were 109 million workers in manufacturing in China, and this was more than double the combined total of 53 million in all of the G7 member countries (cited in Bernard, 2009, p. 6). This current construction of global labour has contributed to greater imbalances of wealth between richer and poorer countries, in addition to widening gaps at home (Lichtenstein, 2007).

Between 1998 and 2004 the share of manufacturing jobs in the Canadian economy fell from 14.9 percent to 14.4 percent, and then fell sharply again between 2004 and 2008 to 11.5 percent (Bernard, 2009, p. 7). Interestingly unionized jobs in manufacturing disappeared between 1998 and 2008 at twice the rate of non-union manufacturing jobs, thereby impacting on union density overall (Bernard, p. 9). This reflects the pattern of higher paid union jobs being outsourced to the Global South or more generally to lower wage areas.

While almost all manufacturing industries have been falling since 2004, a number of industries experienced very significant losses. Among the hardest hit have been textiles and clothing, traditionally one of the largest manufacturing sectors. Almost half of the workers lost jobs between 2004 and 2008 in clothing, textiles, and textile products (Bernard, p. 7). Significantly, "good" jobs for both men and women have disappeared. Clothing and textiles has traditionally been female-dominated manufacturing and the job losses in this industry have been most significant for women. However, as relative newcomers to the traditionally male-dominated spheres of auto, steel, and equipment manufacturing, along with their male co-workers, women have faced layoffs and in many cases, as "last hired" have little hope of recall. As a group, the gains women have made overall in higher-waged, unionized sectors may now be in jeopardy.

JOBS THAT BOOMED: SERVICE McJOBS

Despite the decline in recent years in manufacturing jobs, between 2004 and 2008 the rest of the economy saw an 11-percent growth in the number of jobs (Bernard, 2009, p. 5). Losses in manufacturing coupled with swelling ranks of retail workers means that each of these industries today employs 2 million workers (Lin, 2008, p. 6). The growth in the service sector, however, is a signal for economic woe and decline. Despite the significant growth in recent years (2002–07) in retail trade, only 68 percent of workers received benefits, compared to 81 percent in manufacturing, 90 percent in education, and 79 percent in health care (Lin, 2008, p. 12). Not only is a significant percentage of service work poorly compensated but it also lacks opportunities for advancement and security. At the lower end, service work—particularly retail work—is often part-time, and dominated by women and racial minorities (Williams, 2006, p. 49). **Part-time work** is the proverbial "McJob," with little job security, low rates of unionization, and all the attributes of a "bad job" (Duffy & Pupo, 1992; Pupo & Duffy, 2000).

Currently, competing with, or more accurately trotting behind Walmart, is the order of the day. As Canadian Tire assesses the viability of restructuring its stores to include groceries, along with other retail outlets, it is following the "generalist" superstore model, moving away from the specialty market, where consumers expect to pay premium prices in exchange for service along with the goods. The one-stop shopping experience popularized by Walmart means that under one roof, consumers may buy a number of services, including automotive repair, hairstyling, dry cleaning, photography, or along with their groceries may buy wines, specialty coffees, flowers, videos, eye glasses, and travel packages; and they may have a snack at the McDonalds or Tim Hortons kiosk as well. Giant big box stores employ hundreds of interchangeable, low-wage workers—primarily women and students working part-time. Although they offer convenience along with a wide variety of goods and services, the workers are incidental to the sales, functioning primarily to maintain the flow by keeping the sales floor clean and well-stocked, and by moving customers smoothly through the check-out lines. Workers are expected to engage only in minimal exchanges with customers, finishing with a scripted "thank-you." As a measure of quality control, sales "associates" and warehouse employees are highly monitored and face severe penalties for even slight infractions (Adams, 2006).

In 2008 approximately 5.2 percent of all workers in Canada earned the minimum wage (set by their province) or below (Gougeon, 2009, p. 2). Not surprisingly almost half of all minimum wage earners are teenagers between 15 to 19 and 60 percent of those earning minimum wages are under the age of 25 (Gougeon, 2009, p. 3). Another 29 percent of minimum wage workers are between the ages of 25 and 54, and the majority of those in this group were women. What is most disconcerting about this group is that these workers are in their core or peak earning years and may be permanent employees while those in younger age groups may be attending school and working in minimum wage jobs temporarily. Minimum wage work is concentrated in the service sector and typically does not require special skills, has low rates of unionization, and is often part-time (Gougeon, 2009, p. 4). Part-time workers were almost seven times more likely to work at the minimum wage than full-timers (Gougeon, 2009, p. 5). In 2008 about one-third of full-timers compared to one-quarter of part-timers belonged to a union (Statistics Canada, 2008a, p. 6).

For a number of years growth in service sector employment and in self-employment far outweighed growth in the goods-producing sector. In 2008 the retail sector passed the manufacturing sector as the largest employer in Canada, clearly marking the shift away from an industrial-based economy. This also means declines in jobs that are traditionally better compensated, pushing Canadian workers into the age of wage deflation. Statistics Canada reports that on average manufacturing workers earn $21.66 per hour compared to $14.87 for retail workers, or in other words workers in manufacturing earn an average of 46 percent more than their counterparts in retail work (Scoffield, 2008, p. B1). Given that retail workers are often part-time employees, their take-home pay is a fraction of manufacturing workers who primarily work full-time. The difference in wages and hours worked affects buying power and the overall health of the economy. In 2008, for example, the average weekly earnings including overtime of factory workers was $950.84 compared to $488.58 for retail workers (Scoffield, 2008, p. B1). Among retail workers, those working in general merchandise stores (like Walmart) on average have the lowest wages, earning approximately $357.73 a week (2007) compared to workers in clothing stores, health and personal care stores, sporting goods, electronics, and so on (Statistics Canada, 2007).

The majority of workers in the services-producing sector are women. Overall women hold 55 percent (2007) of jobs in this sector and in contrast women hold 23 percent of jobs in the goods-producing sector and about 28 percent of manufacturing jobs (Statistics Canada, 2008). Among service jobs, there is a great range of skills, educational levels, wages, and working conditions. Whereas women outnumber men in most services categories, men outnumber women in higher wage occupations including professional, scientific and technical services, transportation and warehousing, business and finance.

The shift to a service-dominated economy has affected hours worked and the degree of **hours polarization** in Canada. In the 10-year period from the mid 1980s to the mid 1990s the Canadian labour market was characterized by growing inequality of earnings and polarization of work hours (Morissette in Usalcas 2008, p. 5). However, between 1997 and 2006 the gap in work hours contracted somewhat as fewer worked especially long hours (49 or more). This notable decline in the hours polarization gap reflects losses in the goods-producing sector among both production (blue-collar) workers and managers and gains in the service sector where hours are characteristically more flexible and varied with regard to shifts and required hours (Usalcas, 2008, p. 14). The overall downward shift in the number of hours worked in recent years is also reflected in earnings. Between 1997 and 1998 and 2006 and 2007 in most regions of Canada the average wage in manufacturing saw only mild growth and the median manufacturing wage saw relatively little change[6] (Morissette, 2008, pp. 14–15). However, there have been significant losses in manufacturing jobs since 2004. For example, between 2004 and 2007, the number of manufacturing jobs in both Ontario and Quebec fell substantially by at least 14 percent. However, the fact that earnings remained relatively unchanged indicates that firms responded to a declining market for products manufactured in Canada by laying-off workers rather than adjusting wages (Morissette, 2008, p. 18). Further, with the exception of Ontario and British Columbia, in most provinces the number of manufacturing jobs paying less than $10 per hour fell[7] (Morissette, 2008, p. 19). The service sector remained the repository of so-called low-paid, low-skilled "bad jobs." On average in Canada 49 percent of jobs paid less than $10 per hour in 2006–07, declining only slightly from 51 percent in 1997–98[8] (Morissette, 2008, p. 19).

Despite shifts in the Canadian labour force in terms of swelling numbers of part-time and temporary workers, researchers suggest that it is difficult to conclude with assurance that good jobs are disappearing although wages of new employees appear to be declining (Morissette & Johnson, 2005). However, between 1981 and 2004, there is substantial evidence that the wage gap between young and older workers has grown and that the wages of both males and females with less than two years **seniority** have fallen substantially relative to workers with more than two years experience (Morissette & Johnson, 2005, p. 13). In addition, the percentage of new employees hired in temporary jobs has grown dramatically from 11 percent in 1989 to 21 percent in 2004 while among those with one year of seniority or less, the number of temporary workers was even greater—14 percent in 1989 compared to 25 percent in 2004 (Morissette & Johnson, 2005, p. 18).

Another indicator of declining standards is that pension coverage has fallen for men of all ages and for females under 45 (Morissette & Johnson, 2005, p. 20). This pattern seems to point to losses in men's traditional work sectors, where union coverage is typically relatively high and the employment of women in part-time and temporary work where there are few benefits and typically no pension coverage.

"DONE DIRT CHEAP": IMAGES AND REALITIES OF SERVICE WORK

The service sector thrives on image. Retail, hospitality, and entertainment industries are unrivalled in their ability to create, maintain, and reinforce positive, friendly images. Yet, some of these industries house blatant contradictions between their images of service, comfort, cleanliness, and well-being, and the conditions provided for their labour forces. In these low-waged and predominantly non-unionized workplaces, managements have diligently sought to keep their workers smiling up front to avoid tarnishing the image that has been carefully crafted and meticulously maintained. Walmart reinforces this image with its use of a yellow smiley face. Yet, behind the clean, happy, and healthy images is a workforce left vulnerable and unarmed without collective agreements, and in many cases, without job descriptions. Most recently, Walmart has marketed itself as a forerunner in eco-consumerism, pressuring detergent manufacturers by carrying only concentrated laundry detergents in its stores as of May 2008 (Rinehart, 2007, p. E1). Such diligence in boldly declaring support for a greener economy in the Global North is not matched in the Global South in manufacturing sites where workers labour in toxic environments and live in communities enveloped in dense yellow smog and very poor air quality.

Behind the façade, scores of service workers—most of them women working part-time—are expected to maintain the image despite despicable, dirty, and frequently unsafe conditions. In these contexts, management—front-line supervisors, store managers, assistant managers—often exercise their authority inappropriately, pushing workers to engage in activities well beyond what one might expect if a job description or union representation were available. Workers refusing or failing to do what is asked of them may face dire consequences, despite the lack of rewards if they comply. On a boss's whim, a worker may be dismissed.

Stories from the shopping mall and retail sector expose ways in which workers' contributions along with their health and safety needs and their overall welfare are ignored. It is not surprising that Walmart workers are routinely locked in during overnight hours, despite fire safety procedures. Retail workers are expected to "keep house" by cleaning washrooms, sweeping the floors, tidying up, taking out garbage, and climbing ladders to stock shelves or retrieve merchandise. "Dirty work" faced by retail workers is extensive. Some of it is obvious, but much of it is hidden, taking place out back in storerooms and employee-only areas. Some of it is abusive, as for instance when workers are expected to ignore racist or sexist comments, and to continue smiling and uttering pleasantries while quelling negative emotions (Williams, 2006). The workers who tell these stories are frequently asked to do the company's dirty work and they do so for minimum wages.

The declining manufacturing sector in Canada and the Global North along with the growth in poorly compensated low-end service impacts quality of life and community well-being. This process is one of the most profound aspects of the "shifting landscape" of work. It involves bustling retail centres against a backdrop of rusty and abandoned factories, scores of workers juggling multiple part-time or poorly compensated jobs, declining rates of unionization and standards of living, and heightened levels of insecurity. For many workers the changing terrain of work has clearly been a downhill slide.

ENDNOTES

1. Walmart's record of moving into a community and contributing to bankruptcies among small local businesses is so well-known and widespread that it has been satirized in videos and television programs, such as *South Park,* among others.

2. Interestingly, even where companies are required by law to recognize and "live with" unions, Walmart attempts to ignore the rules. In Germany, for example, Walmart repeatedly clashed with the system of co-determination whereby unions are given a say in matters affecting working conditions (Ewing, 2005). Perhaps not surprisingly, given Walmart's flagrant disregard for the system of labour relations in Germany and ignorance of local customs, the retail giant failed there. Among its blunders in Germany were its use of "American-style" management techniques, its insistence on video surveillance of workers, its threats of store closures, and its clashes with trade unions (Schaefer, 2006).

3. In 2005 when Walmart workers in Jonquiere, Quebec, certified the United Food and Commercial Workers (UFCW) to represent them, Walmart closed the store, citing financial reasons for their decision, putting 190 workers out of work. Jonquiere represented the first successful union drive at a Walmart in North America and the company argues that it did not close the store simply to crush the union.

4. In the fall of 2009 by a majority decision the Supreme Court of Canada ruled that when a business is closed in Quebec in order to avoid a union, under Section 15 of the Quebec *Labour Code* the employees who were dismissed cannot seek reinstatement. In addition, the Court also held that Section 17 of the *Code,* which assumes that the dismissal of employees involved in unionizing drives is an anti-union reprisal unless the employer provides sufficient reason, does not apply in this case. Rather, the Court ruled that

closing the store in itself is "good and sufficient reason" for the dismissal (Lancaster House, 2009).

5. Recently Benetton has considered putting Radio Frequency ID Chips (as big as a grain of sand) in their clothing in order to track inventory. Since these chips remain active after purchases are made, consumer activists have called for a boycott of Benetton's goods, arguing that such technology is an invasion of privacy. (See http://www.boycottbenetton.com/PR_030407.html.)

6. The exceptions were Alberta where manufacturing wages increased on average by 9 percent and British Columbia where they dropped by 3 percent.

7. In Ontario and British Columbia about 10 percent of manufacturing jobs paid less than $10 per hour, reflecting little change between 1997 and 1998 and 2006 and 2007 (Morissette, 2008, p. 19).

8. Here the exception is Alberta where there was a 12-percent decline in low-wage employment during the same period.

Neoliberalism, Families, and Work–Life Balance[1]

Kate Bezanson

DISCUSSION QUESTIONS

1. What are the main problems with the neoliberal market model as it was applied in Canada?

2. How does Jade's story reveal the tensions families face putting together a living in a neoliberal period?

3. To what extent do you think that the dominant economic model can be forced to change given the current financial crisis? Can neoliberalism be confronted and changed?

INTRODUCTION: A WILE E. COYOTE FALL

In the late summer of 2008, classes were resuming and a federal election was in full swing. Canada seemed poised to continue its decade-long pattern of economic growth, high employment and a general mood of prosperity. The crisp autumn air would bring more than a change in seasonal climate: the overheated Canadian economy was about to feel a chill like none experienced since the Great Depression of the 1930s. As the realities of the global economic crisis began to sink in, the scaffolding that had held together the expansion of the 1990s and 2000s was exposed and was found to be weak and built on unstable ground. This scaffolding was a neoliberal market logic. Like Wile E. Coyote suspended in mid air with his legs still running before realizing his predicament and dropping like a stone, the contradictions and problems with **neoliberalism** reached an inevitable crash in the fall of 2008.

The consequences are deep and far-reaching. This chapter asks some fundamental questions about the economic crisis and its implications for work and families in Canada. It argues that the protections that might have shielded families and workers from the worst effects of this crisis were dismantled in the "Road Runner" capitalism years leading up to the fall of 2008.

The chapter proceeds in five stages. First, it explores what has happened in Canada since the crash of 2008. Second, it explains neoliberalism, and how the logic of this kind of economic model left workers and families on shaky ground. Third, it considers social supports in the Canadian welfare state and argues that *before* the crisis of 2008, there were few supports to balance work and family and to offset income insecurity or shortfalls. Fourth, it profiles one family's story from a longitudinal case study of 49 families in Ontario who are balancing significant work and caregiving responsibilities. Lastly, the chapter concludes with a discussion of the future of work and family. It suggests that far from learning from the errors of neoliberal market rule, we have entered into a new era of "strategic" neoliberalism, intensifying the existing problems families face.

THE STORMY PRESENT: WHAT HAPPENED IN THE FALL OF 2008?

In late September 2008, two headlines stood side by side and could not have been more at odds with one another. On the cover of the *Globe and Mail* (Scoffield, 2008, p. A1) was a photo of an oil rig in full production, with the caption: "Canadian Economy Booms in July." Directly underneath was the headline "Bush Urges Congress to Support Bailout" (Feller, 2008), with text describing the collapse of major financial institutions such as banks and insurance companies. In the United States and Europe, panicked discussions about economic bailouts by governments were underway. The doldrums between the sunny past and the stormy present were short-lived. For several months Canadians felt somewhat insulated from the effects of the meltdown in financial markets, mostly due to the more stringent regulatory environment in Canadian banks. Prime Minister Harper showed little concern in the early days of the economic meltdown when he stated during an election interview with the Canadian Broadcasting Corporation's flagship news program *The National* that "there are probably some great [stock] buying opportunities out there" (CBC Television, 2008). But by January 2009, layoffs were almost daily announcements and Ontario was particularly hard-hit as the meltdown in the U.S. auto sector travelled north. There were 387,000 full-time jobs lost in the seven months after the initial crash (Yalnizan, 2009, p. 4). By the new year of 2009, there was no doubt that the effects of the economic recession were going to be devastating for Canada. This was underlined by the Harper

Conservatives almost losing their minority government over their handling of the economic situation. In spite of the mounting evidence of Canada's economic vulnerability, in their fall 2008 economic update, there was no response to the global crisis to stem the tide of job loss and support industry, as other countries were doing. Almost overnight in the fall of 2008, banks in the United Kingdom and the United States were virtually nationalized and stimulus packages planned—by governments who days before would have laughed at the idea of deficit spending. In Canada, the opposition parties were so alarmed by the total lack of response on the part of the minority Conservatives that just weeks after an election, the government looked poised to fall over the issue of the handling of the economy. The opposition parties formed a coalition and called on the Governor General to recognize such a coalition in place of the Harper Conservatives. Rather than face the opposition, within weeks of the House of Commons resuming post-election, Prime Minister Harper asked the Governor General to suspend parliament. When the House returned in January 2009, Prime Minister Harper introduced a new budget, heavy on spending and more in line with the kind of responses governments of wealthy nations took around the world to attempt to remedy the crisis.

At the heart of this crisis was an under-regulated credit market that treated debt as assets. This played out most dramatically in the subprime mortgage market where the artificially inflated prices of homes allowed owners to access large amounts of credit (for a useful, easy to read review of the crisis, see http://www.economicshelp.org). It is hard for most of us to understand how bad mortgages in the U.S. could lead to a global economic meltdown. The organization of these mortgages and the more general level of credit offered by mortgage companies can be thought of as an elaborate house of cards. Once one or two cards at the bottom of the house became dislodged, it was not long before the building itself began to tumble. The house was built over a long period of time, but the biggest building boom happened in the early 2000s, after September 11, 2001 and the crash of Internet stocks. The U.S. economy, among others, faced the prospect of a recession (Canada also faced confirmed mad-cow cases beginning in 2003 along with Severe Acute Respiratory Syndrome in the same year), so interest rates were dropped dramatically. When interest rates drop, it is much cheaper to borrow money and to buy or refinance houses. More people bought houses and housing prices started to go up. Banks eased their lending policies. People with poor credit histories were able to get mortgages much more easily. People were able to leverage their homes to either purchase property or other goods, so they had huge debts. People were also given mortgages with great rates for the first one or two years. Counting on the continued appreciation of value in homes, financial institutions continued to buy up unsecured debt.

When interest rates rose in 2006, many people were not able to meet their payments. New home construction continued while house prices started to drop and so the value of houses fell, although they were still mortgaged for more money than they were now worth and banks could not recoup the loans by selling the houses (*Guardian Weekly*, 2008; *New York Times*, 2009).

If we move up from the houses that are at the bottom of the proverbial house of cards, we find that reckless mortgage companies were backed by banks and other financial institutions. Big financial institutions like Bear Sterns, Morgan Stanley, AIG (an insurance company), and Lehman Brothers owned a lot of the bad debt. The U.S. Federal Reserve bailed out AIG in September 2008 to the tune of $85 billion but stock prices fell dramatically nonetheless (*New York Times*, 2009, p. 2). Banks could no longer lend money to one another as they normally did, and they began to sell off assets, making the problem worse. Confidence in the economy plummeted. Governments tried to buy up bad assets to get the financial system moving again. The U.S. government proposed a $700-billion plan to buy "toxic assets" from the affected banks (*New York Times*, 2009, p. 2). The toxicity spread across the globe, trade dropped, and the credit crisis decimated economies, notably those of Iceland and various Eastern European countries. According to an International Monetary Fund Estimate in April 2009, "writedowns of bad financial assets could reach $4 trillion worldwide, with two thirds of this incurred by banks" (IMF, 2009, p. xi). To illustrate what this number represents, consider that Canada's GDP for 2007 was just over 1.3 trillion (World Bank, 2009). In April 2009, at a meeting of the Group of 20 (G20) in London, leaders pledged $1.1 trillion to tackle the global financial crisis.[2] The public, contra the logic of the market rationally spreading risk and reward, is the backer of last resort for irresponsible financial practices and policies, the rebuilder of the house of cards.

There is much debate about what to do, what this means for workers, for families, and for entire sectors of the Canadian economy. What is clear that the causes—which were not new nor were they unforeseeable—lay not only in the lack of regulation of financial capital but also in the widespread and widely accepted idea that markets would sort themselves out and that intervention meant interference. At the heart of the crisis is the question of neoliberalism.

WHAT IS NEOLIBERALISM?

As with understanding the house of cards built on risky credit, it is hard for most of us to understand how an economic and political *theory* can be the chief cause of massive job losses and the collapse of major banks and companies worldwide. Theory applied to practice—praxis—is powerful. Its power can be seen when praxis leads to a sense that there is no alternative to neolib-eralism, and when the key ideas of neoliberalism come to be accepted by gov-ernments and citizens from across the political spectrum as common sense or **hegemonic**. Everyday experiences of neoliberal theory are not abstract, although trying to understand the big picture of the historical, economic, and political forces at play can seem daunting.

There is a lot of debate about how to define neoliberalism. Some argue that it is the catchphrase that has replaced globalization in discussions about economic policies, ideologies, and practices in the new millennium (Clarke, 2008). Others use it to refer more precisely to policies associated with organi-zations like the World Bank and International Monetary Fund that favour export-led growth and deep cuts in government spending (Stiglitz, 2008). Some (see Peck & Theodore, 2007) speak of it as an uneven and incomplete process—as neoliberalization rather than neoliberalism—to reflect its adapt-ability and variety. For our purposes here, we can talk about neoliberalism as an approach that elevates the free market and advocates individualism and individual rights over any collectivism or group rights.

The kind of neoliberalism that we must grapple with in trying to under-stand how we got to our stormy present is one rooted in the ideas of scholars like von Hayek and later Friedman and the Chicago School (see Braedley & Luxton, 2010; Connell, 2010). These thinkers, whose ideas were initially experimented with and in some cases brutally imposed on Latin America and later all over the world, were deeply opposed to government intervention in the economy in ways that they argued constrained choice and trade. They were anti-regulation in the sense that they argued that constraints on markets crippled and distorted them. The kinds of regulations now being developed in response to the current crisis, like banking and credit oversight, are seen by neoliberals as abhorrent, and even socialist. Nice catchphrases like "free mar-kets create free people" (see for example, Lott, 2007) linked the neoliberal approach with democracy. Those who argued that markets were *not* self regu-lating and that these markets often destroyed workers, communities, and cul-tures were positioned as somehow against freedom and democracy.

What made neoliberalism such a risky approach, leading to such chaos? Neoliberalism is about re-regulation, not de-regulation or self-regulation. What I mean here is that certain regulations—keeping wages low and making work more insecure, or making it easy to move capital out of countries—are very much a part of the project, but regulating *how* capital moves and how credit systems are overseen is interventionist because it is viewed as constraining to the goal of capital accumulation. Neoliberalism is imposed by crisis and by force. It is opportunistic. It is in no way linked to democracy or freedom. The basic neoliberal approach proceeded as follows through much of the 1980s, 1990s, and 2000s. A nation, say an African or a Latin American one, suffered an economic recession or crisis (there were many throughout this period). An international agency—usually the International Monetary Fund—would come in with loans, tied to conditions. These conditions were neoliberalism in action because they hemmed the choices available to governments and created markets that usually did not serve the needs or interests of the country receiving the loans. The conditions included cutting social spending (reducing government and social services), reducing regulations on industry and trade (reducing particular kinds of regulation), usually focusing on export-led growth (so selling products on the world market, often of crops or other goods that might otherwise be used to feed people or at least diversify the economy), and generally disfavouring policies and practices that were social investments aside from infrastructure like roads for business purposes. **Privatization**—not collective ownership—was the mantra, so water, hydro, even education came to be delivered by for-profits as ways to put short-term cash into government coffers. The logic of neoliberalism spread with a consensus emerging that free trade was good, and that the kinds of shocks and adjustments to neoliberal policies would even out and create better lives for most people. This is the house of cards, built on a greed-is-good model of capitalism.[3]

WHAT HAS HAPPENED TO THE WELFARE STATE? HOW WERE WE FARING BEFORE THE CRISIS?

In Canada, in the 1990s in particular, the logic of neoliberalism was embraced as the federal and provincial governments faced a recession and began to privatize industries, cut social spending, and change labour laws. As McBride (2006, p. 260) aptly notes, for neoliberalism "the chief impediment to the free operation of markets is the state, and a number of measures have been advanced to reduce its role." Government transfers and entitlements were cut over the 1990s and 2000s: family allowances were eliminated, Employment Insurance was made significantly less accessible and worth less money, transfers to provinces for housing, welfare, health and education were altered significantly and supports, such as training, were reduced (see Rice & Prince, 2000). There were some positive developments, such as the creation and expansion of the Canada Child Tax Benefit (Battle, 2006, 2008), but there was virtually no sustained movement on childcare and early learning (see Mahon, 2006). All of these elements—the fabric of the Canadian welfare state—matter enormously in buffering people against the unpredictability of capitalist crises and matter because they express a collective desire to share the risks and thus the costs of getting sick, being poor, or losing a job. This fabric was shredded by the logic of greed-is-good neoliberalism and a shared social solidarity or sense of bringing up the floor was trampled. Political economist David Harvey (2006, pp. 154-56) contends that neoliberal states like Canada transfer resources from those with less money to those with more money through means such as privatization, cutbacks in supports for things like social wages, and by changing tax codes and investment structures. "The state," he argues, "once transformed into a neoliberal set of institutions, becomes a prime agent of redistributive policies, reversing the flow from the upper to the lower classes that had occurred during the era of social democratic hegemony." (2006, p. 155).

In people's work lives, a neoliberal logic also played out. We now live in what one sociologist called a "political economy of insecurity" (Beck, 2000). The labour market of the 2000s is very different than the one of the 1970s and 1980s. Non-standard work, a term referring to work that does not match the post–World War II norm of a 40 hour per week full-time, full-year job, became increasingly normative (see DiCaro, Johnston, & Stanford, this volume; Vosko, 2009). Beaujot (2000, p. 129) asserts that by the mid 1990s, "only one-third of workers ha[d] what might be considered to be a typical pattern of one job, 35-48 hours per week, Monday to Friday during the day, working on a permanent basis for an employer at one place of work." The labour market in Canada since the 1990s has been characterized by significant increases in **multiple job holding** and in part-time, temporary, casual/on-call, and self employment (Vosko, 2009). In its important review of labour law, the Law Commission of Canada (2004:5) reflected on the problems with the rise of **non-standard work**:

> Among the problems associated with non-standard work are the following: poor pay, little job security, a lack of access to important statutory benefits and protections (such as Employment Insurance, employment standards protections, workers' compensation, the right to collective bargaining) and a lack of access to employer provided benefits such as dental, life and disability insurance.

As governments weakened labour market protections and supports making work lives more precarious, and as globalization altered the kinds of jobs and sectors in which people in Canada worked (increasing especially the service sector), the conditions under which most families were able to put together a living became more challenging. Moreover, women entered the labour market in record numbers, with 73 percent of all "women with children less than age 16 living at home ... part of the employed workforce" (Statistics Canada, 2007, p. 7) in 2006. There remain huge inequalities in the labour market, and many of these have intensified during this period of neoliberal restructuring. Women and people of colour in particular are concentrated in low wage, insecure, and often part-time work (Galabuzzi, 2006; Statistics Canada, 2007).

In Canada in the 2000s, a two earner model is the norm. In 2008, 68 percent of couples were dual-earners in Canada (Marshall, 2009, p. 12). Yet while men and women are called into the labour market in order to meet their household income needs, the distribution of caregiving is not at all equal. **A dual earner-female career model** prevails (see Bezanson, 2006). What is particularly striking about this arrangement is that Canada has an abysmal record of investment in early childhood education and care (see OECD, 2006, for example). To illustrate, in 2004, for every 100 Canadian children requiring daycare, there were spaces for 12 in Canada (CCSD, 2009). In terms of early childhood services, Canada ties with Ireland for last place among economically advanced countries (see Table 4.1). Further, the combined effects of the gutting of social welfare supports like Employment Insurance and the neoliberal push to get more people working and in more flexible arrangements have meant that work–life conflicts are especially high for women. Economic insecurity was already widespread even in a booming pre-2008 economy. The logic of the kind of neoliberal restructuring of work and the welfare state meant that more work was shifted onto families, and usually onto women's labour within them. When services, like home care for the ill, were downloaded to lower levels of government or cut entirely, the need for the care did not disappear, but it was absorbed usually by women's unpaid work. As British economist Diane Elson (1998) has argued, this assumes that women's unpaid labour is infinitely elastic and can expand to meet needs given various states of social investment. The result is not simply much greater stress, anxiety, and imbalance in people's lives, but also a marked deterioration in the most important relationships in people's lives (see Bezanson, 2006; Luxton, 2006). Relying on loved ones for care can strain key relationships. Some carework simply does not get done, and the consequences are dire. The processes of neoliberalism as they unfolded in Canada in the 1990 and 2000s, then, left many families in a precarious and stressed position before the market crash.

TABLE 4.1

EARLY CHILDHOOD SERVICES AMONG ECONOMICALLY ADVANCED COUNTRIES (2008)

Benchmark	Number of benchmarks achieved	1 Parental leave of 1 year at 50% of salary	2 A national plan with priority for disadvantaged children	3 Subsidized and regulated child care services for 25% of children under 3	4 Subsidized and accredited early education services for 80% of 4 year-olds	5 80% of all child care staff trained	6 50% of staff in accredited early education services tertiary educated with relevant qualification	7 Minimum staff-to-children ratio of 1:15 in pre-school education	8 1.0 % of GDP spent on early childhood services	9 Child poverty rate less than 10%	10 Near-universal outreach of essential child health services
SWEDEN	10	✓	✓	✓	✓	✓	✓	✓	✓	✓	✓
ICELAND	9		✓	✓	✓	✓	✓	✓	✓	✓	✓
DENMARK	8	✓	✓	✓	✓		✓	✓	✓	✓	
FINLAND	8	✓	✓	✓		✓		✓	✓	✓	✓
FRANCE	8	✓	✓	✓	✓	✓	✓		✓	✓	
NORWAY	8	✓	✓	✓	✓			✓	✓	✓	✓
BELGIUM (FLANDERS)	6		✓	✓	✓		✓			✓	✓
HUNGARY	6		✓		✓	✓	✓	✓		✓	
NEW ZEALAND	6		✓	✓	✓	✓	✓	✓			
SLOVENIA	6	✓	✓	✓		✓	✓				✓
AUSTRIA	5		✓		✓	✓		✓		✓	
NETHERLANDS	5		✓	✓		✓	✓	✓			
UNITED KINGDOM*	5		✓	✓	✓	✓	✓				
GERMANY	4		✓		✓		✓	✓			
ITALY	4		✓		✓		✓				✓
JAPAN	4		✓		✓	✓					✓
PORTUGAL	4		✓		✓	✓	✓				
REPUBLIC OF KOREA	4		✓			✓	✓				✓
MEXICO	3		✓			✓	✓				
SPAIN	3			✓		✓	✓				
SWITZERLAND	3						✓		✓	✓	
UNITED STATES	3			✓			✓		✓		
AUSTRALIA	2			✓			✓				
CANADA	1						✓				
IRELAND	1						✓				
Total benchmarks met	126	6	19	13	15	17	20	12	6	10	8

*Data for the United Kingdom refer to England only.

Source: Adapted from Figure 1 in "The Child Care Transition," *Innocenti Report Card 8*, 2008, UNICEF Innocenti Research Centre, Florence.

CASE STUDY: PUTTING TOGETHER A LIVING AND BALANCING SIGNIFICANT CARE RESPONSIBILITIES

In 2006, along with a team of researchers, I began interviewing people with significant paid work responsibilities and significant caregiving responsibilities. The study, called "Ensuring Social Reproduction," aimed to uncover the gaps and tension in social and labour market policies and how these played out in people's day-to-day lives. Using a snowball sampling technique, we selected participants who lived in 49 households from a range of income backgrounds, household structures, geographic locations, ethnic/cultural origins, and caregiving types. We oversampled people with children under age six, creating a subcategory of women who were pregnant so that we could track them as they made decisions about parental leaves and childcare. We also interviewed people who were providing significant elder care. We did not include those caring for a dependant with a disability. We asked all members of the household to participate in the interviews if possible so that we could get a robust picture of a typical day, work lives and schedules, and how people reflected on their work–life balance. In most cases, where there were two adult members, only one (usually a woman) participated in both rounds of interviews. The interviews took place on average 12–18 months apart. Interviews were recorded, transcribed and coded.

Participants were selected from four locations in Ontario—17 households lived in the Niagara region, 18 in the Greater Toronto Area (GTA), 13 were in central-north Ontario and one was from eastern Ontario. We made efforts to include rural as well as urban households in our sample. We categorized the interviews conducted with the members of 49 households into three areas—30 had significant childcare responsibilities, 16 had significant elder care responsibilities, and three had both significant child and elder care responsibilities. The structure of the households also varied. As Table 4.2 shows, most lived in common law relationships or were married. Income spreads among the participating household members ranged from very low income to very high income. Table 4.3 shows the income distribution for the 49 households for 2006. As a point of comparison, for Canada for 2006, average income after tax for families was $67,500 (Statistics Canada, 2009).[4] In our study, when those households with elder care responsibilities, who tend to be comprised of older participants with more years of labour market experience, are removed, the number of participating households below and marginally above the Statistics Canada Low Income Cut Off rises to almost 50 percent.

TABLE 4.2
HOUSEHOLD STRUCTURE (2006)

HOUSEHOLD STRUCTURE*	NUMBER OF HOUSEHOLDS	PERCENTAGE
COMMON LAW/MARRIED	34	69.39
SINGLE PARENT	4	8.16
MULTIGENERATIONAL	9	18.37
OTHER	2	4.08

* We followed Statistics Canada definition of economic family in determining household
categories, with several deviations based on how people identified the composition of
their households and the pooling of resources.

TABLE 4.3
HOUSEHOLD INCOME (2006)

INCOME RANGE	NUMBER OF HOUSEHOLDS	PERCENTAGE
BELOW LICO*	9	18.37
MARGINALLY ABOVE LICO (WITHIN $5,000 PER ANNUM)	5	10.20
MIDDLE INCOME (> $5,000 ABOVE LICO TO $100,000 TAKING INTO ACCOUNT COMMUNITY AND HOUSEHOLD SIZE)	25	51.02
HIGH INCOME (>$100,000)	10	10.41

* LICOs are Low Income Cut Offs. We used 2006 Statistics Canada LICOs, which take into
account community size and household size to determine low income.

We also asked people to *self report* their cultural or ethnic heritage. Table 4.4
shows the heritage of the primary respondents. Where there was more than
one primary respondent in the household, both are reported, thus totalling
more than 49 responses.

The collection of stories reveals a mixed and layered picture of love and
devotion to children, parents, or friends alongside stress, sleeplessness, and
worry. They depict the kinds of crises, particularly around finding and keeping
good childcare, that can make or break paid work decisions and options. They
also reveal that control over paid work and worktime is a crucial element for

ETHNIC/CULTURAL HERITAGE, PRIMARY RESPONDENTS

ETHNIC/CULTURAL HERITAGE	NUMBER
EASTERN EUROPEAN	3
EASTERN EUROPEAN/JEWISH	1
FIRST NATIONS	2
FIRST NATIONS/IRISH/SCOTTISH	3
FIRST NATIONS/FRENCH	1
JEWISH	2
ANGLICAN	1
AFRICAN	1
BLACK/CARIBBEAN/ENGLISH	1
CAUCASIAN	3
SOUTHERN EUROPEAN	2
NORTHERN EUROPEAN	13
SOUTH EAST ASIA AND CHINA	3
FRENCH CANADIAN	3
CANADIAN	7
OTHER	1
NO ANSWER	3

women in particular in order to meet caregiving roles. Social supports, especially extended kin providing assistance with unpaid work, were very significant in managing multiple roles. For the purposes of this chapter, and to illustrate how families were faring in the lead-up to our stormy present, one household's story is profiled below. Jade and her family give a glimpse into putting together a living in the Niagara region of Ontario while on maternity leave and subsequently, while re-entering the labour market with a small child in need of care, two school aged children, and two careers. It shows how the need for childcare determines worklife and consequently, income and divisions of labour. None of the adults in this household have significant job security nor do they have much control over their work hours or conditions of work.

Jade

In 2006 when we first met, Jade, a white woman who describes her ethnic origin as "Canadian," was living with her husband, two sons (7 and 9 years of age), and infant daughter.

Jade was on maternity leave from a permanent, full-time retail position. Jade had an arrangement with her employer in which she worked part-time while on maternity leave to, as she put it, "bank hours" because she anticipated that she would need days off to care for sick children and go to appointments when she returned to work. She began banking hours when her daughter was four weeks old. Her job had no benefits and she did not get paid for sick days. Her husband also worked in the service sector full-time, 40 to 60 hours per week. He had no dental or health benefits associated with his job and Jade said that his job was not terribly secure. Their combined household income for a family of five was about $60,000 for 2006. Jade had enough paid work hours to qualify for Employment Insurance (EI) while on maternity leave. EI covers 55 percent of earnings up to a maximum of a little over $400 per week. For Jade, this meant that for her year of leave, she received about $10,000. She decided to take the leave herself instead of sharing it with her spouse because she considered her job to be more secure and because her husband earned more money. While on leave, she worried and tried to plan about what she would do for childcare when she returned to work full-time.

> ... Just for (the baby), the only person I know is like thirty bucks a day, and that's a lot. My pay cheque is only ... under four hundred dollars a week ... I'm gonna do about half of it in child care. Just over a hundred and fifty a week, just for her, and then there will be something for the boys for after school care.

The year she gave birth to her daughter, the Harper government was elected. They eliminated the proposed national system of childcare and replaced it with a *taxable* monthly cheque worth $100 per child under six. Jade said the money—after taxes about $60 for her household—was handy for diapers. It could not make a dent in the cost of childcare nor was it sufficient to allow her not to work for pay.

By the second interview in 2007, Jade had changed jobs. Her employer, for whom she had been banking hours, did not have a full-time position for her because the business was not doing well. She took a position that paid a bit more and had benefits in another company, and had daytime hours that more easily accommodated childcare, but had less flexibility in terms of taking sick days or providing other kinds of care. She continued to work on Saturdays at her previous job, extending her workweek to six days. Her spouse stopped working on Saturdays to provide childcare, but often worked 12 hours days until 8 p.m. to make up for lost worktime, so Jade managed pick-ups, sports, homework, meal preparation, and bedtime. Getting childcare for her one year old was very hard, as most centres don't have spaces for children under 18 months of age, despite the fact that maternity leave eligibility is 12 months. When she did find a space for her daughter with a home-based provider, she lamented that her prediction about the cost of childcare was accurate: "Half of my paycheque every week … goes to childcare," she said. On days when her daughter was sick, she had to pay for daycare her daughter was not attending *and* hire a sitter to care for her daughter, thus negating her entire paycheque for the day. She reflected that despite this, she needed to work. During her maternity leave, she told us that:

> I had to borrow money from my aunt because our gas was disconnected. Twice. Which was hard … Christmas was stressful until we had the flood … that helped actually … because a lot of the things that we got paid [from the insurance company], like that got damaged, we didn't replace. [Borrowing money was] embarrassing. Stressful. Hard. Very hard. Because my income wasn't a lot to begin with, so when it's cut in half, it was nothing every two weeks.

Even with two adults working full-time, they live paycheque to paycheque. Jade tells a story of her husband not getting a paycheque one night when it was expected and not being able to buy groceries.

Jade does the bulk of the household work, manages the household finances, and arranges childcare. She barters and trades household items and clothes, and worries constantly about meeting expenses. She notes that despite their total household income, she cannot pay all the bills each month so she alternates and carries household debt. She finished the last interview saying that "I wish we could be like Quebec and have … $7 a day childcare … That under an hour's worth of work, paid for me … I'd actually *make* some money, instead of just squeak(ing) by."

Discussion

Jade's family's story is a typical one for those interviewed with middle incomes in the sense that concerns about money and balancing work with caregiving are all being juggled at once. Despite their financial challenges and difficulties with childcare, however, they fare better than many middle income households and most low income households. Because self-employment has risen considerably since the 1990s in Canada, fewer Canadian women and men have insured earnings under the EI system and thus *do not qualify* for EI benefits for maternity/parental leaves. Jade has health benefits at her new place of employment, which offsets some household costs. Jade and her spouse also both have full-time hours mostly at one place of employment, though both work very long hours to make enough money to meet their family of five's needs. Their work is more *standard looking* than many Canadians' work, but it is characterized by Jade's having two jobs and her husband working 12 hour days so that she can work a six-day week. The supports that they need—quality, affordable childcare, well paid parental leaves, more flexible work arrangements—are not available to them. The legacy of neoliberal welfare restructuring and the effects of the last decade or so of changes in labour markets due to globalization have left this family without a strong net as the economy teeters.

NOT SO DIFFERENT AFTER ALL: THE FUTURE OF WORK AND FAMILY IN A NOT-SO-POST NEOLIBERAL ERA

As the economic recession drives onward, a host of proposals are forwarded to redirect its course. None, thus far, proposes real investments in people, their worklives or their caregiving roles. After decades of retrenchment and rescaling of the Canadian welfare state and increased flexibility and precariousness in the labour market, Canadians face this downturn with the lowest level of protection in at least the last century (CCPA, 2009). Recall that one of the key features leading to the crash of 2008 was record levels of household debt. This debtload compounds and makes even more intractable the economic risks families face.

There have been significant responses on the part of governments and international institutions, many hastily thrown together. At the core, however, are supports for financial institutions. The International Monetary Fund continues to respond to the economic crisis as it unfolds in developing countries with loans that are almost exactly the same as the structural adjustment policies that led to such massive debt crises throughout the developing world (Stewart, 2008). Moreover, the aim of investment is to return to an economy like the one that fell so spectacularly in 2008, by freeing up credit and getting people borrowing and buying again. Because neoliberalism thrives on crisis, the time is ripe for a new variant of what seems like a particularly versatile virus.[5] Governments in Canada are not investing in building strong public sectors, childcare programs, or even in education spending, but rather in buildings and roads. The people who will clean the buildings, teach in them, or those who will drive the buses on the roads are not part of the equation. The stimulus is stimulating male employment in the construction trades, with some obvious spill-over into other kinds of jobs that support this industry.

One of the questions that has emerged in Canada as this particular recession has taken hold has been about the future of families. Many of the job losses thus far have been in traditionally male jobs. This is especially true because so many of the jobs have been lost in sectors related to the auto sector. Some have gone so far as to call this a "he-cession" (Pelieci, 2009). Will men, some wonder, become stay at home dads, and will roles reverse? While it may be the case that some men will do this, there are several problems with this logic and the question is too optimistic given the weight of evidence on the subject. This is the first recession in which women, and especially women with children, are already in the labour force in record numbers and most households rely on two incomes (see Yalnizan, 2009). In past recessions, women often were called *into* the labour market to offset income shortfalls. Women are already in the labour market and thus this kind of buffer is reduced. It may be more likely that youth are called into the labour market in greater numbers, returning to a family model of work more characteristic of the early part of the last century. Further, the weight of evidence from economics, sociology, and anthropology indicates that during periods of economic downturn, men do not in significant numbers take on a greater share of **social reproduction** (see for example, Elson, 1995; Scott, 2008). It would appear that absent any real investment in childcare, and given that the current session of parliament has already seen the Harper Conservatives rejecting as socialist efforts to make EI more accessible, the depth of the effects of income insecurity and family stress is only beginning to become plain. Successive neoliberal governments who gutted income supports, labour regulations, failed to invest in carework, and failed to regulate risky credit markets, have left families facing a fraught future in what remains a neoliberal political economy of insecurity.

ENDNOTES

1. The author wishes to thank the Social Sciences and Humanities Research Council for funding the research (grant number 410-2004-1786) reported on in the fourth section of this chapter. I also wish to thank Renee McKinley, for her assistance with data analysis.

2. According to its website, the "Group of Twenty (G20) Finance Ministers and Central Bank Governors was established in 1999 to bring together systemically important industrialized and developing economies to discuss key issues in

the global economy." Canada is one among the 20 nations in the group. See http://www.g20.org/about_what_is_g20.aspx

3. In 2008, Australian Prime Minister Kevin Rudd said, referencing a 1980s film about a Wall-Street investment banker named Gekko: "It is perhaps time now to admit that we did not learn the full lessons of the greed-is-good ideology. And today we are still cleaning up the mess of the 21st-century children of Gordon Gekko" (Rudd, 2008, retrieved from http://www.theaustralian.news.com.au/story/0,25197,24450662-7583,00.html).

4. As with LICOs, this number refers to economic families as defined by Statistics Canada. Average income after tax refers to total income, including government transfers, minus income tax (Statistics Canada, 2009).

5. As Klein (2007) and others (see for example, Harvey, 2005 and Peck & Theodore, 2007) have powerfully illustrated, the adaptability and opportunism of the mechanisms inherent in a neoliberal market logic make it particularly able to dramatically alter regulations pertaining to ownership, working conditions and protections, and wages in contexts of crisis. Klein uses the examples of massive privatization post Hurricane Katrina in the United States and of the selling off of industry and financial systems in Iraq as part of the U.S. occupation strategy to map how expediently neoliberalism approaches crises.

WORKING THE MARGINS

Jim West/Alamy/GetStock.com

5

Trapped in the Shadows: The Working Lives of Invisible Minorities

Gerald Hunt

DISCUSSION QUESTIONS

1. What are some of the positive consequences of disclosing an invisible stigma?

2. How might a workplace determine the level of stereotyping that is occurring?

3. Think of some aspect of yourself that you have not revealed at work. Why? Does it matter?

4. Given the fact there are a wide range of human rights protections in Canada, why would some people still feel it would disadvantage them to reveal a hidden identity in the workplace?

5. Return to the four stories outlined at the beginning of the chapter. What advice would you have for the person in each story?

BOX 5.1

FOUR STORIES

Charles was a well-liked and respected member of the middle management team, as department head in Accounting. A few people he worked with knew he was gay, and some suspected that he was gay, but they also knew that he did not wish to have this part of his life made public, especially to upper management, since he feared it would prevent him from being promoted. Only a very few people knew that Charles had been living with another man for nearly a decade. When his domestic partner died suddenly of a brain aneurysm, he opted not to reveal his "secret" and booked a "fictitious vacation" to deal with the funeral. A couple of people did know the truth, and they felt very awkward about having to perpetuate a lie, but felt they could not betray his confidence by telling others. They knew that many people in the organization would want to offer support and express their condolences if they had been made aware of what happened. At about the same time, a senior executive's wife was killed in a tragic car accident and the entire organization closed down for half a day to allow people to attend the funeral and pay their respects.

Marla, a 55 year old woman, does not like anyone to know that she recently became completely deaf in one ear, and was left with only about a third capacity in the other ear, following a severe ear infection. She feels that revealing her hearing loss might mean she would be thought "old" or "disabled" and by-passed for important assignments and projects. On several occasions she has pretended she has heard something but has not, resulting in serious and costly mistakes.

Alwana quickly removes her head scarf each day as she pulls into the company's parking lot. She got the job a week after the 9/11 terrorist attacks, and felt it would be best not to wear anything that would identify her as a Muslim. Her husband is unaware that she is removing her head scarf at work, and would be very annoyed if he found out. She has overheard anti-Muslim remarks since joining the company but has not responded lest she "out" herself.

John has had chronic irritable bowel syndrome for a decade. Most of the time he has it under control and it rarely interferes with his work. He estimates he might take one sick day a year to accommodate flare-ups. No one at work knows he has this medical condition, and he wants to keep it that way.

INTRODUCTION

The above stories are based on true situations, and serve to illustrate some the scenarios that might take place when a person opts not to disclose a characteristic that is hidden or "*invisible*" to others.[1] In the first case, Charles was unable to access support and sympathy from others when his same-sex partner died suddenly because he had chosen to keep this aspect of his life private. He had also put himself in a position of misrepresenting or falsifying important aspects of his life, and forcing others to pretend they did not know the truth. Marla feared a recent change in her hearing would have negative career consequences and created a fiction that resulted in serious mistakes for the workplace. Alwana opted not to reveal her religion at work, putting her in the very upsetting position of hearing negative comments about Muslims, not to mention the potential problems she might face at home if her secret became known. John, on the other hand, manages his long-term medical condition quite well and does not want his co-workers to know about it. And, we might ask: why should they?

This chapter considers some of the problems, dilemmas, and concerns that emerge relative to invisible differences in the workplace. In the chapter,

I begin by considering the various types of invisible differences people may bring to the workplace. I then assess the reasons why people may or may not opt to reveal these differences, and the consequences this can have for both the workplace and the individual. In conclusion, I consider some of the actions organizational leaders might take to be more welcoming to all workers.

The chapter takes as its starting point that people have a right to choose what they reveal or disclose to others, including their employers and co-workers. Both in law and social codes, people *do* have a right to privacy and protection from discrimination. Legislation in Canada forbids most differences (visible and invisible) from being a cause for discrimination. Cultural norms in Canadian society reinforce the idea of differentiating between public and private domains, and most Canadians would agree that others have a right to keep certain aspects and characteristics hidden if they wish to do so. Within this framework, some people guard their personal lives very carefully; other people feel completely comfortable with others knowing a great deal about them. By the same token, some workplaces welcome and embrace difference and diversity, and offer considerable freedom and latitude for workers to be open; other workplaces make it clear in all kinds of overt and subtle ways that it would be best to blend-in with a dominant framework of what is considered "normal" or acceptable. The important turning point relative to the workplace, however, is when individuals, co-workers, or the organization itself, are put at risk or disadvantaged because of possible misinformation, lies, falsehoods, or fabrications. Equally important, is the reverse. Some people fear the consequences of being exposed as different, and with good reason. If an individual is likely to be put at risk or disadvantaged because they reveal a hidden aspect such as being gay, belonging to a particular religion, or having a disability, there is also a serious problem. Consequently, when thinking about invisible human factors in the workplace, it is important to think about the balance between public and private life, safety and risk factors for the individual and the organization, personality and individual differences, as well as the legal framework and organizational climate or culture.

WHAT IS THE SCALE OR SIZE OF INVISIBILITY FACTORS?

There is a large range of human difference that can remain hidden until a person opts to reveal or disclose this dimension to others. Factors related to sexuality, religion, ethnicity, race, national origin, as well as marital relationship or family status, along with illness and disability, can be aspects of a person that might be invisible. Therefore these characteristics require some sort of revelation, disclosure, or declaration, before they are known. In other words, we all have some factors by which we are visible, such as sex, race, sexual orientation, physical appearance, speech patterns, and a different set of characteristics that are not visible or easily detected by others. All workers bring characteristics to the workplace that are readily visible, and some that are not readily apparent.

A 2001 survey by Statistics Canada found that 3.6 million Canadians reported having activity limitations, representing a disability rate of 12.4 percent.[2] Another survey found that about 10 percent of Canadians had some form of chronic or long term illness, a figure that increases dramatically with age.[3] If we combine the figures, approximately 22 percent of Canadians have some form of disability or chronic illness. Similarly, another survey found that one in five Americans (20 percent) have some sort of disability or chronic health issue, and that at least 40 percent of these disabilities could be invisible to others (Mathews & Harrington, 2000). This would mean that close to 10 percent of disabilities and long-term illnesses could be hidden from others.

The number of gays and lesbians in society is hard to estimate because of the invisibility factor. In his pioneering work on human sexuality, Kinsey (1948) found many Americans had engaged in some form of homosexual activity. To chart this activity, Kinsey developed a scale measuring sexual orientation, from 0 to 6, where 0 was exclusively heterosexual and 6 was exclusively homosexual. He later added a rating of 7 for asexual (i.e., not sexually active). Kinsey's work suggested that about 10 percent of the adult male population rated 5 or above and were therefore predominately homosexual. Recent research, though, has found this figure to be a bit high, and studies now find that 5 to 6 percent of the population is predominately homosexual and identify exclusively as gay or lesbian. That percentage rises to as high as 13 to 15 percent when bisexual and transgendered people are included (Bagley & Tremblay, 1998). By comparison, the total visible minority Chinese population in Canada, according to the 2006 Census, is just under 5 percent, the total Black population is under 1 percent, and the number of Jewish people is around 1.2 percent.[4] The number of gays, lesbians, bisexuals, and transgendered people (**GLBT**) who remain invisible at work is unknown, but it could be as high as half of that population. John Amaeichi, for example wrote a book about his closeted life as a professional NBA player (Amaeichi & Bull, 2007). Most Jewish people opt to be open, but again, it is not known with any reliability how many remain invisible.

The prevalence of other invisible human factors is harder to track. The number of people who keep such things as their national origins, ethnicity, and religion invisible from others in the workplace is not known with any dependability, but one could imagine it to be as high as a third of the workforce. Most adults who are married or living in a committed relationship tend to be open, but a small percent opt to keep this information private when at work. A single parent may decide not to be open with his or her status. A person of mixed race may opt not to reveal his or her racial complexity. A person of one race who can pass for a member of a different race may allow this to happen. See Tables 5.1 and 5.2.

WHY WOULD PEOPLE OPT TO LET A CHARACTERISTIC REMAIN INVISIBLE?

Even when we account for individual differences—some people are just more private than others—the overwhelming reason people choose not to reveal an **invisible characteristic** is because they fear being judged negatively. In other words, they fear the stereotype or **stigma** that might be attached to it, and the

TABLE 5.1

RELIGION IN CANADA: MAJOR RELIGIOUS DENOMINATIONS IN CANADA (1991 AND 2001)

2001	1991*	PERCENTAGE CHANGE 1991–2001			
		NUMBER	%	NUMBER	%
Roman Catholic	12,793,125	43.2	12,203,625	45.2	4.8
Protestant	8,654,845	29.2	9,427,675	34.9	–8.2
Christian Orthodox	479,620	1.6	387,395	1.4	23.8
Christian, not included elsewhere**	780,450	2.6	353,040	1.3	121.1
Muslim	579,640	2.0	253,265	0.9	128.9
Jewish	329,995	1.1	318,185	1.2	3.7
Buddhist	300,345	1.0	163,415	0.6	83.8
Hindu	297,200	1.0	157,015	0.6	89.3
Sikh	278,415	0.9	147,440	0.5	88.8
No religion	4,796,325	16.2	3,333,245	12.3	43.9

* For comparability purposes, 1991 data are presented according to 2001 boundaries.

** Includes persons who report "Christian," as well as those who report "Apostolic," "Born-again Christian," and "Evangelical."

Note: 2007 Census data not available.

Source: From Statistics Canada: www12.statcan.ca/english/census01/Products/Analytic/companion/rel/tables/canada/cdamajor.cfm

TABLE 5.2

RELIGION IN CANADA: PROJECTED PERCENT CHANGE IN RELIGIOUS AFFILIATION (2001–2017)

MUSLIM	145%
HINDU	92%
SIKH	72%
BUDDHIST	36%
JEWISH	10%

Source: *Canadian Diversity* 5, no. 2, Spring 2006.

negative consequences that will result if it is revealed. Dovidio et al. (2000, p. 3) characterize stigma as "a social construction that involves at least two fundamental components: (1) the recognition of difference based on some distinguishing characteristic or mark; and (2) a consequent devaluation of the person." As Beatty and Kirby (2006) note, stigmas are enduring social categorizations; they cannot simply be legislated away.

Irving Goffman, a Canadian sociologist, and one of the first to highlight the role stigma plays in creating and maintaining social boundaries, argued that stigma encompasses a reaction by others that "spoils identity" (Goffman, 1963).

Not all stigmas are created equal. Beatty and Kirby (2006, p. 34) offer a useful framework for understanding the relative intensity of stigma within a workplace context, based on the focus and context of the stigma and how others respond to it. They propose four dimensions to stigma that are particularly relevant in the case of invisible characteristics: the person's perceived responsibility for the stigma by others, the course or trajectory of the stigma over time, the perceived moral threat of the stigma, and the perceived effect of the stigma on performance. Responsibility refers to the degree to which the person has or is seen to have control over the stigma. A good example would be **HIV/AIDS**, where a person might be thought to have brought the disease upon his or herself, even though this would be a stereotype or irrational thinking. The trajectory of the stigma over time refers to how permanent, temporary, or transient the stigma is perceived to be. In other words, how likely is the person to "recover" from the stigma? An example would be a medical condition that can reasonably be expected to improve, versus a chronic condition that may get worse over time. A stigma can have a high or low degree

THE STIGMA OF MENTAL ILLNESS

In 1850 the city of Toronto proudly opened the first permanent psychiatric hospital in Canada called the Provincial Lunatic Asylum. Citizens feared the residents of the facility so much that a wall was built around the compound to make sure the patients did not escape. Since then, society's approach to mental health care has changed dramatically. Now, most people are not hospitalized and are encouraged to remain active in society and keep their jobs if at all possible. Still, the stigma associated with mental illness continues.

The Canadian Mental Health Association estimates that 1 in 5 Canadians experience a serious mental health problem at some time in their lives, and that about 10 percent of the population have mood disorders and 12 percent have anxiety disorders serious enough to warrant treatment. The Association suggests that people with mental illness face a very high degree of stigmatization in the workplace, and experience significant barriers to employment. At the same time, they note that productive work has been identified as a leading component in promoting positive mental health and in paving the way for a rich and fulfilling life in the community.

Source: http://www.cmha.ca

of moral threat, reflecting the intensity of the social-political attitudes others have about the characteristic. For instance, gays and lesbians might be perceived to constitute a high moral threat in some settings, but not in others. Finally, a stigma is more intense if it affects or is seen to affect performance-related outcomes. If a stigma is likely to mean that others must pick up the slack, or that it will interfere with the social process necessary to get work done, then its intensity increases. In other words, if one has a disability that could mean absences from work, it would be perceived as performance limiting. Similarly, if a stigma is such that people do not want to work with a particular person, productivity is at risk. Figure 5.1 illustrates and summarizes this framework.

The entire framework of stigma is negative and pejorative. As Paetzold, Dipboye, and Elsbach (2008, p. 187) point out, stigmatized individuals may be denied opportunities, and may be subject to bullying, harassment, and social rejection. They go on to suggest that a stigmatized person may even develop self-identities that become self-fulfilling prophecies by becoming the stereotype that is inherent in the stigma. Consequently, stigmatization can be personally and socially costly—no wonder people fear it, and opt not to reveal an invisible characteristic that might lead to being stigmatized. Fear of stigma and stereotyping is not the only reason people make choices about whether or

FIGURE 5.1

RELATIONSHIP BETWEEN DIMENSIONS OF STIGMA AND INTENSITY OF STIGMA

DIMENSIONS OF STIGMA

1. Perceived recovery potential (by others)

2. Perceived performance disruption potential (by others)

3. Perceived moral threat (by others)

4. Perceived individual responsibility (by others)

LOW TO HIGH

INTENSITY OF STIGMA—Low to High

Source: Beatty, J., and S. Kirby. (2006). "Beyond the Legal Environment: How Stigma Influences Invisible Identity Groups in the Workplace." *Employee Responsibilities and Rights Journal* 18(1): 29–44.

not to reveal an invisible characteristic at work, but it is a powerful restraining force for many people.

WHAT INFLUENCES WHETHER PEOPLE WILL DISCLOSE?

As I have already pointed out, the perceived intensity of the stigma associated with a hidden characteristic plays a vital role in shaping the decision to disclose, but this is not the only reason. Clair, Beatty, and Maclean (2005) have produced a very helpful model of the reasons people opt to reveal or disclose hidden characteristics in the workplace (see Figure 5.2). They suggest there are two categories of factors that affect the disclosure decision: (1) individual differences, and (2) interpersonal and organizational context.

Individuals vary in the amount of information they disclose. This reflects personality differences, propensity toward risk taking, developmental stage, and personal motives. Some individuals are more extroverted with outgoing personalities, and might not think twice about revealing a hidden characteristic. Others will avoid revealing to others if at all possible. Some people are risk-takers, while others shy away from revealing information for which the reaction might be unknown. Individuals with a sense of pride and self-confidence about an invisible

FIGURE 5.2

A CONCEPTUAL MODEL OF THE DECISION TO REVEAL INVISIBLE CHARACTERISTICS

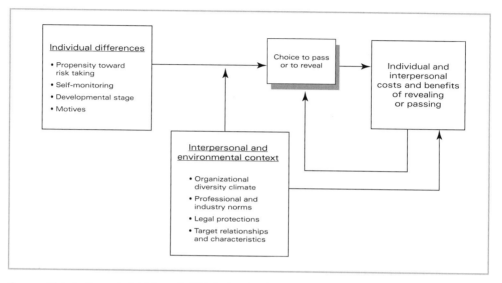

Source: Clair, J., Beatty, J. & Mclean, T. (2005). *Out of Sight But Not Out of Mind: Managing Invisible Social Identities in the Workplace*. Academy of Management Review 30 (1), 78–95.

characteristic such as a biracial background or religious affiliation would probably be more likely to make it known. People with multiple, potentially stigmatizing characteristics (visible and or invisible), may be less likely to reveal an invisible characteristic since they believe they already face enough potential bias. A person with a visible mobility disability, for instance, might be reluctant to reveal that they also have a hearing impairment, or some other characteristic they feel would stigmatize them further.

Contextual conditions that influence the decision to disclose include the organizational climate, industry norms, legal protections, and importance of the relationship (Clair, Beatty, & Maclean, 2005, p. 84). Perhaps the most important is the overall diversity and equity climate in the workplace. Organizations that place a high premium on diversity and equity, and follow through with anti-discrimination policies and practices that reinforce the value of differences are more likely to feel like a "safe" environment for a person contemplating a disclosure decision. Professional, sector, and industry norms also play a major role in shaping the disclosure decision. For example, workplaces in the construction industry or police force, or a school run by a

BOX 5.3

HIV/AIDS DISCLOSURE

An estimated 58,000 Canadian were living with HIV/AIDS at the end of 2005 compared with 50,000 at the end of 2002. An estimated 2,300 to 2,500 new HIV infections occurred in 2005 compared with 2,100 to 4,000 in 2002.

How likely is it for people with HIV/AIDS to disclose? A British study involving 79 men and 16 women being treated for HIV/AIDS, reported a mean disclosure rate of 68 percent. Self-disclosure was highest for partners and friends and lowest for family members and work colleagues. Five individuals had not disclosed their HIV status to anyone.

Sources: Public Health Agency of Canada 2007, "HIV/AIDS Update," accessed on-line at http://www.phac-aspc.gc.ca/aids-sida/publication/epi/pdf/epi2007_e.pdf; and Petrak et al., 2001, "Factors Associated with Self-Disclosure of HIV Serostatus to Significant Others," *British Journal of Health Psychology* 6, no. 1: 69–79, p. 69.

religious order, might have anti-discrimination policies in place, but have organizational cultures that create more restrictive environments. In such settings, coming out as gay or lesbian might not be welcomed, and could have negative consequences in terms of camaraderie or career success, so a person would be more likely to remain hidden. On the other hand, a workplace in the social or health services sector might have norms that project a strong positive message about the value of differences and diversity, making it easier for a person to reveal. Perhaps the best known example of this is the American military, which has an official "don't ask, don't tell" policy for gays and lesbians. The cost of breaching this code is dishonourable discharge (Herek, Jobe, & Carney, 1996). Even though gays and lesbians are legally entitled to enlist and serve in the Canadian military, social codes may in effect create a don't ask, don't tell norm.

HOW DO PEOPLE MANAGE HIDDEN IDENTITIES?

Opting to keep a hidden characteristic invisible requires some sort of management strategy. In some cases, this might be as simple as never mentioning it to someone else. For example, a person with a health condition that is under control would simply choose to keep this private (such as John, who had irritable bowel syndrome, did in the story at the beginning of the chapter). Other people might choose to keep their faith traditions private. These sorts of situations are probably common, and often have little bearing on individual or organizational well-being and performance. Many invisible characteristics, however, are of a kind that requires escalating degrees of premeditation and management to keep them from being exposed. Management of these kinds of invisible characteristics usually involves something more than simply not mentioning it, including lying, creating falsehoods and fictions, leading a double life, misrepresentation, and deceit.

There are interesting stories about how people manage hidden characteristics and identities. Some of the earliest stories come from historical literature looking at Black Americans "**passing**" as White. Conyers and Kennedy (1963, p. 215), define passing as "negroes who are accepted and identified as Negro in their home communities, who themselves accepted this identification and who at some point in their life sought to be accepted as white in some or all life roles." In a study they completed in the early 1960s, they found the top reasons people would undertake to pass were to secure equal cultural, social, recreational, and economic advantages, facilitate an interracial marriage, help hide a past life, and for the simple psychic thrill of fooling Whites. These reasons are not hard to imagine given the high level of racial intolerance in much of America at the time. One hopes that a rise in Afro-American pride since then, along with increased human rights protections, has made passing less relevant for Black Americans today.

Similarly, in a landmark study, Woods (1993) looked at the strategies gay men used to try and remain invisible or appear to be straight in corporate America. After interviewing gay surgeons, lawyers, chief executive officers, among others, he found their concealment strategies ranged from appearing to be asexual to creating complete falsehoods, including fictionalized relationships and marriages. Overall, he found the men he studied used two common strategies to manage being in the **closet.** The first was that they attempted to pass as heterosexual by projecting a heterosexual image in a variety of ways, such as taking a woman to company events and pretending they were dating or in a relationship. The second was to avoid and evade the issue through telling lies, half-truths, and censoring information.

As Clair, Beatty, and Maclean (2005) point out, fabrication, concealment, and discretion are common mechanisms for hiding, but people also use more psychologically complex ways to remain in the organizational shadows. Some people employ what is termed "impression management" to give the appearance of being something they are not, or to be in agreement with something that is contrary to what they actually believe. An example might be a teacher working in a Catholic school who was brought up as a Catholic, but who has become an atheist or nonbeliever, giving the impression that they continue to agree with the doctrine of that faith in order to avoid conflict or potential job

BOX 5.4

COVERING

Kenji Yoshino's book, *Covering: The Hidden Assault on Our Civil Rights* takes as its premise that everyone is involved in "covering" (his term for passing). By this he means that we all have some unpopular or disfavoured trait that we tend to downplay or hide completely in order to blend into the mainstream. In other words, we all experience pressure to conceal one or more aspects of ourselves because we feel it will be perceived negatively. Yoshino argues that the costs of doing this are too high. He says that even though we have laws against penalizing people for differences based on race, sex, sexual orientation, religion, and disability, we still routinely deny equal treatment to people who refuse to downplay differences along these lines. Racial minorities are pressed to "act White" by changing their names, languages, or cultural practices. Women are told to "play like men" at work. Gays and lesbians are asked not to engage in public displays of same-sex affection. The devout are instructed to minimize expressions of faith, and individuals with disabilities are urged to conceal the paraphernalia that permit them to function.

Yoshino argues that human rights law has generally ignored the threat posed by these covering norms and demands. In his book, he shows that the work of human rights will not be complete until it attends to the harms of coerced conformity.

Source: *Covering: The Hidden Assault on Our Civil Rights* by Kenji Yoshino, published by Random House (www.randomhouse.com)

loss. In other words, people may go to considerable lengths to give a sense of conformity to values and norms, but in fact hold views that might be quite the opposite.

WHAT ARE THE COSTS OF INVISIBILITY?

The actual costs of remaining invisible are hard to assess. In some cases, there is unlikely to be any harm to either the person or the workplace, but in other cases the costs might be quite high. If an individual believes that he or she cannot be his or her true self at work, it may provoke discontent and low morale, a desire to change jobs, failure to promote the organization in a positive light, and a general disconnect between what people see and who the person really is. An organization that does not embrace its workforce in all its multidimensionality is not in a position to capitalize on their unique strengths and talents, nor is it in a good position to attract potential employees who may have an unusual trait or characteristic. In other words, a workplace that is not embracing and welcoming differences is at risk of running a human capital deficit because it is insufficiently accessing the internal and external talent pool.

Some of the potential "costs" associated with invisibility would include the following:

- A person may think of changing jobs in order to locate somewhere more inclusive. In other words, an employer may not be thought of as an employer of choice

- Individuals may act out against the workplace in negative ways such as stealing or calling in sick when they are not ill

- A person may only partially invest in the organization, operate within a work-to-rule mentality, and fail to perform at a high level

- An individual may be less likely to make a commitment to the workplace

- Someone may become obsessively preoccupied with his or her invisible issue and with ways to keep it concealed

- Individuals may use time and energy to cover-up and mislead; energy that would be better used in the performance of job functions

- A worker might avoid activities where his or her status could be discovered, and as a result, turn down a promotion or special assignment

Ragins (2008) proposes a model that isolates the antecedents and consequences of disclosing invisible stigmas in work and other life domains. She argues, similar to others, that the intensity of stigmas varies, and that the decision to disclose is related to a person's internal psychology, the anticipated consequences, and the environmental support that is available. She adds to our understanding by highlighting the fact that disclosure decisions vary across work and non-work domains, and the more there is a gap the more possibility there is for a person to have identity disconnects, and have to manage their identity differently in different parts of their life. This lack of integration can lead to a variety of psychological problems and disorders, impact health, career success, and organizational performance.

DeJordy (2008) also offers an overview model of the consequences of remaining invisible, concentrating on the intra and interpersonal outcomes of passing. He suggests that passing involves a lack of self-verification, and that can easily lead to isolation, alienation, ego depletion, and what he terms "taxed information management." These factors can in turn lead to emotional exhaustion, burnout, stress, and decreased decision-making capacity. Ultimately, these stresses may lead the individual to disengage from the organization (mentally, emotionally, or physically), leading to productivity and performance issues. Of course, not all situations lead to these outcomes, but the model highlights the potentially devastating impact that passing can have on the individual, and eventually on organizational performance.

In the end, an individual must weigh the benefits of remaining in the shadows of invisibility versus costs and consequences of stepping out. Croteau et al. (2008, p. 542) rightly summarize the dilemma this way: "the risks associated with revealing include experiencing stigmatization, prejudice, and workplace discrimination. Potential benefits of revealing include feeling more authentic, establishing closer interpersonal relationships, and contributing to organizational change."

WHAT SHOULD ORGANIZATIONS DO?

So far, I have highlighted the human characteristics, traits, and identities that are invisible from others unless exposed voluntarily or by some sort of action that forces a disclosure. Unlike visible differences, a person with invisible difference must decide whether or not to reveal or disclose. I have considered some of the reasons individuals opt to keep these characteristics hidden, but the burden and costs of keeping secrets can be high for the individual and ultimately for the organization. It makes very little sense for an organization's workforce to expend energy worrying about being found out, or to maintain and perpetuate a fiction; it is far better that workers devote their talent and vigour to healthier and productive ends.

How might an organization keep the negative aspects of invisibility to a minimum, be perceived as inclusive, and assist people in being whole and integrated at work. The important point to be made is that workplaces should not aim to force everyone to reveal, since people retain the right to disclose as they see fit, but rather, remove barriers that keep people from functioning at their full potential. The underlying issue is this: when some aspect of an individual is important enough to affect their integrity and productive worklife, or requires an accommodation to ensure their dignity or safety, but it is not revealed for fear of the negative, prejudicial, or harmful outcomes that might ensue, then the organization and the individual have a problem in need of a solution.

There is a broad consensus that the best strategy is for a workplace to create what Thomas and Ely (1996) call an **"integration paradigm"** rather than an assimilation or differentiation paradigm. They characterize an assimilation paradigm as one in which employees are viewed as all the same at the core, a differentiation paradigm as one in which difference is celebrated, and an integration paradigm as one that enables employees' differences to matter. By this they mean a paradigm that not only promotes equal opportunity, but capitalizes on difference, and they suggest three strategies for achieving this:

1. Encourage open discussion of cultural, ethnic, religious backgrounds

2. Eliminate all forms of dominance by race, gender, sexual orientation, religion, etc.

3. Create a climate of trust and acceptance

   The key point is that they recommend building on differences rather than merely celebrating them. They argue that by opening the door for the unique contribution that can be made by everyone, the workplace can reasonably expect people will showcase rather than hide their differences, talents, and abilities. Obviously, if a workplace is seen to be diverse and valuing of diversity, it makes it easier for an individual to reveal a difference or hidden dimension since the consequences appear to be positive.

   The International Personnel Management Association also suggests the key is to make diversity an asset for the organization. The Association suggests that **diversity management** requires attention to the mindset and climate of the workplace in order to leverage the different perspectives and talents people bring to a workplace due to such things as race, disability, and sexuality.[5] Similarly, the Nova Scotia Public Service Commission indicates that organizations must work toward an environment of fairness, equality, mutual respect, and understanding if they are to achieve a climate that celebrates diversity. They suggest that a model workplace values diversity as a strength and strives to remove barriers that exclude or disadvantage employees, ultimately with the goal that no one is excluded from employment, promotion, and input for reasons unrelated to qualifications.[6] A benchmark organization would at the very least have the following:

- Job postings that encourage people from diverse backgrounds to apply

- Selection panels with diverse membership

- Extensive diversity training for all employees

- An employee orientation program that provides clear information about the organization's commitment to equity and diversity

- Zero tolerance of harassment and discrimination

- Appropriate accommodations for people with disabilities

- Ongoing surveys to take the pulse of the workplace on diversity issues

- Inclusive messages in newsletters and other internal publications

- Inclusive messages in announcing events to which spouses or partners will be invited
- Inclusive messages in external publications such as annual reports
- Support groups for minority groups
- Mentoring programs that account for diversity
- Exit interviews that ask questions related to experience around diversity

CONCLUSION

Workers bring a variety of invisible characteristics to the workplace, reflecting differences related to religion, sexuality, ethnicity, race, ability, and relationship status. The choice to reveal or pass in the workplace is related to a variety of factors including individual differences, organizational climate, professional or industry norms, and the anticipated consequences of disclosure. There are many reasons why a person would choose not to reveal a hidden dimension to others, but it is often because they fear the stigmatization that might be attached to the characteristic if it became known. Some people also fear that revealing a hidden dimension might hinder their organizational and career opportunities. This is often the case for people who have invisible disabilities or chronic illnesses. In some cases it makes little difference if a person keeps some personal aspect of their life private while at work, but in other situations, the consequences of concealment can be serious for the individual and the workplace. Individuals will sometimes go to great lengths to manage their "secret," often at a high psychological cost, and often with the parallel outcome of negative feelings about the workplace and job. This might be especially the case in examples such as these: someone trying to keep an illness a secret, a lesbian devoting energy to keep this

BOX 5.5

ON THE DIVERSITY BANDWAGON

For decades, IBM was considered the role model of a traditional organization. Its nickname was "Big Blue" to depict its insistence that its almost entirely male workforce wear a dark blue suit, white shirt, and dark tie. But over the years, IBM has transformed itself into an organization widely known for its diversity and equity initiatives. In the decade 1994 to 2004, IBM increased its number of female executives by 370 percent, minority executives by 233 percent, its GLBT executives by 733 percent and the number of executives with disabilities more than tripled (Thomas, 2004). As one measure of IBM's new image, it has a human resources global manager, whose entire portfolio is GLBT issues worldwide.

Most other large organizations in both the public and private sectors also have large equity and diversity programs. Xerox Canada, for instance, has a number of programs designed to build a more inclusive culture. Some of these include, balancing work–life demands; developing and valuing women's leadership attributes; developing inclusive managers; recognizing, rewarding, and promoting inclusive managers; benchmarking best practices; gender awareness; and a zero tolerance harassment policy. As a result, Xerox has been recognized as one of the "50 Best Companies to work for." Canadian banks have also moved away from the stodgy image of the past and now have departments devoted to diversity initiatives, and also sponsor a range of activities to help create a profile in diverse communities. In 2008, TD Canada Trust was a lead sponsor of Toronto's GLBT pride, and Scotia Bank was a lead sponsor for the Toronto Caribbean carnival called "Caribana."

Labour **unions** in Canada are also more and more active around diversity initiatives. The Canadian Union of Public Employees, the largest union in the country, has a number of national committees devoted to equity and diversity concerns. Among them are the Pink Triangle Committee (GLBT issues), the Women's Committee, the Committee on Racism, Discrimination, and Employment Equity, and the Persons With Disabilities National Working Group. Other unions such as the Canadian Auto Workers and the Communication, Energy, and Paperworkers' Union have taken similar steps.

Obviously all of these initiatives and programs are only as valuable as the difference they make on the ground. The real measure is whether or not organizational members feel sufficiently valued and empowered to make their maximum contribution without being weighed down by concerns about potential prejudice or stigma.

part of her identity unknown, or for someone who feels compelled to misrepresent or conceal a racial or religious background. There can also be disconnects between "hide-able" characteristics that are known in some settings but not at work. This kind of psychological fragmentation can lead to mental health problems. The cost to workplaces when workers are using energy and time to manage a hidden characteristic can be high.

Leaders can take a number of initiatives to create an environment where human diversity is seen as a strength, and make the transition out of the shadows easier. Overwhelmingly, the most important is for the organization to create a climate where difference is seen as normal. To do this, an organization must encourage and support people by providing role models, support groups, and diversity education. On top of this, recruiting and hiring strategies must target diversity in order to access the best available talent.

It should also be noted that many organizations "talk the talk" but fail to "walk the walk" when it comes to valuing diverse populations. Substantial improvements need to be made in many workplaces. In fact, many workplace gains have been "bottom-up," i.e., initiated by workers demanding/requesting accommodations, rather than by organizational leaders.

While organizations must recognize the necessity of the right to privacy, they must also recognize the costs associated with people living in the shadows. If workers invest time and energy in maintaining silence or ensuring a closet door remains closed, it will too often be at the cost of productivity and job satisfaction.

ENDNOTES

1. The names and identities of the people in these scenarios have been concealed.
2. http://www.statcan.ca/english/freepub/89-577-XIE/canada.htm, accessed August 5, 2008.
3. http://www.cureresearch.com/c/chronic/stats-country.htm, accessed August 5, 2008.
4. http://www12.statcan.ca/english/census06/data/highlights/ethnic/pages, accessed August 6, 2008.
5. http://www.ipma-aigp.ca, accessed October 27, 2008.
6. www.gov.ns.ca/psc/diversity, accessed August 15, 2008.

The Entrenchment of Racial Categories in Precarious Employment

Kiran Mirchandani, Roxana NG, Nel Coloma-Moya,
Srabani Maitra, Trudy Rawlings, Hongxia Shan,
Khaleda Siddiqui, and Bonnie L. Slade[1]

DISCUSSION QUESTIONS

1. What is meant by the notion of racialization and how does this relate to "race" and "racism"?

2. What are the employment dynamics and micro politics that foster the racialization of precarious work?

INTRODUCTION

Much of our understanding of the racialized nature of **precarious work** to date has been based on demographic data, which reveal the predominance of immigrants and people of colour in temporary, short-term, and contract work. This provides an important understanding of the racialized nature of precarious work. At the same time, an examination of the hiring practices and the subtle, often invisible play of **power** in the workplace are crucial in shedding light on *how* **racial fixities** are entrenched in the labour market and in Canadian society. Our chapter focuses on the employment dynamics and micro politics that foster the racialization of precarious work. Drawing on interviews with 50 women workers from three occupations where precarious working conditions prevail in Toronto, we document the ways in which people and work are racialized through the relations established within workplace cultures of contingency. Drawing on the research focusing on the social construction of race we show how, through various employment practices, racial categories are produced and entrenched. Once fixed, these categories render groups of people as inferior, thereby justifying their marginalization and exploitation.

Precarious workers are at the forefront of the **post-Fordist** economy characterized by labour market restructuring bolstered by **neoliberal ideologies** (Padavic, 2005; Szabó & Négyesi, 2005). Precarious jobs encompass "forms of work characterized by limited social benefits and statutory entitlements, job insecurity, low wages, and high risks of ill-health" (Vosko, 2006, p. 11). Several studies have documented the increasing rise in various forms of precarious work[2] around the world. For example, in spring 2004, there were about 7.4 million people in **part-time work** in the U.K. (Francesconi & Gosling, 2005), including 5.8 million women (78 percent) and 1.6 million men (22 percent). This means that about a quarter of workers in the U.K. in 2004 were working part-time (Millar, Ridge, & Bennett, 2006, p. 20). In the U.S., Mastracci and Thompson (2005), based on Bureau of Labor Statistics study, revealed that as of 2001 individuals under non-standard work arrangements accounted for one-third of the workforce. In Canada, between 1997 and 2003, temporary work increased almost twice as fast as permanent work (ACTEW, 2007), and in 2004, 37 percent of the workforce were either self-employed or in part-time or temporary jobs (Toronto Training Board, 2005).

Evidence indicates that post-Fordist work arrangements and work relations are highly gendered (Bakker, 1996), and increasingly becoming racialized (Breitbach, 2001; Rawlings, 2005; Vosko, 2006). As summarized by Teelucksingh and Galabuzi, "the labour market is segmented along racial lines, with racialized group members overrepresented in many low paying occupations, with high levels of precariousness" (2005, p. 6). This is in the context of the rapid growth of racialized groups, which has far outpaced the average in recent years in Canada. According to the 2006 Statistics Canada Census, between 2001 and 2006, Canada's foreign-born population increased by 13.6 percent compared to 3.3 percent for the Canadian-born population (Statistics Canada, 2007), with "visible minorities" comprising 16.2 percent of the total population (Statistics Canada, 2008a).

This chapter is based on data from 50 semi-structured, in-depth interviews in five languages (Cantonese, English, Hindi, Mandarin, and Bengali) conducted with women precarious workers employed as call centre telemarketers (which includes market researchers) (n = 20), supermarket cashiers (n = 15), and garment sewers (n = 15) in the Greater Toronto Area (see Ng and Mirchandani (2008) for a further discussion of our methodological approach).

All but eight of the interviewees were immigrants to Canada, and a majority (n = 28) immigrated more than three years ago from China, Hong Kong, Pakistan, India, Tanzania, the Philippines, Jamaica, Bangladesh, West Indies, Nigeria, and Sri Lanka. Overall, 62 percent of the women had university-level education. The level of education varied between jobs, with 40 percent of the cashiers, 53 percent of the sewers, and 85 percent of the call centre workers having a university degree. With respect to income, 80 percent of the women earned $20,000 per year or less; 36 percent of the women earned less than $10,000. These women all worked in part-time, seasonal or temporary jobs. None of the garment and call centre workers were unionized; however, many of the cashiers worked in supermarkets that were unionized. Out of the 15 cashiers we interviewed 12 were working in unionized stores and two were also union representatives. By and large, however the presence of **unions** seemed to make little difference to the poor working conditions, low pay structure, or hazardous health effects compared to those stores that were not unionized. Elsewhere, we have explored the ways in which women are siphoned into precarious jobs and how their skills are diminished rather than enhanced through the training they receive (Mirchandani et al., 2008). This chapter focuses on the processes of racialization through which their precariousness is entrenched.

We begin by describing studies that show that immigrants and women of colour often occupy precarious jobs in Canada and explore how the notion of racialization can further our understanding of the processes through which this trend occurs. Drawing on our interviews, we explore the work cultures in three types of jobs within which precarious work is prevalent—telemarketing, cashiering, and sewing. By examining employer work practices such as fluctuating wages and work schedules, and the health impact on precarious workers, we identify and contextualize the processes of racialization which structure women's work in precarious jobs, specifically, competition, favouritism, and silencing. These processes form the racialized culture of precarious work. They entrench racial categories, which in turn serve to stereotype workers and their skill sets, organize their access to and exclusion from certain types of jobs, and impose cultural rules and norms that classify and essentialize workers in terms of race, language, and ethnicity.

IMMIGRANTS AND WOMEN OF COLOUR IN PRECARIOUS JOBS

Precarious jobs in Canada have been increasing since the 1990s and it is currently estimated that almost one-third of Canadian workers are employed in precarious jobs (ACTEW, 2007; deWolff, 2000). Census data reveal that "visible minority" women are more likely than "non-visible minority" women to be in part-time jobs (for example, in 2001, 55 percent "visible minority" women worked as part-timers). Part-time employment is particularly prevalent among West Indian (65 percent in 2001) and Arab women (64 percent in 2001) (Statistics Canada, 2006). ACTEW (2007) similarly demonstrates that 43 percent of "visible minority" women are employed in precarious work compared with 37 percent "non-visible minority" workers. Cranford and Vosko refer to this as the **racialized gendering of jobs**" whereby "women of colour are the most likely to be in and out of work, and to have less than a year on the job—two important indicators of contingency" (2006, p. 65). As de Wolff notes about Toronto, "the city's economy relies on an underemployed immigrant labour force to fill low waged precarious jobs" (2006, p. 185).[3] This concentration of immigrants and women of colour in precarious jobs is not new. Das Gupta argues that "people of colour were, historically, allocated to jobs that were the least desirable—jobs with low pay, insecurity, and gross exploitation" (2006, p. 320). Further evidence of the demographic predominance of people of colour in precarious jobs is provided by Galabuzi (2006), who demonstrates that a third of recent immigrants are in sales and service jobs compared to just over a quarter of all Canadians and that low-paying occupations such as clothing have an over-representation of people of colour.

Other studies also note that immigrants, a majority of whom now originate from Asia (Zietsma, 2007, p. 7), have a greater likelihood to be working in sales, service, or manufacturing occupations (Statistics Canada, 2006, p. 237). As our interviews revealed, precarious work arrangements pervade these very occupations. These arrangements are in fact the predominant labour practice in parts of the service and retail sectors (Hipple, 2001; Theodore & Mehta, 1999). For example, call centres in Canada that have experienced a rapid growth rate since 2000 (approximately 26 percent or 570,000 jobs) (Abraham, 2008; Steedman, 2003). Many have a predominance of women and youth as workers (Buchanan & Koch-Schulte, 2000). This racialized division of labour is a national phenomenon. In Manitoba, Aboriginal people and people of colour are utilized to boost the exponential growth of this sector (Guard, 2003). Call centre jobs are characteristic of precarious work; they are routinized part-time and low paid (Buchanan & Koch-Schulte, 2000).The retail industry is another major site of precarious work, and has a large number of young female workers. Supermarket cashiers, especially, are mainly women (MacIvor, 1996). Similar to the call centre industry, jobs in these positions are part-time, requiring relatively little experience or training, and have irregular work hours—on evenings, weekends, and holidays (Usalcas, 2005). While there is a paucity of studies on racialized workers in the retail sector in Canada, Ng et al. (2006) in their study of professional Chinese immigrant women, indicated that labour market barriers forced these women to take up jobs as cashiers and servers in grocery stores and fast food chains. This diversion of immigrant women into the service sector contributes to the increase in employment by 1.8 percent a year on average in the retail trade between 2000 and 2006, or a total of 255,899 workers. According to the 2006 Census, among women, the most prevalent occupation reported in 2006 was retail salespeople and clerks, at just over 400,000, followed by cashiers at 256,000 (Statistics Canada, 2008b).

Similarly, the garment industry is also heavily dependent on the labour of immigrant and ethnic minority women (MacIvor, 1996; Ng, 2002). It is internally differentiated along gender, ethnic, and racial lines, with men occupying the more skilled positions as cutters, and immigrant women of colour occupying the semi-skilled positions as sewers or packers (Ng, 2002). The garment industry is also one of the largest employers of unregistered contractors and home-based workers who do not appear in official statistics; these workers are mainly immigrant women of colour (Yanz et al., 1999). According to existing statistics, 76 percent of all garment workers are women, 50 percent are immigrants, and almost 30 percent are people of colour (Ng, 2002; Yanz et al., 1999). Similar to the two sectors mentioned above, the industry itself is unregulated, offering low pay, irregular work, and no benefits or job security (Yanz et al., 1999). This is one of the reasons why many scholars (for example, Gannagé, 1986; Ng, 2002) have raised concerns about the proliferating oppression and exploitation that immigrant women experience as precarious workers in Canada's garment industry. Given the gendered and racialized structure of precarious work in Canada that depends on a steady supply of cheap and docile labour (Gannagé, 1999), it is evident that these three occupations (call centre work, cashiering, and sewing) derive immense benefits from hiring particular groups of vulnerable workers.

PROCESSES OF RACIALIZATION

Clearly, then, there is substantial evidence of the gendered and racialized nature of precarious work in Canada. Our research focuses on the *processes* through which precarious work is racialized, by examining the mechanisms through which racial categories are fixed and entrenched irrespective of the colour of the people who are in precarious employment. Our argument draws on the notion of "racialization," rather than of "race" (e.g., Hall, 1980, 1996; Miles, 1989, 1993). There is now agreement among analysts that "race" is a socially constructed category based on the supposed biological or "natural" characteristics of groups of people for the purpose of establishing social hierarchies. The term "racialization" focuses on the process of classification, representation, and signification used by various groups to distinguish themselves from the "other" (Armstrong & Ng, 2005, Mirchandani & Chan, 2007). Phoenix, for instance, argues that racialization does the work of putting race in quotation marks and draws attention to the fact that "race does not have a biological basis but that it becomes significant through social, economic, cultural and psychological practices" (2005, p. 8). This notion shifts attention away from individual, trait-based conceptualizations to a focus on ways in which people are *produced* as different. It enables us to see that racial differences are not the only means of signification. Not only have racial categories changed over time in different historical periods and under different socio-economic conditions; racial differences also intersect and interact with other axes of differentiation (such as gender, age, class, etc.) to demarcate groups of people from each other. For example, in 19th century Canada, White Irish immigrants were considered to be a different "race" from the English immigrants, and as a result they faced discrimination in all aspects of their life in Canada (McLean & Barber, (2004). While Irish people are now considered as White, at one time in Canada they were "near the bottom of the social ranks" (p. 154). Axes of difference establish hierarchical, dominant-subordinate relations that across time serve the interests of the dominant groups.

Following from this process of differentiation, the term "racism" names the process of inferiorization, exclusion, marginalization, and subordination. Concepts of racialization and racism, therefore, enable us to examine practices that produce dominant-subordinate relations that become fixed and entrenched as systemic properties of our society; they place social structures at the centre of the analysis (Murji & Solomos, 2005, p. 11). This understanding of racialization and racism challenges the fixity assumed to exist within racial groupings. It draws attention to how processes of racialization, and therefore forms of racism, change across time and space in relation to groups of people and changing material conditions (Armstrong & Ng, 2005, p. 36). It directs our gaze toward the actual practices of people as they navigate changing economic and social conditions.

Proceeding with this understanding, our study examines how precarious working conditions are organized and enacted through the activities of people as they attempt to maximize profit (in the case of employers) and survive (in the case of immigrant workers) in the current climate of post-Fordist economic restructuring. We discovered that the jobs within which precarious work is prevalent focus on lowering labour costs through labour practices such as **just-in-time management practices** and fluctuating wages. Workers are constructed as disposable and renewable labour, and gendered and racialized immigration policies ensure the availability of such a labour pool (Galabuzi, 2006). Three common conditions prevailed in the jobs that our respondents occupied. First, women's incomes were highly variable and overall wages were extremely low. It was not uncommon for workers to earn different amounts from week to week depending on the number of hours they worked, which was determined by the scheduling needs of employers. Second, jobs were structured with the assumption that workers were always available for work and that workers could be and were scheduled for work with little notice or consistency. Workers experienced periodic layoffs, last minute changes in work schedules, and sudden requests for additional work. Finally, the work processes and physical environments in the three occupations we studied put workers at great risk of job-related ill-health and stress. Constructing racial difference on the basis of skin colour, language, and appearance (i.e., racialization) is key in facilitating the conditions of precarious work.

Wages and Wage Instability

On average, the women in our study earned $8.10 per hour. Although some had over 10 years of work experience, they were still making less than $10 per hour. As the majority of the women were not guaranteed a minimum number of weekly work hours, their jobs did not allow them to earn enough to meet their basic needs, and that it was a constant struggle for them to survive. In the call centre, the worker could never be sure of how long they would be working on any given shift. One call centre worker discussed her frustration with her wages:

> Many times, initially like, I go home after three hours. I was really frustrated, because for me traveling is one hour. Because I travel by subway, I take TTC, it is for me like one hour going to work and one hour back home. So it was really frustrating. And also they pay really low. Initially they pay only $7.75. After 9 weeks, they increase 25 cents to make it $8.

Another call centre worker complained about the uncertainty of her income:

> Yes, and then you don't even know how much money you'll be making in a month, because sometimes if they have work, that's too much work, they call you to fit it, and if you have no work, you don't get any job. So sometimes we are, like, in a week we only work 2 days, so that's … you know, like, our money is not constant.

The same dynamics existed in the garment factories:

> (Sighing). I think it is money issue. Actually, for any career, you would care about money and want to know how much you would earn. But for sewing career, we would not know it until our pay cheque comes out. We do not know how much we earn until one or two days before the pay cheque comes out. So, there is pressure here since you would worry about how much you could earn this time and if this is enough to support your family. For example, you expect to get $600, but you actually get $400.

Sometimes, women had to fight with management or company owners just to get paid. One woman who worked as a sewer was fired because of her "low productivity" and was owed three days' wages: It took six weeks for me and them to battle for just ninety-six dollars. The last time I went, I went with my daughter, I stood in the cold for one and a half hours.

Erratic Scheduling

A second feature that characterized the jobs of many of these women is the constant flux in work schedules. Garment sewers, in particular, bore the brunt of the cyclical/seasonal nature of the industry, and reported great variations in their earnings from month to month. Several women noted that they experienced annual layoffs. One woman described the cyclical nature of the work:

> Each year [the company] lays us off almost for half a year. I was once laid off for one year … For the first year, I was laid off for 6 months … They wrote a paper for you to go to apply for EI … They would call us back when they had work to do again.

Supermarket cashiers were scheduled for shifts on a weekly basis and were often asked to report for work at the last minute. Workers were told to wait at home for a call from their employer. While they might be working only a few hours, *all* their time was structured by employer's demands; this feeling of time constraint was noted by many of the women we interviewed. According to one call centre worker:

> They do fix the schedule, they'll be like 'Come from this time to this time,' and then someone might call in sick or whatever, so they'll tell you to come earlier … They do call me and they're like 'Come to work today, come to work tomorrow', whatever, but I can't make it there. There has to be a schedule, you can't just call people at any time, people have other things to do.

Call centre workers also experienced uncertainty in their work schedules and reported being sent home after three hours if there was insufficient work or if the productivity rate of the day was not high enough. This extended quote from a call centre worker details the high levels of uncertainty built into her work schedule:

> Before, we used to get enough hours … for me, it was good because I only wanted to work part-time, 5 hours, but now they've changed the rules, and in that case, sometimes … they have this production rate, like every hour gets one survey, depending on what survey you're doing. So in 5 hours, they expect 5 completes from you, and if it's not quite, you don't get it, you're below the production rate, then they send you home after 3 hours. Minimum, you stay 3 hours; they can't send you home before that … Oh, yes, they cancel many times, and say that they don't have enough work, and they don't want that many people scheduled. Say about 20 people have scheduled and they don't have work for 20 people, then they phone you in the morning and tell you, or sometimes an hour before, they tell you. Like, the work starts at 5, and we leave the house around 4, so they just call you, maybe 15 minutes before that, and tell you not to come in.

For all the women interviewed, this constant shifting of schedules forced them to make their low-pay unstable jobs their priority. They continually had to rearrange other commitments such as family responsibilities, childcare, community work or schooling:

> Oh! It is hard. If anyone asks me I won't say it is hard It's the situation. Either you do that or you don't have money to pay to school. I don't have money to go to school and I don't get a lot of hours so that means I have to split it. If I only work at [the store] they won't give me all the hours I want so I have two jobs and I do then I have to go to school and I have to arrange for the money that I need for school and my own. And also I go to school every week, so I need money every week.

Precarious work thus becomes a way of life—a culture—where insta-bility in job schedules and wages shapes all other aspects of the women's lives. This kind of work environment is stressful for workers, and many of the women in our study experienced significant ill-health and stress as a result of their jobs.

Ill-Health and Work-Related Stress

The third feature of this culture of contingency is the ill-heath and work-related stress experienced by many of the workers. To varying degrees, women in all three occupations had experienced physical problems, mental pressures, and emotional strain. The unpredictable working hours (hence unstable income), workers' lim-ited autonomy in decision making, intense workloads, abusive employers and cus-tomers, alienating working environments, and haphazard working conditions had all contributed to the negative experiences of women at work.

In each of the occupations, women complained about physical problems and mental stress at work. In the garment sector, workers developed headaches, including migraines, eye problems, stress, sleep disorders, and tension. The following quotes illustrate their work-related problems.

> Eyes would have pain too. Sometimes when you keep too focused on sewing, your eyes would have tears.
> I could not sleep for doing such job. I had headache and sore eyes. I had pain in my shoulder muscles. My fingers became stiff and felt much pain. While I was working, my fingers could not stretch straight to work. I had to always bend my fingers. So the joints of fingers had much pain.

These problems often developed as a result of inadequate physical space, poor conditions of work, and deplorable/intolerable working arrangements in the garment factory. One worker described the harsh factory conditions:

> … That factory was horrible. It was dark. Once you entered there, you could feel like you might enter the hell. The workplace was not so clean as the workplace in my first factory. The first factory had bigger and brighter workplace. But this one was dark and it had men too. I was very tired and exhausted working in this factory. We were working like a machine. We did not seem to use our brains … My whole body became exhausted and stressed out.

Another woman complained about the impact of her work setup, "I have to stand for 8 hours for embroidering each day. It's very tiring". The pace of work was also a stressful part of the work. One woman made links between the pace of work and worker stress:

> … So, those knitting workers were extremely stressed and uneasy. Even before they could finish eating, still with the food inside their mouth, they had to start to work again … Even if you go to washroom more than one time, they would blame you.

Whereas the sweatshop conditions of the garment sector might not be exactly replicated in other sectors, work arrangements engendered significant stress. For the cashiers, having to work in standing positions, lifting heavy items, and the constant pressure of scanning items often led to back pains and other health problems. The women reported getting migraines, eye problems, and rough hands from the cleaning solutions used in the stores. One woman reported having developed arthritic knees and carpal tunnel syndrome in her right wrist from constant scanning and standing. The following quotes describe the health problems and mental stress experienced by the women working as cashiers:

> My hands hurt and my arms. I think … they are repetitive tasks [that's why] it hurts. That's why I can't even work too many shifts. Standing part you feel it when you go home you stretch. I stretch for a moment when I am on cash. I find it is very dehydrating when I am at cash. Sometimes I feel thirsty and sometimes headache.

It is stressful for me not physically but mentally and emotionally, emotional labour that's involved ... You sort of feel the same kind of stress ... when you have to do 30 scans per minute or how much you are voiding into your account ...

... there is so many people you don't have time to relax. You are constantly scanning or like punching codes, so it can, you know, get like your shoulders starts aching, in the code scanning and stuff those are kind of heavy, some people are like buying stacks of stuffs, I don't know what they do with that but you know I'm trying to put that and constantly scanning and just like because there are so many things to do, I don't know, your shoulders starts aching your fingers sometimes goes numb.

The call centre workers shared similar experiences as the garment workers and cashiers. In our interviews, problems revealed by call centre workers were related to workers' lack of control over their work processes, working hours, and the repetitive nature of work. One worker summarized, "Here, for 3 days, the [supervisor] is pushing, pushing, mentally, physically, emotionally 'Oh, you have to get it, you have to get it'." Others revealed:

Frankly speaking, non-stop calling the people and talking, surveying the people, it's terrible. Physically very stressed but continuously three months non-stop working and it was stressful.

. ... Yes, sometimes, I do get headache. Looking constantly at the screen and constantly dialling, I get headache. Because sometimes when I do double shifts, I cannot sit, because you have to sit for 12 hours, 11 hours. You have to constantly look at the screen and constantly dial. So ... this whole side pains. This whole side pains.

Sometimes, yes. My eyes, my eyes give me a lot of problem, and I close my eyes and my boss shouts at me. I can't do anything about it!

The majority of the workers did not mention their health-related problems to their employers because they feared that they would be fired. Instead, some workers used their personal funds to purchase work aids that helped ease the physical discomforts associated with their jobs to some extent:

> [In this job the management] don't [give us] head sets, [but in] the other job where I worked before, they used to give head sets, I think they should, because if you have to keep putting down the phone and picking it up and if you are on the phone for like 20 minutes, 25 minutes … It's very hard for me to hold a receiver to my ear, you know? All the time like that, so I used to have pains in my shoulder, so I went and got a head set [myself].

Additionally, call centre workers and supermarket cashiers reported emotional strains caused not only by the workplace or the employers only, but also from abusive customers. For example,

> Yesterday this man picked up the phone and I said I'm calling from such and such. And he said, F-Off! You know, he used the word! I don't use those words. I mean that can make you feel angry or sad or whatever, but I mean because I've had those sort of encounters on the phone for so long I don't feel that much. I don't have such a feeling about it, although I'm really saddened that people would say things like that to me on the phone when I call. And there are other things [customers say]—Woman go and look for a job! And don't call back here! And they scream at you, and they slam the phone in your ear. Those are things I don't like.
>
> I know some of our girls have gotten into fights with customers. They have been slapped by customers. They have products thrown at them. A friend of mine had a cake thrown at her face. It was all over her.

When women were exposed to harassment or verbal abuse from the public, they were told by employers or supervisors: "you have to be polite, even if some of the people are rude" as "it was part of our work." None of the workers mentioned that neither the management nor the union had taken any note of the health problems and work-related stress of which their workers faced. None of the women resorted to other mechanisms to address their health problems. In fact, most of the women did not even have health insurance to fall back on.

As a captive labour force, essential yet disposable in the capitalist labour market (Ng, 1993), individual women workers were pulled into and left with little protection within the culture of contingency, which provided optimal conditions for employers to reduce production costs and maximize profits. These manifestations of the culture of contingency—wage instability, lack of control over work scheduling, and work-related illness/stress—were beneficial to employers in their quest to augment profits, but they also produced a sense of insecurity and anxiety among the workers. These features form the conditions within which racist and sexist practices occur.

FIXING RACIAL CATEGORIES

The concept of racialization allows for a deconstruction of the ways in which race is often seen as static and fixed. Focus on the constructed nature of race serves to unpack the processes through which racism is enacted. While **racialization** (the process and practice of attributing biological and social differences to groups of people) is not identical to **racism** (the ideology and practice of inferiorizing groups of people who are racialized), it sets the stage for racism; that is, for the negative and demeaning treatment of people. Below we describe the ways in which employers and workers themselves often fix and entrench racial categories through three work processes—competition, favouritism, and silencing—which are normalized. These processes serve to stereotype workers and their skills sets, organize their access to and exclusion from certain types of jobs, and impose cultural rules and norms that classify and essentialize them in terms of race, language, and ethnicity. These work practices serve the interests of the employers in maximizing profits; by employing strategies of competition, favouritism, and silencing, the owners are able to keep workers divided.

Workers in our study noted that they were confronted frequently with gross generalizations where particular ethnic groups were associated with certain skills but not with others. These generalizations affected the allocation of positions and responsibilities meted out to the workers by their employers. Workers were told, for example, that "Vietnamese are not nice" or "[t]hose Cantonese were loud and aggressive," or:

> Black women are very confrontational. They will talk right back at you. Asians have nimble fingers. They are so gentle with things, they can do that paper thing like origami.

Such ideological construction of skills and stereotyping paved the way for discriminatory work practices founded on perceptions of racial and cultural differences. A garment sewer related:

> Filipinos are not allowed to sew just because they don't like it. It is not that we don't know how to sew but the employers do not like us Filipinos to sew. So the sewing jobs were done by the Chinese people. We used to do only folding, pinning and trimming.

Similarly, in the supermarket sector, work was allocated by the perceived skills of racial groups. One of the interviewees pointed out:

> In the bakery there are no Black people, in the nursery there are no Black people, and in produce there are no Black people—all Chinese, all Oriental people. For Black people it is just front-end deli and cashier.

A few other cashiers observed that their workplaces were organized hierarchically, with White people in charge with preferential working schedules. One cashier commented, "[t]hey are all White … The White ones are at the top, they get like, 40 hours a week." This segregation on the basis of colour and perceived cultural differences forms the foundation upon which competition, favouritism, and silencing is exercised.

Competition

Racialization goes beyond cultural perceptions, however. We found that workplace segregation was both a result and a prerequisite of the precarious organization of production. In the garment industry, for example, because of the piece rate system and the unstable workload, workers were compelled to compete for work. One garment worker complained, "[t]hey [another ethnic group] always competed with me to grab more work to do." As garment work production is organized by a hierarchical division of labour, some workers reported that workers in the upper strata would hand down jobs to people of the same ethnic groups as themselves in the next stage of the production process. The atmosphere was such that some garment workers retreated into individualism where they felt that they had to survive by protecting their knowledge or skill, "afraid that you might take their work to do, if they told you how to do it and even might do it better than themselves." This "individualization of work" (Carnoy, 1999) has become a hallmark of restructured flexible work.

Competition among ethnic groups for work was not always purposefully designed by the employers. Small contractors, who were the employers of the women we interviewed in the garment industry, had little control over the unstable production cycles themselves. However, workers reported that some of the employers and their representatives on the shop floors, such as supervisors, purposely created conflicts and segregation among the workers. One garment sewer noted, "Workers fight one another and could not get on well with each other. I had the feeling that she [supervisor] deliberately did this ... the whole factory know this."

What was accomplished in this particular case is that the potential for solidarity, community, and cooperation among the workers was disrupted and undermined. Whereas competition for work was most pronounced in the garment sector, the lack of sociability among workers was not unique to the garment sector. Few workers regarded their workplace as a social space. In fact, the precarious nature of call centre and cashier work was such that the women rarely had time to unite across different backgrounds, which thwarted the bargaining power of workers as a whole, and maximized profits for the employer.

Favouritism

Women also experienced blatant favouritism on the basis of perceived racial and ethnic differences from employers or their representatives. They reported that workers of different heritages were treated differently in the workplaces. For example, a call centre worker mentioned: "[h]e [the supervisor] would be different with White people and different with all other types." A Canadian-born White call centre worker noted that she was able to request for an ergonomic work station after she complained. The cashiers we interviewed reported racial discrimination even in the unionized stores. In one case, a cashier mentioned that her sister was not hired by one of the unionized retail stores as she was wearing a hijab. Across jobs, women noted that work was often allocated to workers based on employers' personal and ethnic/racial preferences. The experience of a woman of colour being discouraged from applying for other types of work on the supermarket shop floor is a blatant example. She said:

> I wanted to do the photo lab but they won't put me into that. I thought about it and how come there are no Black people at the front desk ... I heard that positions were opening and people were leaving and they

> needed help. I went and spoke to my supervisor ... She said, 'O.K. When the time comes we will let you know,' and all of a sudden I saw a bunch of people around the photo lab and I thought what's going on. They said, 'oh, we are training.'

A worker from the call centre stated that as a woman of colour, she was assigned difficult market research projects while White workers were given the easier projects. In the garment sector, workers reported that the division of labour between lighter and heavier jobs was sometimes determined by level of proficiency in English language. In some cases, those with English language facility were given lighter work while those with low proficiency in English were assigned heavier work, even though there was no ostensible connection between the degree of difficulty of the work and the ability to speak the English language. That is, language as a criterion for job assignment was not neutral, as it disadvantaged non-native English speakers in varying ways. Furthermore, this practice was arbitrary and inconsistent, as one garment worker observed in the case of "a Vietnamese [who] could also communicate and interact with the supervisor well. But still, the supervisor would give her heavier work than the White co-workers."

Silencing

Language was one of the key dynamics that organized the experiences of the women in our study. It is through constructions of the "right way to speak" that silencing is enacted in precarious work. In the call centres, for example, some immigrant workers reported encountering prejudice and abuse from customers because of their accents and the pronunciation of their names. Workers reported angry and aggressive customer responses to their accents. In the face of racism and a work system that diminished their dignity, most immigrant workers kept quiet, acquiescing to the status quo. In call centre work, some women were instructed by their supervisors to use pseudonyms when talking to people on the phone. They were told that by using an Anglicized name they would not alienate the potential market research respondents. Some women were angry about this management request. One woman voluntarily changed her name, saying: "What difference does it make whether you're Nancy or Namisha?" In other instances, they were made to take on a Canadian identity—"[m]y supervisor told me to change my name."

Although some garment workers made special efforts to study English, most of them did not have the opportunity to do so. For example, many of the sewers we interviewed did not have the time to gain fluency in English and spoke of being "trapped" in the garment sector. The lack of English proficiency led to feelings of inferiority, embarrassment, and fear:

> In the beginning I was timid and would not say any-
> thing to them. I felt a lot of stress. I felt afraid. I was
> worried that I wasn't doing well enough. I would not
> know how to say anything to them. Say I want to take
> a day off tomorrow, I would not know how to ask
> them. I would ask other people but I did not feel com-
> fortable to be always asking others to help … After a
> while I felt embarrassed. I felt the stress that I should
> have put more effort into learning English. But it was
> not really possible. When I went home I had to look
> after the kids. There was no time. That is another kind
> of pressure for me.

Some supermarket workers were of the opinion that the stores they worked in tended to take advantage of those women who were new immigrants and did not speak much English well. One worker who was active in the union and had a strong critique of management practices reported:

> People who have now come to this country and are afraid
> to kind of go [on] their own, they're going to have prob-
> lems like if they speak English but not very well they kind
> of need help, they [management] tend to take advantage
> of the person. They appear to be helping the person but
> in reality they are not. So the people who are nice and
> gullible they are going to be taken advantage of.
> Sometimes they are asked to do the reduced staff's work
> you know, like that they are taken advantage of.

Although many immigrant women workers wanted to improve their English, this desire was not always in line with the employers' interests. Employers did not offer English language training to those with minimal English language skills. Consequently many workers, especially those in the garment industry, spoke and associated only with people who spoke the same language, which further hindered their ability to secure better work opportunities and integrate into the mainstream labour market. While the women's official qualifications and credentials were not recognized in the Canadian labour market, employers never hesitated to appropriate their prior education and skills where it was effective and profitable to do so (Mirchandani et al., 2008). What is more, some call centre workers were streamed into work talking in their own language on overseas calls.

What is evident here is how racialization serves to stereotype immigrants, devalues their skills and abilities, and silences them on the basis of appearance and language. Language is a key component in the maintenance of **hegemonic relations**, which preserve the domination of certain groups over others. Constructed as deficient in English and therefore inadequate in their communication and other skills, immigrant workers of colour, regardless of their former education, training, and experience, were assumed to be less skilled and proficient than their White Canadian counterparts.

CONCLUSIONS

While demographic and statistical analyses are useful in revealing the composition and gendered and racialized character of the precarious workforce, this chapter deepens our understanding of racial hierarchies by examining the actual conditions and practices that produce and reinforce racial categories. We pinpoint the work practices in three jobs—garment sewing, call centre telemarketing, and supermarket cashiering—through which workers were constructed as different and inferior, so that they could be marginalized and exploited to augment profit in a post-Fordist restructured economy. Without adequate protection, the current economic uncertainty will likely further impact immigrants and women of colour in precarious jobs as employers face severe pressure to reduce labour costs.

ENDNOTES

1. This paper is based on a research project funded by Social Sciences and Humanities Research Council of Canada. Kiran Mirchandani was the Principal Investigator on this project and Roxana Ng was the Co-Investigator. The remaining authors were collaborators and are listed in alphabetical order. Other group members involved in this project include Jasjit Sangha and (late) Karen Hadley. We would like to thank Patricia E. Simpson and Anke Allspach for research assistance.

2. In this paper we use the terms "precarious" and "contingent" interchangeably. The term "contingent" was first used by Audrey Freedman in 1985 to refer specifically to "conditional and transitory employment arrangements" (see Hipple, 2001, p. 3). Subsequently, it was developed by other scholars to exemplify part-time, temporary work, seasonal work representing **non-standard employment**, just-in-time work (Hipple, 2001), and work that is low paid,

without security and benefits (ACTEW, 2007). For further discussions on the various forms and definitions of contingent and precarious work see Mirchandani et al. (2010) and Vosko et al. (2003).

3. Not only do immigrant women predominate in poorly paid jobs, but many are excluded entirely from the formal economy. One study shows that "immigrant women in the 25 to 54, or 'core' working-age group, had much higher unemployment rates and lower employment rates than both immigrant men and Canadian born women, regardless of how long they had been in Canada" (Zietsma, 2007, p. 6).

Work, Living, and Learning within Canadian Guest Worker Programs

Peter H. Sawchuk and Arlo Kempf

DISCUSSION QUESTIONS

1. What do you feel may be the current and future economic impacts of the growth of guest worker programs in Canada, and how might the limitation of workplace rights for guest workers affect these?

2. Countries like Canada and the United States are often thought to be examples of a modern knowledge economy. In what way does the rapid growth of guest worker programs in both of these countries fit with this depiction?

3. What do you feel are the most important "lessons" that guest workers and their allies are learning today in Canada?

INTRODUCTION

Lack of oversight by the federal government has allowed foreign workers to be abused by their employers, Auditor General Sheila Fraser says in a scathing report on Canada's immigration program. Lower-skilled temporary workers are particularly at risk of these problems because of "their economic conditions, linguistic isolation, and limited understanding of their rights. … " (*Toronto Star*, November 4, 2009).

Over the past 20 years, various authors from different disciplines have written about **guest worker programs** (GWPs). Although many different names are used to describe these programs they all generally refer to the importation of temporary workers under specific conditions of employment in specifically selected types of work. In a number of different forms and across an expanding set of industries, these types of programs are currently on the rise in many countries around the world. These programs deeply affect the "sender" or "origin" countries as well as the "host" countries. And, looking to the future, the role of GWPs in the national economies of North, Central, and South America as well as around the globe is poised for explosive impacts. In the European context, where types of GWPs have been in place since the end of World War II, racial, cultural, and ethnic conflicts between visiting workers and their "hosts" have erupted. Indeed, GWPs have played a major role in shaping race and class relations in numerous European countries. The growth of such programs in Canada demands that we pay close attention to their development, as well as to the resulting cultural and economic effects that are frequently negative and contradictory.

There is a significant body of research on various forms of guest work, migrant work, and **transnational labour.** Our focus, however, is the relations of work, living, and learning of guest workers. Guest worker experiences of work, living, and learning remains virtually invisible in the literature, but even still, at first glance, this focus may still seem odd to some. After all, from a narrow perspective, the work, living, and learning of guest workers simply represent a highly exploited form of labour and learning that involves little, if any, skill, knowledge, or learning of consequence to the evolving future of work or workers in the 21st century Canada. How, it might be asked, can such experiences with echoes of decades if not centuries past be considered a relevant topic in the 21st century? Our argument is that in a rapidly *globalizing* and just as rapidly *polarizing* world guest work is every bit as definitive of work as these other forms. And, that a focus on the relations between the work, living, and learning of guest workers anticipates the fact that no social change occurs in the absence of people's learning; that the most powerful learning of all is the learning that comes from experience, and that guest worker experiences are becoming increasingly central to globalized labour markets and economies.

In light of these and other issues, in this chapter we consider the following types of questions. What are guest workers learning in their work lives here in Canada? What are they learning about Canada and Canadians? What are Canadians learning about the cultures and countries from which guest workers originate? Here at the beginning of the 21st century, these and other related questions are becoming increasingly important as guest work has continued to spread to touch virtually every region of the globe including Canada.

GUEST WORKER PROGRAMS: A PRELIMINARY FRAMEWORK

Below we begin with a brief historical overview, which reveals a long pattern of what we call GWP "infra-structure building" in Canada and the United States. This refers to a long process taking place in both countries that has established, in our view, the virtual inevitability of a continued, massive expansion of GWPs across all of the Americas and beyond. In short, although some resistance to the growth of these programs exists, the continuation/expansion of guest work is a sure thing in North America. We also claim that the situation in Canada cannot be adequately understood without awareness of some of the military, political, and economic dynamics that have played an important role in shaping how GWPs have enveloped the Americas over time. When looking at the Mexican guest workers in Ontario for example, it is important to consider NAFTA and the effects it has had on each country's economy. Looking even further back in history how did the relationship between Canada and the Caribbean and, in particular, among the United States, Canada, and Mexico come to be what it is today in terms of GWPs? We then discuss some of the relevant dimensions of transnational work, community life, and learning relationships. Finally, we undertake a brief secondary analysis of **popular education** materials based on Mexican guest workers in Southern Ontario in order to gain a better appreciation of how these workers are experiencing GWPs themselves.

The Historical Roots of Guest Worker Program Expansion

In Canada, guest worker programs were originally established with the Caribbean through the British colonial network. With origins in the 17th century, both Canada and several Caribbean countries were part of the broader British Empire, and eventually through this developed types of national interrelations establishing an independent, Caribbean-Canadian agriculture-based GWP in the 1960s. Since the 1980s, however, Canadian GWPs have increasingly followed the United States dominated policy, and as we shall see, this has shaped the growth of total and proportional numbers of Mexican workers in its agricultural GWP.[1] Below, we look at the nature of this long-term synchronization of Canadian policy to that of the United States.

In many ways, to understand the contemporary nature of North American GWPs we need to examine the long infrastructure-building process that began with the Mexican-American War (1846–48) (see Chacón & Davis, 2006). Massive land seizure by the United States at the end of this conflict re-drew the map of nine U.S. states[2] and strengthened the United States' capacity for establishing what are known as peripheral,[3] or secondary, labour market supply sources in Mexico. A pattern soon emerged that shaped the economic as well as cultural fabric of the United States, Mexico, and more recently Canada. This pattern featured periods of what we might call "official" migrant labour policy as well as periods of more indirect, hidden, or "unofficial" migrant labour policy. In both instances, however, it is important to keep in mind that migrant labour policy can be seen to have actively shaped how control over workers is exercised by employers and government and the subsequent experience of work, living, and learning for workers themselves.

More specifically, throughout the 20th century we can chart this pendulum of official/unofficial migrant labour policy. It is characterized by active, official state experimentation with various models of migrant labour programs, e.g., during World War I with programs to fill labour shortages; the inter-war period when migrant labour policies became more indirect and unofficial due to public pressure; the World War II era Bracero[4] program, which once again provided official programming in the area of migrant labour policy; and, more recently the establishment of the North American Free Trade Agreement (NAFTA)[5] and Maquiladorization of the U.S.–Mexican border; and the types of border control measures that increasingly are discussed in U.S. politics (see Chacón & Davis, 2006). We should note, for example, that since the discontinuation of the United States' most ambitious guest worker program—the Bracero Program—American government policies have allowed the expansion of peripheral labour markets by doing relatively little to limit the illegal immigration of millions of undocumented people who once across the border, work in low-paid, high-risk jobs with few if any rights and benefits. Although American politicians have certainly made a lot of noise about undocumented workers, the sheer volume of traffic speaks for itself. Richard Vogel (2007) refers to this government approach as "official grandstanding to cover an unofficial open border policy demanded by American capitalism" (p. 8). In this context we can also see that American policies have increasingly incorporated Canada over the past 25 years. Canada's involvement comes not simply through its participation in Mexican debt re-structuring via the World Trade Organization (WTO)[6] but also through Canada's involvement in NAFTA. The result has been Canada's movement away from its original migrant labour programming.

GWPs in Canada Yesterday and Today

Economically, the agricultural sector has traditionally been at the centre of GWPs in both the United States and Canada. In Canada specifically, such programs flourished under long established labour codes that excluded farm workers from trade **union** organizing (sections of the labour code first enacted to protect against "communist" labour organizers moving onto the "family farm"). Despite the dramatic decrease in the number of family farms over the last half century, these sections of labour code, until just recently,[7] remained firmly entrenched. Under competitive pressures and with the virtual demise of the farmer cooperative movement that helped to protect family farming, over the course of the last 40 years agri-business and factory farming became well established setting the stage for broader support of migrant labour policy and contemporary GWPs such as the Seasonal Agricultural Workers Program.

Recently however, GWPs have expanded into a variety of new sectors: oil production, hospitality, transportation, meat processing, as well as light manufacturing and even elder care. Obviously the economic effects on broader labour market conditions are multiplying rapidly and will likely continue to spread. Indeed, where major segments of industries incorporate increasing numbers of guest workers—under the current conditions—we can expect a variety of startling downward pressures: on wages, on rights, and expectations (e.g., Vogel, 2007). These sectoral expansions aside, for now the current phase of this long history requires the completion of a "clamp-down" exercise to dismantle the unauthorized migrant labour flows of the past 25–30 years. As the United States begins more effective and earnest efforts at closing its borders to undocumented (illegal) workers, the resulting labour shortage will be filled by guest workers. Again, this is in part a response to American public outcry. According to Vogel (2007), the clamp-down phase was initiated by the U.S. Senate in 2003 and slated for completion by 2012. Strangely enough, it has become intertwined with the "War on Terror" and the establishment of the U.S. Department of Homeland Security (DHS), which allows for the flow of enormous amounts of funding that, justified in terms of national security, easily avoids public debate. In one form or another, the coming of an expanded GWP initiative to Canada is now well underway in part due to Canada's participation in trade agreements such as NAFTA, WTO, and GATS to which both the United States and Canada are signatories.

Although the push for corporate profits drives this process, the process itself relies upon a solid bedrock of worker insecurity as well as traditional nativist xenophobia and racism.[8] Workers are made aware that they are disposable and can lose their jobs at anytime, while it seems that many locals accept the notion that Canadians are too good for such jobs, or that somehow the terrible work and working conditions are justified by the status (racial, cultural, ethic, geographic, etc.) of the workers. The primary goal of such processes, beyond establishing a gateway through which to better control the rich natural resources of Central and South America, has for some time been as we have tried to show to establish a permanent peripheral pool of workers with which to fill low-wage, low-rights, and low-possibility jobs in Canada and the United States.

By looking at the history and contemporary context of GWP expansion over these initial sections, we hope to have established a firm ground for (1) understanding the nature of this evolving form of labour (and labour relations), and (2) for setting the stage for an understanding of the dynamics of the work, learning, domination, resistance, and social reproduction, and their reverberating effects across a range of economic sectors, as well as host/origin country communities.

Canadian Agricultural Guest Work

Without most of the rights other Canadian workers take for granted; and with the help of state enforcement, unannounced cancellations of contracts with few avenues for appeal, guest workers' experiences in North America offer perhaps the closest modern version of the American system of chattel slavery. Moreover, as researchers beginning in the 1970s (Burawoy, 1976) have shown, migrant labour systems generally function like parasites: families and communities in origin countries bear the costs of social reproduction[9] while certain groups in the host countries claim the profits and enjoy almost total control over the workers, their work, and their outputs.

From its inception Canadian immigration policy revolved around the targeting of specific national/racial/ethnic groups. However, by the early 1960s, having experienced competitive pressures on markets for their products hand-in-hand, which led to the temptation to compete based on reduced labour costs, and seeing the more general national pressures to reform its immigration system, Canadian agri-business demanded changes. In 1967, Canada's entry requirements for immigrants changed, with a new focus on the educational and economic background of prospective immigrants (rather than simply on the applicant's race, ethnicity, and national origin). The agricultural sector anticipated this change, and correctly understood immigrants with stronger formal educational backgrounds and more money would be less likely to do poorly paid manual labour on Canadian farms. In preparation for this change, the Canadian government instituted its Seasonal Agricultural Workers Program (SAWP) in 1966. The SAWP brings particular groups of foreign workers to Canada for periods of six weeks to 10 months. Built on formal agreements with origin countries, the agreements are spun as a win/win whereby growers in Canada get low-wage workers delivered to their doorstep and pay less than what was required to employ Canadian citizens; and, workers from the Global South earn relatively high wages in relation to local alternatives (Preibisch & Binford, 2007, p. 9). Largest in the provinces of Ontario and Quebec, the SAWP is now established in nine of 10 provinces. It is expanding at an enormous rate. In 2001 it included 20,000 workers (Weston & Scarpa de Masellis, 2003) and according to Human Resources and Skills Development Canada over 192,000 guest workers arrived in 2008.

As indicated earlier, building on its roots in the British Commonwealth, SAWP originally targeted Caribbean, and specifically Jamaican, men to come and work on fixed-term labour contracts on Canadian farms (see Satzewich, 1991). Caribbean men constituted the bulk of these workers until the late 1980s when the state, alongside eager growers, established Mexico as the soon to be dominant origin country for SAWP (Preibisch & Binford, 2007). This transformation, from Caribbean to Mexican workers, has not gone unnoticed. Binford (2002) argues that fuelling this change is a two-part, race-based assumption on the part of the employer, regarding the submissiveness of Mexican workers on one hand, and the feistiness of Caribbean workers on the other. Binford points to a culture of (albeit limited) empowerment developed among the English-speaking Caribbean workers, who may demand their employers stick to the contract, and who may be unwilling to work hours not mandated in that contract. Conversely, Mexicans are relatively new to the terms of work and, facing a substantial language barrier, to date have often come unprepared to negotiate the informal cultural contract that governs much of the day-to-day life of a guest worker.

Canadian-based scholarship in this area began to emerge about the same time as this shift, and has developed since (Basok, 2002; Binford, 2002; Bolaria, 1992; Cecil & Ebanks, 1991; Preibisch, 2004, 2007; Sharma, 2006; Smart, 1998; UFCW, 2002). Early research focused on migration experiences and the dual social and economic effects on origin and host countries. Joined by both broader international economic analysis, which revealed the contradictory, transnational economic compulsions and results (e.g., Stasiulis & Bakan, 2005) and analyses from the field of migrant studies, basic research on guest workers has reached a critical mass as far as scholarship that looks simultaneously at class, race, and gender issues (as well as the way these issues relate to one another). The work of Satzewich (1991) for example, was one of the earliest to highlight the effects of social class as well as the racial dimensions of the SAWP program.

Support for the program is found among growers. Local businesses in the host communities also see economic benefit, with some guest workers noting instances of price gouging. Activist and organized labour in Canada see a serious violation of social justice as well as serious organizing challenges interwoven with concerns that wages for Canadian workers will be pushed downward as a result of the relatively low wages paid to guest workers. Because of difficult economic conditions in their home countries, Caribbean and Mexican guest workers are forced to embrace the opportunity to work and send money home to family. Although they occasionally make sustained community connections in host communities and nearby cities, most workers experience a profound alienation from their surroundings, employers, and work. When thinking about the hard work and low wages in Mexico for example, it is important to remember agreements such as NAFTA, which actually contribute to these limited local options. As a signatory to, and co-author of NAFTA, in this sense Canada is partially responsible for limiting local options and pushing wages downward in Mexico. Through programs like SAWP, Canada benefits from the insecurity and destabilization it creates. Guest work is framed by health risks, loneliness, harsh conditions, instances of poor treatment, lack of citizenship and worker rights, as well as pronounced feelings of alienation. This system has, not infrequently, led to divisions between guest workers and the local communities in Canada near where they work, and in some cases forms of racial violence directed at workers.

We argue that it remains important to look at the experience *and* the learning associated with guest work itself, and here there are few sources of research on which to draw. Our own observational and literature research along with our discussions with workers in the Southern Ontario region show that at the level of the work process, traditional divide-and-conquer strategies are common throughout the SAWP in Canada. The roots of these strategies are found in both personal racism (of the growers), and pseudo-genetic assumptions that become intertwined with a basic business management logic that play out in the relationships between growers, workers (both new and returning), workers' families at home, and the local communities of both the host and origin countries. A core feature of divide-and-conquer strategies in practice is race/ethnicity-based organization of work and the workplace. Workers are separated by culture and language. Pseudo-genetic formulae are invoked, e.g., Caribbean workers for the tree-picking and sustained ditch work versus Mexican workers for weeding and planting and low crop harvesting (see Preibisch & Binford, 2007). Workers are also separated based on assumptions regarding their ability to understand and work well with one another. Language use is regularly the object of control in guest work (i.e., employer controlled "back-chat"), as English speakers will regularly supervise Spanish speakers, or vice versa, creating a language and culture-based division between supervisors and workers, and between one cultural group and another.

These structures and resources for the control of guest work and guest workers are powerful. However, we can also see that groups of guest workers can and do generate and maintain cultures of solidarity and resistance on a local scale, with a few instances of open revolt in B.C., Ontario, and Quebec. Moreover, with the aid of local community groups and activist organizations such as Justicia/Justice for Migrant Workers (J4MW),[10] as well as with the support of organized labour (e.g., the United Food and Commercial Workers (UFCW)), there is a developing potential for expanding support, resistance, and organization. In short, guest workers and their allies are learning through their experiences of work and living in Canada a variety of important lessons.

Deepening the Analysis of the Work, Living, and Learning Process of Guest Working in Canada

We begin by outlining the basic dimensions of what we feel is a complex circuit of communication, participation, and learning that shape Canadian guest work as a type of transnational work, living, and learning process. As we have said, there is in fact very little prior research on this particular complex of concerns; particularly so when we include the notions of work and learning. The presumption, in this sense, would appear to be that there is very little to know about the work, living, and learning process. Thus, in the context of little if any guidance from earlier research of this type, establishing a way to think about this complexity is important as a means of better recognizing and developing positive changes in these experiences.

Organized training in guest worker production is virtually non-existent. Thus, we can begin by noting that ongoing, worker-to-worker on-the-job training and direct supervision provide the primary production-based learning opportunities. In a broad sense, the degree to which guest workers are skilled (and to which they become skilled on the job despite the absence of formal training) is recognized concretely by the employers who according to the most recent measures recall experienced workers, by name, at a rate of 70 percent each year (see Binford, 2002). But these practices represent merely the tip of the work, living, and learning ice-berg. Intertwined with immediate production learning, there is a second dimension in the form of the dense fabric of "**inter-cultural learning**" surrounding guest work. This learning is multidimensional and can be broken down into a series of mutually constituting learning dynamics across the following six sets of relationships:

1. Between workers and growers

2. Between bureaucrats from both Canada and origin countries

3. Between workers and residents of host communities (although there are some examples of cross-cultural benefit[11] here, these relations are for the most part conflictual)

4. Between workers from different regions, cultures, and countries

5. Between workers and host country activists (such as those from J4MW or the UFCW) as well as community and university-based organizations

6. Between communities in Canada and communities in origin country, compared with family and community units across borders and, with the passage of time, generations

Together, across these six sets of relationships we find what could be called a "curriculum of experience" generated, redeveloped, stored, taught, and learned.

These six interlocking sets of relationships of the living/learning circuit form a basic means of understanding the experience of guest work.

As we have noted, there is very little research that looks at the intersection of work, living, and learning in Canada. Thus, having established a basic framework of relationships, we now turn toward a brief, secondary analysis of some of these learning relationships based on popular education research on work and learning carried out by J4MW (Hinnenkamp, 2004).[12] Limited in its empirical scope, in conjunction with our own research it nevertheless provides one of the only empirical points of access to the phenomena at hand currently available. Yet understood against the backdrop of the variety of additional, broader research studies that confirm similar conditions across SAWP work sites, it is possible to draw some initial conclusions from it.

What becomes clear in both Hinnenkamp's research and our own is that to understand the work and learning dimensions of guest work, it is vital to first address the role of material conditions.[13] Although traditional forms of workplace control are in full force within guest work (including divisions of labour for a divide-and-conquer strategy), additional physical conditions shape the experiences, interests, and learning needs at the centre of guest work. **Workplace learning** within guest worker programs in Canada is experienced through the raw conditions lived through both on and off the job: being too cold, being too hot, being too wet, using outdated or broken tools, and having poor housing. In other words, this is learning motivated and shaped by substandard equipment, clothing, boots, transportation, and pesticide protections. Workers in Hinnenkamp's discussion groups, for example, clearly articulate how acute injuries and chronic health dangers stand as a central theme around which their thinking, reaction, and strategizing revolves.

The method that Hinnenkamp (2004) used is based on the work of popular educator Paulo Freire.[14] It involved the workers selecting pictures (from magazines, etc.) from a large set (or creating pictures themselves) in order to facilitate dialogue with each other and the researcher as a means of better understanding their experiences and concerns. One example was the selection of a picture of a marathon runner. This formed the basis for dialogue about their experience, learning, and living associated with the work process. Looking as a group at the picture, one worker commented: "This also represents a job. Some people work in this way and others—the Mexicans—that come here, we do it in a different way, helping Canada to progress." This statement, Hinnenkamp reports, suggests at least two possible work/living/learning themes for our consideration here.

The first theme involves how Mexican workers bring with them specific patterns, points of reference, and cultural understandings of worklife that are likely distinct from Euro-American work processes and workers. One way to understand this may be to think of these views in light of the research themes related to the notion of "over-worked workers," "work–life balance," and so on. According to these Mexican workers, they have a different approach that, while clearly not eschewing hard work, nevertheless may consider paid labour as only part of the fulfillment of individual and collective needs—only part of what is needed to be happy. Hinnenkamp's focus groups also reveal another theme. It is based on a specific understanding that differences among workers in terms of skills, abilities, and work interests should be taken into account in the design and execution of the work process. This would seem to run against how most workplaces are designed in North America where the worker accommodates the work, rather than the work accommodating the worker. This approach stands as an alternative to the manic neurosis and insecurity that many workers feel today in countries like Canada. A quick look at the over-worked and over-stressed North American workforce that has been well-documented over the last two decades tells us that such an approach is certainly absent and perhaps desperately needed. These points suggest that there are likely specific forms of work-based experience, knowledge, skill, and self-understanding—to this point hidden from academic research—concerning guest agricultural work that are distinct from what now constitutes the dominant experience of employment for many North Americans.

Additional themes about work, living, and learning that emerge from this section of Hinnenkamp's work deals with the conflict between newer, often younger workers, who in classic sociology of work literature would be called "rate-busters"—working particularly fast to garner supervisory approval. Hinnenkamp's research specifically comments on this, noting that workers were hesitant to fully explain these dynamics. Although the learning of how fast to work, and of how to subtly resist and control production speed is by no means new to the field of sociology of work, unique aspects of guest work may allow us to expand our understanding of these dynamics. In response to resistance, growers may choose to "country surf" for whole new intake communities—thus terminating all members of the community participating in the resistance (Preibisch & Binford, 2007). Further shaping and sharpening these relations of control is the broader poverty of Mexico that has been actively constructed, as we saw earlier, across an almost two-century trajectory of concerted political decisions within which, in the last few decades, the Canadian state has played an active part. Here we see a structure that sets specific patterns of labour, living, and learning in a new more understandable light. It is a system that is both archaic and contemporary.

The knowledge and skill that stems from workers' needs and interests rather than the needs of employers and production are still far too often ignored in research on guest work. The most intense and obvious examples of these are the moments of resistance—both organized and spontaneous resistance—to the content and structure of work and working life. Further fuelling conflict and resistance for guest workers is cultural alienation and a racialization of exploitation. One group of workers in Hinnenkamp (2004) argued, "[i]n Canada they like dogs better than they like Mexicans." Others went on to describe their treatment as "animals," as "machines," and so on. Outright racism deeply shapes many of these experiences, both within the production process and within the experiences in the surrounding communities. The ethno-linguistic differences—revolving around the absence of Spanish-language capacity of the supervisory staff for example and the racist ideas that continue to replicate this inadequacy—produce a very negative and debilitating feedback-loop of events where English-only instructions, half-understood, ineffectively direct work. Workers in any context, understandably have a difficult time doing their jobs when unable to fully understand the supervisor's instructions. This is followed by supervisory criticism (and not infrequently racist statements about laziness and lack of care). Workers meanwhile, become increasingly frustrated, and on it goes. More and more frequently, these negative experiences are giving way to forms of guest worker resistance. Reflecting on poor conditions, a worker comments: "[I wonder] if this is really what the Canadian people or the bosses we have want us to do—hold a demonstration … to express what's wrong with our houses, how we are treated, and the benefits that we should have a right to?" (quoted in Hinnenkamp, 2004, p. 19).

CONCLUSIONS

Guest worker programs are poised to undergo significant expansion, implicating a host of countries across the Americas and beyond. In this chapter we have sought to establish a historical foundation for understanding the work, living, and learning processes that shape these programs in Canada today. These dynamics have radiant causes and effects on workers, employers, origin and host communities, and will undoubtedly reverberate across labour markets more broadly in the short and long term.

Our goal in this chapter was to begin to develop a preliminary framework concerning not simply the historical origins but the contemporary, complex dimensions of work, living, and learning of Canadian guest work. We argued that cultural, political, and economic forces are important factors at play within a broad "curriculum of experience" that is contemporary guest work.

We have offered a means of beginning to understand this complexity as well as explored some core themes drawing on a brief (secondary) analysis of related themes based on previously published, popular education work in the farm fields of Ontario that is consistent with our own preliminary research efforts.

We maintain that these dynamics, far from being isolated, unrepresentative, and unimportant, will increasingly play a role in defining the nature of work in the 21st century. Although reflective of the labour processes of previous centuries, the implications for the 21st century are paramount, particularly as far as these dynamics are shaped by the difficult and powerful intersections of race, social class, and citizenship. How workers and their allies experience these processes and how they learn their way within and beyond them is likely a definitive element of future change.

ENDNOTES

1. In addition to Mexican and Commonwealth Caribbean nations, Canada now draws guest workers from countries around the globe, including Thailand, Guatemala, Sri Lanka, India, Haiti, Somalia, and others.

2. For the low price of troop withdrawal and $15 million, this treaty established, redefined, and/or enlarged the territories of California, Arizona, New Mexico, Nevada, Utah, Colorado, Wyoming, and Oklahoma—as well as settled contestation over the Texas border (Chacón & Davis, 2006).

3. Generally speaking, the terms "peripheral" or "secondary" labour markets refer to types of employment that feature lower wages, lower benefits, and that are often part-time, contingent, or temporary as opposed to what most people think of as stable, full-time employment with acceptable wages/benefits. This term was established in economics and sociology literature that identified clusters of what are typically referred to as either "good" and "bad" jobs.

4. The Bracero Program (rooted in the Spanish word "brazo," meaning "arm(s)"—as in manual labour) was the first large-scale, overtly supported, guest worker program in the U.S., operating between 1942 and 1964.

5. Indeed, the Central America Free Trade Agreement (CAFTA) is designed to recreate and extend the basic pattern further.

6. Canada is further implicated by its support for initiatives such as the General Agreement on Trade in Services (GATS) at the Organization for Economic Cooperation and Development (OECD).

7. In June 2007 the Supreme Court of Canada overturned the old law with a ruling that allows, in principal, the right to organize labour unions inclusive of farm workers. The province of Manitoba, under New Democratic Party governance, was the first provincial jurisdiction to apply this to their own labour code, extending rights to migrant/guest workers. With a range of court challenges pending, the United Food and Commercial Workers (UFCW–Canada) has been particularly active in these issues. In Ontario,

which is home to the largest proportion of migrant farm labourers, the Agricultural Employees Protection Act 2002 (Bill 187) was passed on November 18, 2002. It allowed farm workers to form associations, though not the right to unionize or the right to strike. The *Fraser v. Ontario* case (2009) appeared to extend the right to unionize, however at press time this judgment is still under appeal in front of the Supreme Court of Canada.

8. In Canada, these dimensions are particularly well laid out in Sharma (2001, 2006) wherein she examines Bill C 11 —Canada's border security and citizenship law that was actively debated and that laid bare the active racialized and gendered construction of "preferred citizens" and their others.

9. The term "social reproduction" refers generally to how individuals, families, groups, and communities sustain and reproduce themselves in terms of material standards of living as well as culturally.

10. For more information on the important work of J4MW, see their website at: http://www.justicia4migrantworkers.org

11. According to Hinnenkamp (2004), learning about Anglo-Canadian culture is one of the enjoyable features of guest work for workers; and according to Preibisch (2004) there are similar examples of enjoyment for host community members. These instances are largely overshadowed, however, by ethno-racial-class conflict.

12. Sessions were held in Southern Ontario and involved Sunday meetings held over the course of four weeks. They involved 18 male and three female farm workers, aged 20 to 60. All were citizens of Mexico and part of the Canadian government's SAWP. The project eventually produced not simply data but striking artwork, dramatic scripts, and highly informative interpretation.

13. The term "material conditions" refers to matters related to resources such as time, space and shelter, food, clothing, etc. Having adequate material resources in this sense means having enough of the basic necessities to live and work.

14. For more information on this method visit the Paulo Friere Institute website at: http://www.paulofreireinstitute.org/

©*Left Lane Productions/Corbis*

8

The Lengthening Shadow of Employment: Working Time[1] Re-examined

Ann Duffy

DISCUSSION QUESTIONS

1. How is an average day in your life structured around work and how much of your "awake" time is devoted to paid work, unpaid work, leisure (active and passive), and non-work? What are the societal implications of the ways in which you organize the time of your life and do you feel time-crunched?

2. In what ways have workers as individuals as well as workers' unions struggled to wrest some control over their time at work and what are the prospects for future struggles?

3. Do you agree or disagree that the microtechnology revolution (computers, cell phones, and so on) is as momentous a shift in the lives of average workers and their families as the industrial revolution?

4. What are the negative consequences of the current imbalance between "work and life" and what benefits (social, institutional, and personal) might accrue from a more open and flexible approach to incorporating work (paid and unpaid) into our lives?

5. Why is the lack of non-worktime in our lives a public issue with enormous societal and cultural consequences rather than a personal trouble in need of an individual solution?

> It is the time dimension of the new capitalism, rather than high-tech data transmission, global stock markets, or free trade, which most directly affects people's emotional lives outside the workplace. (Sennett, 1998, p. 25)

INTRODUCTION

Work as a feature of human existence has been central in sociological analysis for many decades and a wide variety of topics and perspectives—worker alienation, the bureaucratic structures of work organizations, work-family conflict—have been examined. While this scrutiny has contributed significantly to our understanding of work processes and workers' lives, it would appear from recent economic and social developments that the very fundamentals of work and its location in our lives are increasingly at issue in post-industrial societies. In particular, a number of analyses arguing that workers are devoting too much of their lives to paid employment seem to have resonated powerfully with North Americans and Europeans. Notably, Juliet Schor's *The Overworked American* (1992) struck a chord and lent support to a variety of analyses and social movements that critiqued paid work's domination of personal life and the erosion of "free" time (Hayden, 1999; Hochschild, 1997; Lewis, 2003; Menzies, 2005; Roxburgh, 2002). Here, I will argue that there is considerable evidence, despite the 2008 economic crisis, suggesting that the time out of our lives that is devoted directly and indirectly to paid employment continues to expand and, for many workers, challenges our personal as well as societal well-being.

Time devoted to work—on a daily, yearly, and lifelong basis—seems to be in the midst of significant transformations. In particular, the 40-hour standard workweek along with lifelong job tenure are increasingly anomalies. The dramatic expansion of **non-standard**, **part-time**, contract (**fixed term work**) and other forms of employment, the extensive elimination of **mandatory retirement** and, finally, the reconceptualizations of work and **non-work** all suggest a dramatic shift in both our understandings of and our experiences with worktime. In particular, these shifts suggest, ironically, an intensification of our worktime obligations. Preparing for work (education, training, and retraining), searching for work, commuting to work, juggling work obligations along with actual on the job activities have expanded dramatically for many Canadians from the 1960s. Worktime—paid, **unpaid**, and anticipated—permeates more and more of our lives; time that is truly outside of and beyond work becomes a more rarefied experience. In this process, our inner lives and emotional well-being are eroded as our abilities and opportunities to live beyond work are undermined (Bailyn, 2006; Wallace & Young, 2010).

A VERY BRIEF HISTORY OF WORKTIME

Time seems to be integral to human experience. Even in the furthest reaches of human history, we assume that as human beings we recognized the passage of days and seasons. Indeed, throughout most of human existence on the planet, it appears likely that human beings constructed their lives relative to seasonal and biological timetables—birth, puberty, pregnancy, death, interspersed with seasonal shifts. Seasons were linked to the intermittent availability of food resources—including game, berries, roots—and necessitated certain activities in order to sustain the group. In this way, throughout most of our history, we have not only been cognizant of the passage of time—for ourselves and others—but have been required by external factors to construct our lives in response to the time-specific events. Of course, not all human experiences were identical since the impact of seasonal changes would vary enormously from the harsh conditions of the arctic to the more forgiving sub-tropics. Further, it is probable that men and women experienced the impact of biological time tables differentially since pregnancy and lactation likely have long had a profound impact on many women's lives.

What is significant in this scenario is that, throughout history, humans have constructed their lives in temporal terms. Within this context, it is possible to talk about working time since the overwhelming majority[2] of humans have always devoted some portion of their daily and lifelong time to "work-related" actions. These work activities were directly connected to the routinized provision of food, shelter, and clothing. While many of these pursuits would overlap with artistic, social, and other categories of actions, it is clear that some endeavours—hunting, gathering food and fuel, preparing food and clothing and so on—entailed work tasks as they are loosely conceptualized today.

Through the course of history, worktime patterns[3] shifted. The first major change entailed the emergence of more complex societies as a result of advances in agriculture, animal husbandry, and weaponry. Typically, these new social forms included ruling classes—pharaohs, kings, queens, emperors, religious leaders, and various aristocrats. These well-to-do and powerful individuals, along with their families, friends, and immediate subordinates, were generally freed from some or all of the drudgery of routine worktime and benefitted from extended **leisure**. Some analysts speculate that this emergence of a leisure society permitted the forming and displaying of identity since for the first time groups of individuals had the time and opportunity to exercise choice and creativity (Rojek, 2001). Meanwhile, those on the bottom end of the social continuum were expected to take up any slack by working more intensely and longer on both a daily and lifetime basis.

The next fundamental shift in worktime was precipitated by advances in both technology and the factory system. Of course, these historical upheavals occurred at different times in different cultural contexts. Indeed, it is important to note that even today there remain significant cultural differences in the experience of both time and worktime. The discussion below briefly sketches the experiences of mostly Western, highly "developed," and more affluent societies. Reflecting fundamental differences in social beliefs and values, traditional cultures that are mostly Eastern, less "developed" and less affluent are often inclined to accept a more time-consuming approach to economic interactions in contrast to the West's preoccupation with speed and efficiency, even at the cost of social relationships (Manrai & Manrai, 1995).

Keeping in mind this historical and cultural diversity, it is clear that technological advances coupled with the factory approach to production altered time relationships and necessitated shifts in traditional approaches to work. Initially, in 18th century Britain for example, the new technology—notably, the cotton ginny—intensified worktime in the pre-industrial economy. In cottage industries, for example, employers would "farm out" equipment and raw materials to workers' home and then pay the head of the family in terms of units of product, for example, cotton spun into thread. Technological improvements both simplified the work process and seriously eroded the value of workers' skills in the productive process. In the process, the new technology increased employers' control over the workforce since it was employers who owned the means of production—the physical equipment being used in cottage industry. In this context, employers were free to demand increased time devoted to productivity.

Soon these changes in workers' lives were overshadowed by the efficiencies and increased profitability provided by the factory approach to production. Bringing workers, raw materials, and technology together in one central location—the factory—dramatically cut transportation costs while providing employers with much greater opportunities to supervise and control their workers. This enhanced domination of the productive process (along with the initial absence of workers' organizations and state regulation of workplaces) meant many employers could demand long working hours on a daily and weekly basis. Many of these early factory employers clearly felt that their investment in the factory and its equipment along with their entitlement to profits meant they could demand very long hours from their employees, even to the point of overwork in the midst of dangerous working conditions.[4]

Many analysts have commented on this momentous historical shift toward industrial production. In particular, for the first time in most social environments, the conflation of family life and worklife was seriously eroded if not ended (Zaretsky, 1986). Previously, for example, in the pre-industrial city, skilled craftsmen typically would work at home—drawing on family members such as spouses and children to provide assistance (Sjoberg, 1965). Work, home, and family were entangled enterprises. While, initially some factory owners hired entire families, soon the atomized worker—male, female, and child—was hired as an employee and paid as an individual.

This dislocation of family, work, and home necessitated dramatic changes and, not surprisingly, numerous social commentators discussed the dire implications for the family and community. However, of particular interest here are the implications for worktime. Particularly momentous was the decoupling of pay and units of production. Once employers began paying workers for tending to particular machines for a set period of time, it became important to extract as much labour as possible from each unit of time being paid for. In this context, control over the workers' time becomes pivotal. They must show up on time, so as not to slow the overall factory process or set a bad example for their fellow workers; their down time—on a daily (lunch breaks) and weekly basis (Sundays)—becomes central to the worker-employer relationship. Nowhere is this domination over workers' time more clear than in the oft-cited banner hung over one early industrial factory's gates: "If you don't come in Sunday, don't come in Monday."

In this splitting of private (personal and familial) and public (paid work), not only did the struggle over the control of workers' time emerge as a central societal issue, the boundaries surrounding worktime solidified. By physically separating activities in the home from work in the factory, time at work emerged as a much more concrete social reality. Far removed from the fuzzy days of hunting and gathering societies where work and artistry and sociality might be coterminous, in the factory era, worktime could be clearly understood to start when the worker entered the factory gates and, similarly, only end when she or he left at night.[5] The workday itself became highly structured, often the ringing of a bell signalled the meal break and failure to show up on time or to work without stopping was punished with fines, dismissals, and even physical coercion (Rinehart, 2001). In this economic configuration, employers were in an advantageous position in terms of determining who was working and how hard.

Of course, as noted previously, the new working reality took hold at different times and in different geographical contexts. More importantly, the process was often contentious and tumultuous;[6] workers and their organizations frequently resisted the new discipline. As individuals they might arrive late, quit without notice, and malinger. More significantly, as groups they formed unions, workers' co-operatives, and protest groups to challenge the controls imposed in the workplace. Canada's history is interwoven with numerous workers' actions. From the Winnipeg General Strike of 1919 to the current (2010) strike by 7,000 workers in Sudbury, workers have struggled collectively and as individuals to improve the content and security of compensation for their time at work. Although workers' organizations, especially unions, have been on the defensive for a number of years, their struggles have succeeded over the course of decades in decreasing the length of the mandated workday and workweek (Keune & Galgoczi, 2006) (see Box 8.1).

RENEWED DEMANDS FOR 30-HOUR WORKWEEK
DURING THE U.S. ECONOMIC CRISIS

The notion of a 30-hour workweek was first suggested in 1922 during a national strike of U.S. coal miners. During the Depression, further efforts were made to reduce the workweek so that more workers could be employed. When the economy boomed in the early 1960s, even a U.S. Senate sub-committee was speculating on a 22-hour workweek by 1985. Of course, by 2000 the average U.S. workers were working 199 hours more per year than they had in 1973. The economic downturn of 2008 and the continued high rates of unemployment throughout much of the United States have lead to renewed calls from workers' organizations for a reduction in the workweek, especially in light of the fact that France had introduced a 35-hour workweek in the 1990s and created an estimated 400,000 jobs. As many others have argued, if the work is shared and/or if overtime is reduced, then there would be more than enough work for all the unemployed. However, employers clearly recognize that training more workers, paying more benefits, and managing a large labour force do not meet their needs for reduced labour costs (Grevatt, 2007; Hayden, 2005; Shillington, 2009)

In 1870 workers in the Canadian manufacturing sector were averaging 64 hours per week. Trade union pressures were directly responsible for reducing the workday to 58.6 hours in this sector by 1901 and to 50 hours in 1921. After World War II, there were further reductions so that by 1957 the average workweek (prior to overtime being paid) was reduced to 40 hours a week (Krahn & Lowe, 1988). Since that time, despite shorter workweeks being established in various European countries and continued pressures from the Canadian labour movement to reduce the workweek, many Canadians, as detailed here, are experiencing an intensification of their paid work obligations.

ARE WE WORKING MORE?

It is hard to believe that in the 1970s, analysts were concerned about Canada's future as a leisure society—what would people do with all their free time? Today, analysts are much more preoccupied with the various ways in which paid employment "increasingly dominates" our lives (Lewis, 2003). Indeed, in the past three decades, almost one-third of Canadian workers aged 19 to 64 (31 percent) have consistently described themselves as "workaholics" (Keown, 2007). Working too much, to the detriment of one's health and personal relationships, seems to be socially acceptable.

Certainly the emergence of the so-called 24/7 global economy is related to changes in employment in many Western societies (Rubin & Brody, 2005;

Lewis, 2003). In this emergent economic context, significant portions of the Canadian workforce by the end of the 20th century found themselves working longer hours than previously. Between 1986 and 2005 men's participation in paid work increased from 6.1 hours per day to 6.3 hours. Women far surpassed this growth as they saw their paid daily worktime increase from 3.3 hours per day in 1986 to 4.4 hours in 2005 (Statistics Canada, 2006c).[7] Predictably, women's workweeks also expanded and between 1997 and 2006 women increased their average weekly hours by 0.6 hours to 33.1 hours. At the same time, a growing majority of women (73.9 percent) were employed on a full-time rather than part-time basis (30 hours or more) basis.[8] Part of this shift towards women devoting more hours to paid work is due to the fact that more and more mothers, even of children under 6 years of age, now hold full-time employment and there is, in fact, very little difference between the full-time employment rates of mothers of young children and mothers with no dependent children at home (Usalcas, 2008).

Youth as a category have also experienced some growth in their paid worktime.[9] Although, between 1979 and 2000, hours for young (16 to 24) male workers dropped by 22.1 percent and for young women by 11.4 percent, much of this apparent drop seems related to increased involvement in education. If students are excluded from these calculations, between 1979 and 2000, work hours for young males fell by 16 percent and for young women they actually rose by 4.5 percent (Heisz & LaRochelle-Cote, 2003). Most recently (from 1997 to 2006), the average paid workweek for all youth (15 to 24) increased by a half hour to 28.8 hours per week and for full-time students with paid employment grew by 1.7 hours to an average of 15.2 hours per week (Usalcas, 2008).

Here once again, women in particular saw their paid work hours (on weekends as well as on school days) increase. Between 1986 and 2005 young women intensified their paid labour force activities by two hours per week and by 2005 young women had a higher daily employment rate than young men (Marshall, 2007). Further, when young women's various obligatory activities are combined—paid work, school work, and domestic chores—they are busy indeed. Research indicates that girls aged 12 to 19 years of age experience a higher total workload (a combination of schoolwork, domestic activities, and paid employment) than comparable boys and these comparable boys have more free time, especially when aged 12 to 14 (Hilbrecht, Zuzanek, & Mannell, 2007).

This gendered pattern is also apparent among older workers. Hours worked per man aged 55 to 69 dropped by 23.8 percent between 1998 and 2005 while they increased by 21.4 percent for comparable women.

In short, there is clear evidence that by the beginning of the new millennium, women in every age group are experiencing increased hours in paid employment. The fact that women, as a group, are characterized by increased paid worktime does not mean of course that all men are enjoying a break. By the late 1990s certain elements of the male labour force, especially in the manufacturing sector, confronted an intensification of paid working hours. Global competition (with poorly paid, non-unionized factories in other countries) encouraged strategies to reduce labour costs. These included downsizing the labour force, introducing more labour-saving technology, and, of course, offshoring production to Mexico, China, etc. A reduced workforce along with the application of technology often translated into increasing time pressures on individual workers.

For example, particularly in the 1980s and 90s, employers used overtime schedules to maximize their deployment of skilled workers. Employers in industrial settings realized that it was both more efficient and cost effective to draw upon their now smaller workforce to work longer hours rather than to hire, train, and benefit additional workers. This pattern was consistent with the **just-in-time** and **flexibilization** management approach to corporate efficiencies. Existing workers could be called upon to work overtime, without incurring additional costs and while maintaining overall flexibility. Overtime schedules could be easily cut in the event of shifts in labour force needs.

Within this economic context, it is not surprising that a significant segment of the male labour force continued to work particularly long hours. In 2001, more than one-tenth of male workers and in 2005 as many as 14 percent were employed 50 hours or more during a typical workweek (Heisz & LaRochelle-Cote, 2006). However, this pattern of long work hours for men appears to now be on the wan in light of the 2008 recession. Coincidental with the steady loss of industrial jobs in the last several years, the numbers of men working very long hours (49 hours or more) have declined from 16.7 percent of men of all ages to 13.8 percent in 2006.[10]

In short, there is evidence indicating that certain segments of the population—notably, men in manufacturing, women of all ages, and youth, especially student youth—are increasing their hours of paid work. It is likely this trend is directly related to efforts on the parts of families to maintain or improve their economic situation by mobilizing more paid workers—mothers and teenagers—into the labour force. Certainly wives and mothers have become a routine component of the employment picture as have youth.

The motivators behind these patterns of increased labour force participation are complex but certainly economic pressures on the household—pressures exacerbated by a burgeoning consumer economy and the stagnation of wages—have propelled more family members into paid work

(Jackson, 2005). However, it is certainly not discretionary spending and lifestyle concerns that are primarily responsible. Dramatic increases in housing costs across Canada, growing pressures for additional educational accreditation (with their attendant financial costs), inflation, and the failure of average incomes to keep up with cost of living have meant that many families had little choice but to make accommodations by having more family members spend time in paid labour (Ashton and Elliott, 2007; Livingstone, 2001). There have been other strategic responses as well, including the tendency of youth to remain in or return to their parents' home as they navigate the "grim" economy (Beaujot & Andersen, 2007).

It may seem ironic that in this context of family mobilization into the paid labour force men of all ages have tended to see their hours at paid work decline. It is also very puzzling that paid work hours have actually increased or declined very little when research continues to indicate that many women and men in the global economy want fewer hours of paid work. Recent research indicates that in the United States and (West) Germany more than one-third of workers indicated they wanted reductions in their worktime and in Japan almost half and in Sweden almost three-quarters indicated they wanted fewer hours of work (Reynolds, 2004). However, these longings do not appear to fit with the ongoing evolution of paid work arrangements.

ARE WE WORKING LONGER?

For a relatively short period of time, following World War II, many Canadian workers worked a 40-hour week and made sufficient income to support a spouse (who worked full-time in the home) and children. For a wide variety of reasons, this social construction of the workday is long past, despite its continuing influence on societal beliefs and values. While in 1978 almost half (47.4 percent) of workers worked between 35 and 40 hours a week, by 2000 only slightly more than one-third (39.4 percent) were working this so-called standard-length workweek. In place of traditional arrangements, a continuing polarization and diversification of worktime arrangements have occurred, with more and more workers employed on a part-time basis or working long hours (overtime) (Heisz & LaRochelle-Cote, 2006).[11]

The dramatic growth in part-time employment was one of the first outstanding symptoms of the revolution in labour time arrangements. From 1953 to 1997, part-time work grew exponentially and by2006, 26.2 percent of women workers and 10.9 percent of men workers were employed on a part-time basis (Duffy & Pupo, 1992; Usalcas, 2008). The dramatic growth in part-time work is, of course, coincident with the availability of a willing labour force and increased demands from growth areas of the economy.

The movement of wives and mothers and youth into the paid labour force in response to family and personal needs was a key ingredient as was the dramatic surge in service sector employment and the equally profound decline in manufacturing sector work.[12] By 2006, 76 percent of employment was in the service sector of the economy and 85 percent of all new jobs created since 1997 were also there (Usalcas, 2008)

While part-time work continues to figure as the most prominent change in the time structure of paid work, a whole range of new variations have also emerged. Fixed term work, **multiple job holding**, shiftwork, **worksharing**, on call positions, and agency work have all expanded. For example, while more than one-quarter Canadian workers are now part-time, more than one in 10 are on fixed term employment (increasing from 9 to 13 percent between 1997 and 2003 and during this period almost one-fifth of all growth in employment was on a fixed-term basis (Saloniemi & Zeytinoglu, 2007).

Of course, these working time structures overlap with one another and change over time. A full-time worker who is also employed part-time is a multiple job holder and may also be a casual employee in one or both of his or her workplaces. Further, there is often considerable movement in and out of worktime arrangements. Full-time employment over the summer months may segue into part-time work in the fall; 2006 was a good year for employment and 2008 was marked by layoffs and reduced hours. As a result, particularly among workers with low-quality[13] and non-standard jobs, there may be considerable variation in annual work hours over time.

An examination of longitudinal data spanning a five-year period reveals that almost one-quarter of Canadian workers experienced an annual variability in worktime of more than eight weeks and the average worker experienced an annual variation of about five full weeks of work. In other words, for one in four Canadian workers, 50 weeks of work one year may translate into 42 the following year and vice versa. In short, many workers in Canada are experiencing considerable unpredictability in their worktime over the years (Heisz & LaRochelle-Cote, 2006).

This longitudinal analysis of changes in worktime, in turn, lends itself to a lifelong perspective on worktime arrangements. Just as the traditional 40-hour Monday to Friday workweek appears to be rapidly evaporating, the 40 or 45 year worklife followed by a hopefully leisure-filled retirement shows growing signs of fragility. The official elimination of mandatory retirement in various provinces has, of course, signalled that age 65 is no longer considered the appropriate time at which to withdraw from the paid labour force (Gillin, MacGregor, & Klassen, 2005). However, even prior to this legislation, there was considerable evidence that older workers and retirees were either remaining in or returning to the paid labour force (Duffy, Glenday, & Pupo, 1998).

Recent research continues to document this trend towards lifelong work. In 2005, two-thirds (68 percent) of men aged 55 to 64 were employed (up from 59 percent in 1998); more than half (51 percent) of same-aged women held jobs, up from 41 percent just six years earlier. Further, both men and women in this age group had experienced an increase in their actual paid worktime since 1998—a 1.2 hours per day increase for men and one hour increase for women. Even senior workers in the 65 to 74 age group experienced a small increase in the amount of paid work they undertook (Statistics Canada, 2006a). Of course, the 2008 recession will likely intensify this trend towards employed seniors, since pension funds have not only been eroded but also confidence in income supports for retirees has been undermined (Duffy, forthcoming).

Just as many Canadians on a daily and weekly basis are spending more hours in the paid labour force, this evidence suggests that over the course of their lifetimes Canadians will be devoting more months and years to paid work. The intensification of our working lives is not restricted to the present; it may extend far into the future. "Freedom 55" appears to be on the verge of becoming as anomalous as the leisure society.[14]

DO WE HAVE LESS TIME AWAY FROM WORK?

Among the most significant recent shifts in our understandings of work has been a re-examination of the lines between work and non-work activities. In particular, the women's movement with its campaign to draw attention to the "real" (and often unrecognized) work in the household challenged the traditional parameters of work. As extensive **feminist political economy** literature points out, domestic labour—food preparation, cleaning, childcare, and so forth—activities that maintain the household and provide for the reproduction of the labour force on a daily and generational basis are "real" work that needs to be recognized and, in some sense, compensated.

This shift from the 1950s ideology of household work as a "labour of love" to contemporary views is also, of course, rooted in the actual work experiences of men and women. As economic and consumer pressures, along with dramatic increases in the numbers of single-parent (typically mother-headed) families, grew through the latter part of the 20th century, families were forced to deploy more paid workers. The massive movement of mothers into paid employment along with the deployment of many teens into part-time work speak to this shift in many families' relationship to the labour market.

The net result was inevitably a shortfall in time available for traditional household responsibilities and a rapidly growing recognition that unpaid activities in the home were inextricably linked to paid work. Such understandings are now embedded in family law, notably divorce legislation, which recognizes the unpaid labour contributions of a spouse who assumes primary responsibility for domestic labour and/or childcare. Similarly, numerous research studies in the sociology of the family indicate that spouses negotiate responsibilities in the family by taking into account the importance of unpaid labour in the home (Wallace & Young, 2010). Finally, the routine collection of census data on unpaid worktime in the home also speaks to the social acceptance of household work as a form of "real" work. While the resulting new unpaid work arrangements in Canadian families may remain inequitable, there has been a social realization that unpaid work in the home is also "real" work and consumes "real time."

This recognition of domestic work as work has been facilitated when the actual labour—care of children, preparation of meals, household cleaning— exists extensively as actual paid occupations in the external economy. More challenging has been the recognition that other elements of family work— emotional support, maintenance of social networks, and consumerism—may be all understood and experienced as unpaid work obligations. Most notably, for example, family members in a consumer society undertake long hours preparing for and engaging in consumer-related activities and, finally, actually making purchases, assembling them, storing them in the home, and disposing of both packaging and household objects that have been replaced. Aspects of these efforts are complexly interwoven with prevailing notions of leisure and choice. For example, is buying a car a choice we make and is it a component of our leisure activities? Certainly, consumer advertising seeks to convince us that this is a pleasurable activity premised on individual choice. While routine consumption obligations (for example, grocery purchases) may now be frequently understood to be "work" and not leisure, there is a wide diversity of contentious household activities that seem to blur into issues of "choice" and "leisure" (Ravenscroft & Gilchrist, 2009).

Volunteerism provides another intriguing example of this blurred line between work and non-work, between "free" time and "obligatory" time and between choice and compulsion. At one point in time, it was perhaps the case that a citizen might (somewhat) freely decide to volunteer in their community. However, in recent years there has been a popular trend throughout the post–industrial West to require, formally as well as informally, individuals to "volunteer" for community service (Warburton & Smith, 2003). These compulsory volunteer programs (a revealing oxymoron) take a variety of forms.

In areas of Canada, for example, young people are required to fulfill 40 hours of "community service" in order to earn their high school graduation diploma. Even the criminal justice and welfare systems have joined the bandwagon by requiring "community service" from their "clients." In addition, of course, every university and college student realizes that the pursuit of employment routinely entails including "volunteer" activities on their resumes and that certain professional programs, notably teaching, prioritize extensive volunteer work. While volunteerism continues to be lauded as an example of Canadians "giving back" to their communities, it is increasingly unclear where these activities should be situated relative to work obligations.[15]

Beyond household chores, consumption, and required volunteering, a wide diversity of compulsory, unpaid activities may be understood as integral to "work" in our society (Lewis, 2003). In particular, workers' short and long-term efforts to prepare for work, though unpaid, are clearly related to the reproduction of the labour force. For example, as increasingly clear in most education institutions, the years of effort spent in acquiring an education and relevant skills are unpaid work in the pursuit of paid work and the number of years required for these efforts are expanding. Indeed, the enthusiasm for so-called lifelong learning in the new economy speaks not only to the desirability of learning but the never-ending obligation to work (unpaid) to satisfy the changing requirements of the **globalized workplace** (Cruikshank, 2007).

The expansion of educational work not only includes more hours in the classroom but also increasing demands for work done at home (homework). This work sent home from the school functions to erode children's leisure activities while also increasing the unpaid work roles of parents, especially mothers. This notion of "work to take home" of course also permeates the realities of paid employment. Advances in technology mean that it is much easier for workers to carry their workplace with them—checking their Blackberry, answering e-mails, preparing documents while at home, on vacation, and so forth. While not unprecedented, it has been dramatically amplified in the digitalized work era.

Along with education-related work, there are a variety of other unpaid work activities that are required to maintain access to paid employment. Preparing a resume (often also part of the educational curriculum), applying for work, scrutinizing the employment websites, networking and so on appear as pertinent to the maintenance of the paid labour force as the household labour that feeds, clothes, and houses workers. This is particularly the case for the numerous Canadians employed in nonstandard work who often must devote considerable energy to pursuing work and sustaining a continuous employment life. In short, it seems reasonable to propose that to the degree to which household labour is conceptualized as unpaid work and an ingredient in our "work" lives, so too should education, training, and the pursuit of work.[16]

Once it is accepted that "work" encompasses both paid and unpaid activities—both of which contribute directly to our paid employment, then it is possible to find considerable additional evidence of the intensification of work demands in Canadians' lives and, implicitly, the erosion of "free" time.

Janet Fast and Judith Frederick (2001) examined Canadians' time use, including paid work, unpaid work, self-care, and leisure. They found that between 1986 and 1998, Canadian parents aged 25 to 44 with children under age 25 actually increased their worktime from 8.7 hours to 9.7 hours a day for women and 9.0 hours to 9.9 hours per day for men. In short, a 7-hour day has been added to parents' workload over the 12 years. Similarly, Martin Turcotte's (2007) examination of family time reported that workers with families increased their time in work and work-related activities from 506 minutes to 536 minutes per day from 1986 to 2005. Indeed, he suggests that this increase in worktime is a key factor in the erosion of the amount of time spent with family members. Between 1986 and 2005, the average amount of time workers spent with their families dropped by about three-quarters of an hour per day. In 1986, 23 percent of workers spent six hours or more with their family but only 14 percent did so in 2005 and those who spent only one hour or less increased from 9 percent in 1986 to 14 percent in 2005 (pp. 2, 5, 11). These findings of dramatic increases in the typical "work day" and the coincidental erosion of non-worktime are, of course, entirely consistent with various research indicating that parents, especially mothers, are routinely experiencing a "**time crunch**" with too little time to do what needs to be done (see Box 8.2).

BOX 8.2

TOO MUCH WORK AND TOO LITTLE SLEEP

Contemporary analysts estimate that Canadians are working (paid and unpaid work) an additional 15 hours per week compared with the 1960s. The 2008 recession simply intensified pressure to work long hours and multiple jobs. According to a 2008 poll, one-third of North Americans employed 30 or more hours a week reported they had fallen asleep or become extremely drowsy at work—an issue reflected in the recent controversy surrounding pictures of Toronto Transit Commission workers photographed sleeping on the job. The U.S. Sloan Work and Family Research Network found that 89 percent of workers agreed (somewhat or strongly) that they work very hard and never seem to have "enough time to get everything done" (Nebenzahl, 2010, p. B8). Not surprisingly, the more you work, the less you sleep. Working full-time, commuting for more than one hour a day, working non-traditional work schedules (on call, casual, shift, split shift, and so on), having a partner, having children, and being "time crunched" all translate into less sleep. Inadequate and disrupted sleep has been associated with cardiovascular disease, hypertension, asthma, diabetes, and depression. Yet, many of these inadequate sleep factors are increasingly commonplace in our society (Hurst, 2008).

Parents are not the only Canadians whose combined burden of paid and unpaid work is experienced as increasingly onerous. Contrary to images of a leisurely retirement, many seniors report heavy work obligations and little in the way of "free" or "leisure" time. Recent research conducted through the General Social Survey distinguishes paid and unpaid work and leisure. Among men 55 to 64 years old, there has been an intensification of paid work between 1998 and 2005 and a not surprising decline in active leisure (30 minutes less per day). Among comparable women, they continue (from 1992 to 2005) to devote an average of 4.8 hours per day to unpaid work and have increased their paid work obligations by an average of one hour (since 1992) with a not surprising 0.7 hours drop in time spent in active leisure.

Older men and women (aged 65 to 74) do experience a decline in their average paid worktime, but the men experience a sharp increase (3.1 hours a week) in their contribution to unpaid work (totalling 3.9 hours per day) while same-aged women continue to spend the same 4.8 hours a day on unpaid work that their younger counterparts as well as earlier cohorts also expended. In short, it would seem both senior men and women are not shedding paid employment for leisure, but rather, continue to shoulder significant daily obligations in terms of unpaid work (Statistics Canada, 2006a).

THE IMPACT OF NEW REALITIES IN WORKING TIME

Many Canadians are experiencing an intensification of their working lives. This includes not only working for long hours, when they are able to secure employment, but also devoting more years to education and training, spending more time travelling to and from jobs, expending more resources juggling non-standard work arrangements, and continuing to work well into their senior years while all the time experiencing reductions in their "non-work" or "free" time. A wide diversity of research suggests that these emergent patterns fail to benefit Canadians in terms of quality of life and, indeed, may be directly associated to physical, mental, and emotional health problems.

Not surprisingly, as wives and mothers have become a more integral element in the paid labour force, more mothers and fathers have reported feeling "rushed" every day. According to 1998 examination of Canadians' time use over the life course, employed parents 25 to 44, more than any other age/family category, reported time scarcity. Mothers in this group are particularly likely to feel trapped by the busyness of their lives (Fast & Frederick, 2004). Predictably, this pattern persists, despite the continuing integration of mothers into paid employment and the proliferation of non-standard work.

Contemporary research reports that Canadians who are juggling heavy paid work responsibilities with family formation and children frequently speak of the stress of being time-crunched and having inadequate leisure time (Holmgren et al., 2009). Working shift or part-time may not only not resolve the pressures but may compound difficulties in terms of scheduling family activities and reducing time available for family roles (when contrasted to full-time homemakers) (Tausig & Fenwick, 2001). The "role overload" employed parents, especially mothers, are subject to along with the lack of control over worktime that they may experience may, in turn, lead to stress and a decline in mental and physical well-being (Beaujot & Andersen, 2007).

Kindred conclusions are suggested by surveys of older Canadians. For example, among older women (but not men) (55 to 74 years old) healthy women were more satisfied with their lives if they spent less time on paid work and more time on active leisure (Statistics Canada, 2006a). Similarly, research indicates that as women age and they spend less time in paid work and more in active leisure, they (55 to 74 years old) report themselves to be more satisfied with their lives (Statistics Canada, 2006a).

Not only does heavy paid work and parental obligations often result in dissatisfaction and stress, some particular forms of non-standard paid employment appear to be particularly linked to worker dissatisfaction, relationship problems, and poor health. Men and women who work evening or night shifts along with men who work rotating shifts are more likely to indicate job dissatisfaction than those with regular day-time schedules. Predictably, dissatisfied workers were found to be more likely to rate their physical and mental health as fair or poor (Shields, 2006; Statistics Canada, 2006b). Some analysts go so far as to assert that working nights can seriously damage your health (Humm, 2009).

Other research indicates that working fixed night shifts greatly increases the rates of separation and divorce for both women and men workers (Presser, 2000). Evening shifts from 4 to midnight are also challenging for relationships. Wight et al. (2008) found that parents who work non-standard evening hours spend less time in some child-related activities, spend less time with their spouse, get less sleep, and watch less television than parents with standard work days. Finally, Strazdins et al. report that when children live in families where one or both parents work evenings, nights, or weekends, parents report worse family functioning, more depressive symptoms, and less effective parenting; the children in these families were more likely to have social and emotional difficulties (Strazdins et al., 2006).

While not as traumatic as evening and night shifts, fixed term employment is associated with very high feelings of job insecurity, which is in turn related to stress. While only 15 percent of Canadian workers in 1994 report their job is insecure, a dramatic 57 percent of those on fixed term contracts perceive their employment to be insecure (Saloniemi & Zeytinoglu, 2007).

Not surprisingly, men and women who work evening or night shifts are more likely to indicate job dissatisfaction than those with regular day-time schedules. Predictably, dissatisfied workers are found to be more likely to rate their physical and mental health as fair or poor (Statistics Canada, 2006b). Along a similar vein, workers who experienced considerable variability in the pattern of their annual working hours report a higher incidence of stress. Some 47 percent of workers with high variability reveal feeling high stress compared with 34.5 percent of those with stable hours (Heisz & LaRochelle-Cote, 2006).

The variability in working time arrangements and workers' dissatisfaction with this reality also speaks to the more general tendency for workers to report they lack control over their work schedules. A wide variety of research, for example, documents that in most European countries, employees spend more hours at work than they would prefer (van Echtelt, Glebbeek, & Lindenberg, 2006). Even if it meant a reduction in income, many workers prefer to work fewer hours and even part-time workers often indicate they end up working more hours than they want.

In short, not only working long hours but being employed in non-standard working arrangements, insecure fixed term employment, working evening or night shifts and having little control over work scheduling as well as numbers of hours at paid work appear to be related to negative outcomes for many workers. These patterns of worktime appear likely to undermine many workers' emotional and physical health, their sense of well-being, their abilities to balance family and work, the quality of gender relations in their families, and their sense of choice and control in the workplace (Boulin, Lallement, Messenger, & Michon, 2006; Vosko, 2000). Nonetheless, it is precisely these worktime arrangements that are currently flourishing.

THE FUTURE OF WORKING TIME

Needless to say, the pressures to mobilize more family members in the paid labour force have been exacerbated by the 2008 recession as concerns about the stagnation of wages, retirement funding, job insecurity, and the need to "invest in" education and training are all intensified. Of course, this has particular implications for women in Canadian society. As indicated previously, it is mothers and wives who have experienced an increase in their overall work load, even in their senior years. This is, in part, a result of the ways in which the new economy and non-standard forms of employment have tended to target women (Messenger, 2004; Vosko, 2000). Women juggle, for example, mothering and paid employment by turning to part-time, fixed term work. While this may make their overall work load more manageable, it often does not allow them to escape the time crunch of combining mothering and paid work and it leaves them vulnerable to the low wages, scant benefits, few opportunities, and generally poor job characteristics that frequently characterize non-standard work (Perrons et al., 2006). These work arrangements simply perpetuate gender inequality (Messenger, 2004).

In the aftermath of 2008, women as wives and mothers will continue to be under considerable pressure to contribute to the economic stability of the family while their economic vulnerability will make it difficult to press for schedule flexibility or control over work. Such ongoing contributions to the persistence of gender inequality are particularly troubling in light of research that indicates not only are women working more, their experiences of free time tend to be inferior to those of men (Mattingly & Bianchi, 2003; Wallace & Young, 2010).

Youth are also likely to be adversely affected by the economic turmoil (see Box 8.3). They will continue to feel pressured to improve their educational qualifications in a highly competitive labour market. Increased educational credentials require financial resources that will necessitate intensified participation in the low-wage segments of the service economy. Of course, juggling paid employment and education will continue to provide an excellent overture to full participation in the labour force. Older workers in their 30s, 40s, 50s, and older who are fortunate enough to achieve employment will also be strongly motivated by fears of job insecurity to improve their training and educational qualifications, thus further encouraging an extended working day. As discussed above, economic concerns will mean that many seniors will stay in or return to paid employment, often in some form of non-standard work.

BOX 8.3

GENME WILL NOT SETTLE FOR A LIFE DOMINATED BY WORK

Recent commentaries on Generation Me (those individuals born between 1982 and 1999), suggest that beliefs and values surrounding work and leisure may be changing. In contrast to the Boomers (born 1946 to 1964), for example, they are seen as interested in "working to live" not "living to work." They prioritize jobs that accommodate their family and personal lives. A recent survey of a U.S. representative national sample reports that GenMe does place significantly greater emphasis on leisure time relative to previous generational cohorts. For example, almost twice as many GenMe's rated having a job with more than two weeks of vacation as very important compared with a similar survey in 1976 and "almost twice as many wanted a job at which they could work slowly." Further, in contrast to previous generations, they were less likely to want to work overtime and more likely to say they would stop working if they had enough money (Twenge, Campbell, Hoffman, & Lance, 2010).

For all workers, increases in job insecurity encourage workers to bow to an intensification of time demands, including unpaid overtime and work at home (especially among non-unionized workers) and to postpone efforts to lobby for more manageable time schedules (such as jobsharing) (Rubin & Brody, 2005; Saloniemi & Zeytinoglu, 2007). Indeed there is some evidence that this may be the case as an Environics poll reported that 21 percent of Canadian workers surveyed were working more hours a week than normal and about 37 percent of these workers were not being compensated (Chai, 2009). Similarly, surveys in Quebec suggest that workers generally believe that arriving early and leaving late are viewed favourably by work organizations and 60 percent of those surveyed felt that their employer expects overtime. With the prospect of continued layoffs, workers may feel compelled to demonstrate workplace commitment through long hours at work (*Globe and Mail*, 2008, p. C5). This pattern of fear and economic insecurity may already be affecting the length of time women take while on maternity leave with women opting to return early to work in order to bring in a "much needed paycheque" (Kopun, 2009) and other women reporting employers eliminated their jobs while they were on maternity leave.

Conversely, worker initiatives to gain control over schedules and working time may be jeopardized. Reports from the United States suggest that flex time, family time and telecommuting are "slipping away." In a recession, employers are under no compulsion to use such methods to retain employees; the spectre of unemployment is sufficient. Workers hesitate to ask for any accommodations out of fear they will appear less committed to their work (*Globe and Mail,* 2009, p. L6). In short, the economic crisis in various ways tends to undermine movement towards worker control over scheduling (Tausig & Fenwick, 2001).

This erosion of control over worktime is also evidenced by increasing pressures to accept government and employer-mandated **job sharing**. Throughout the economy, workers have been asked to work share to avoid layoffs. Rogers Communication asked many of its full-time staff to accept a 20-percent pay cut; Taiwan's Hsinchu Science Park has asked 100,000 to take up to 10 days unpaid leave a month to prevent further job losses. In Utah, 17,000 state employees are now working a four-day week. By March 2009, thousands of Ontario steel workers are on job sharing (Popplewell, 2009). Similarly, in Germany, automaker Daimler AG has reduced worktime for 73,000 workers by as much as five hours a week to save job cuts (*Toronto Star,* 2009, p. B4). In Welland, Ontario, for example, unionized industrial works worked out an agreement with Employment Insurance Canada whereby workers would work four days a week at full-pay and while not working on the fifth day of the week would receive E.I. payments (A. Duffy, personal interview,

May 8, 2009). In this way, the number of layoffs was, at least temporarily, reduced; however, it is likely that in the short run some of these workers will take up additional part-time work on their "free" day.

Some analysts argue that this proclivity towards overwork is built into the structure of the new economy. Although some workers have been accorded considerable autonomy (telecommuting, satellite offices, and so on) they are still competitively evaluated in terms of productivity (for example, task or project completion). In the context of high rates of unemployment, such workers will be inclined to focus on completing the work at hand, despite the time pressures (including unpaid overtime) rather than demanding a reduction in working hours. Even part-time workers will work extra hours as they focus on successfully addressing the work tasks at hand. The very logic of job design in the contemporary economy militates against demands for reduced working time—if workers cannot handle the tasks in the time provided, they are expected to find another job. Predictably such assumptions tend to deflect efforts to reduce the working day or make it more flexible (van Echtelt, Glebbeek, & Lindenberg, 2006).

From a **life course perspective**, the economic recession will reinforce tendencies away from lifelong employment with one employer and toward the growth in non-standard work forms. These worktime structures will in all likelihood necessitate more time spent commuting,[17] navigating, and obtaining employment. Workers with multiple jobs or combining jobs and education will, inevitably, spend more time going from place to place. Workers who see their jobs, as a result of fixed term contracts or layoffs or reduced hours, end will also be likely to travel further afield in search of work and/or education. Indeed, across Canada workers already devote a considerable portion of each day to travelling to and from work and between 1986 and 2005, they significantly increased their daily work commute (Turcotte, 2007, p. 11).

Men and women who form families will increasingly need to intensify their labour force contributions (including multiple job holding and minimal parental leaves) in order to mitigate the impact on the family of any future layoffs. Older workers will likely respond to insecurities surrounding pension funds and the financial pressures on their adult children by prolonging and/or intensifying their paid labour force involvement. All these forays into paid employment necessitate changes in family life and perhaps in the quality of familial relationships (Maher, Lindsay & Franzway, 2008).

Finally, it seems probable that in the midst of a prolonged economic downturn many initiatives such as "worktime reduction" and "downshifting" as well as the increased mobilization of workers' organizations and unions will face an uphill struggle.

However, there is a more sanguine vision of the economic crisis and Canadians' immediate work future. High rates of unemployment along with reduced working hours may free many, at least momentarily, from the heavy time constraints of paid employment, commuting, and much of the extensive unpaid work that supports paid employment. Canadians may have more time for themselves, their families, and their communities. Further, the growing sense of economic and work insecurity may prompt more people to question the consumerism, indebtedness, and workaholic mindset that supports current social arrangements. Indeed, the research supports such a possibility since the time use data suggest that a strong sense of community is indeed associated "with an increase in discretionary time, a decline in time scarcity and a concomitant increase in leisure time" (Fast & Frederick, 2004, p. 30).

E N D N O T E S

1. This discussion of worktime implies a distinction between work and non-work and, as discussed below leads to a discussion of unpaid work (domestic labour), leisure (free time, non-obligatory time, discretionary time), volunteer time, and so forth (Lewis, 2003). The research literature contains a variety of approaches to the operationalization of these concepts. Needless to say, it is enormously difficult to compartmentalize individuals' lives and tally the number of minutes devoted to specific activities. Significantly, many activities overlap or bleed into one another. The driver making a business-related cell phone call or the mother helping her children with their homework while putting away the groceries exemplify the common place multitasking in our society. While acknowledging these complexities and contradictions, the author is commenting on the typical distinctions between paid work/employment (including self-employment), unpaid work (most commonly household maintenance, childcare, housekeeping) and "free" time (time that is freed from any sense of obligation or necessity). For a detailed example of the breakdown of specific activities, see Fast and Frederick (2004, Appendix A).

2. Assuming that human history dates back at least 30,000 years, throughout most of human history the majority of humans alive on the planet would have had to engage in actions to ensure their physical survival. Only in recent years have there been groups of individuals (royalty, corporate, and political elites, and so on) whose privileged social positions removed any necessity to engage in work activities.

3. Anthropologists estimate that prehistoric women and men devoted approximately four hours a day to activities designed to ensure their physical survival—that is, the provision of food, shelter, and clothing.

4. A wide variety of social history documents the horrendous living conditions experienced by many early industrial workers. See, for example, Bradbury, 1982; Copp, 1974; Coulter, 1982.

5. Of course, as Daniel Glenday points out in this volume, workers have long strived to hew out some small "time-outs" from worktime so that they can engage in personal and social activities during the course of the working day.

6. The class struggles over working time took both direct and indirect forms. For example, police and military directly opposed workers' demands in Winnipeg in 1919. At the same period, a mass education program was being deployed across the country that more indirectly socialized young Canadians into their obligations to be punctual, obedient, and drilled.

7. In the United States, employed women worked nearly 20 percent fewer hours per year in 1993 than they did in 1997 and added 233 hours to their average work year (U.S. Department of Labour, 1997).

8. From 1997 to 2006 full-time employment rates among women increased from 70.7 percent to 73.9 percent (Usalcas, 2008).

9. In fact, Canadian teens ranked third among OECD countries in terms of the hours spent in paid labour during the school week.

10. Similarly, workers in Great Britain (which has a reputation for long working hours) has also witnessed a drop in average weekly hours of paid work from 33.2 hours per week in 1994 to 32.6 hours in 2003 (Bonney, 2005).

11. Similarly, in the United States, by the early 1990s only one of three employed Americans aged 18 and older worked the standard shift of days, 35 to 40 hours a week, Monday to Friday and by 2000, workers in non-standard work arrangements (part-time, agency, contingent and temporary) comprised 30 percent of the U.S. labour force (Martin & Sinclair, 2007; Tausig & Fenwick, 2001, p. 102).

12. The availability of a workforce and changes in the economic structure are two key factors. However, social policies are also deeply implicated. Whether or not policies support, for example, the growth of part-time employment and whether or not labour organizations successfully mobilize against part-time work, impact at the national and provincial level the nature of working time. See, for example, Bosch, 2001. For recent developments in the struggle among employers, governments, and workers' organizations in Europe, see Keune and Galgoczi, 2006.

13. Low quality jobs would include insecure, low-wage, low-benefit, dead-end employment.

14. The cover for the October 20, 2008 cover of *Maclean's* asked, "What just happened to your retirement …?"

15. This is reflected, for example, by efforts in 1999 to gauge the contributions to the economy provided by the non-profit sector and volunteering (Statistics Canada, 2004).

16. When U.S. analysts expect that the job search for unemployed executives will take from four to seven months or longer, the time spent on searching for work over the course of a lifetime may constitute a significant investment (*Globe and Mail*, 2009, p. B15).

17. The increasing urban sprawl in Canada has already resulted in longer commutes. Between 1996 and 2001 the median commuting distance for workers increased from 7 km to 7.2 km (Statistics Canada, 2003).

Power and Loose Time: Resistance, Compliance, and the Potential for Creativity in Large Organizations

Dan Glenday

DISCUSSION QUESTIONS

1. What is power? What are the limits to the exercise of power in large organizations?

2. What is loose time? Explain how the uses of loose time can paradoxically both maintain and resist the exercise of power in large organizations while affording opportunities for resourcefulness and creativity?

INTRODUCTION

Why study the managerial uses of **power** at work? For that matter, given the fact that large hierarchical organizations today are dominated by ICT (information and communications technology) surveillance strategies, is it possible to exercise any freedom at work? This chapter examines the differences in how power is actualized in large organizations, how employees at different levels capture labour time ("loose time") for themselves, and the associated negative or positive sanctions they might expect to receive from authorities in the organization.

The author advances the notion of loose time as a theoretical construct and an innovative methodological strategy to study the asymmetrical distribution of power in large organizations and proposes the inclusion of individual innovation and creativity as integral to a practical understanding of how power is actualized in large organizations. Twenty-four interviews (14 women and 10 men) were completed over a six-month period covering employees in a variety of organizational settings. They included high school teachers, call centre employees, human resource consultants and managers, credit union financial advisors, and regional government administrators. The chapter concludes with a discussion of loose time as a conceptual, methodological and empirical modification to the study of power in large organizations.

POWER FOSTERS COMPLIANCE, RESISTANCE, AND CREATIVITY

The Exercise of Power at Work: Resistance as Complicity

Since Weber's demarcation of domination into three distinct subsets: traditional, charismatic, and legal-rational, the concept of power for most social scientists stood for legitimate or legal-rational authority, not war or personal physical prowess (Weber, 1968). This concept of power signified compliance to the will of others holding offices positioned higher than oneself inside the bureaucratic hierarchy. Compliance depended, in large measure, on the belief that the individual is being treated fairly and objectively by criteria outside the purview of personal preference. The fact that legal-rational authority contains a set of canons that are abstract and transmitted culturally assured a sufficient degree of compliance to secure the smooth running of any large-scale organization.

Within the critical social science tradition, however, researchers emphasized employee conflict and resistance to the *actual* unfair practices of individuals who owned or controlled the organization, particularly for-profit companies. Individuals who experienced unfair labour practices, for example, were always "free" to exit the organization and seek employment elsewhere. Or, if the **grievances** were experienced collectively, employees struggled to form organizations of their own that they believed could advance their interests as a whole either within the dominant organizations as trade **unions** or as separate entities such as co-operatives.

If we were to catalogue this vast literature, we would find research studies that confirm both compliance to the rules and regulations of the organizational regime and *resistance* to what is felt or believed to be unfair or inequitable. However, there have been and continue to be those in the critical social science tradition who offer a twist to the conventional view of resistance to the power embedded within the organization. They seek to understand how workplace resistance can result in continuity not the expected disjuncture of organizational life.

Michael Buroway's (1979) ethnographic study of a piece-rate factory system was among the first to point out how an informal system and culture of employee resistance to management's encroachments on their labour time actually *reinforced* the formal bureaucratic hierarchy of management-worker relationships. This process of daily resistance in the workplace with management's tacit approval is what he would call the *manufacturing of consent* to corporate controls.[1] In the end, Buroway and others adopting labour process theory point out that the particular mix of the following ingredients: compliant managerial labour control, workers' resistance, and their social complicity to the organizational hierarchy are necessary to secure the workers' effort bargain with the employer (see for example, Berberoglu, 2002; Braverman, 1976/1998; Wardell, Steiger, & Meiksins, 1999).

Enter ICT in the "New" Workplace

The advent of new *communications and information technologies* (ICTs) in the workplace ushered in futuristic visions of automated factories effortlessly churning out products with little downtime for maintenance and repairs. Freedom from arduous and physically demanding tasks awaited workers. Moreover, many futurists argued that the age of the microchip in the workplace foreshadowed the advent of a shorter workweek and more leisure time for almost everyone (see for example, Glenday, 1997; Gorz, 1985, 1987).

The truth of the matter has been somewhat more ominous. ICTs can render virtually every task more visible to management by monitoring and shadowing employees wherever they are in the organization or even at home. To this end, ICT puts an emphasis on visibility and surveillance as the means of controlling the effort bargain and the mobilization of worker experience, knowledge, and skills. Taken together, some researchers adopted Michel Foucault (1980, 1982, 1989, 1991) and his notion of power as a *Panopticon* to understand the impact of ICT in the workplace.[2]

Researchers were apt to compare the factory or office with the prison. New information technologies and their application to the shop floor and office required a metaphor that captured their pervasiveness and their ability to reveal the hidden talents of employees. That is, borrowing from Foucault's study of the prison, the workplace becomes home to the *Electronic Panopticon*. Sewell and Wilkinson's (1992) examination into JIT and TQC (just-in-time and total quality control), for example, views these as two of several devices in a "tool box" that "both create and demand systems of surveillance which improve on those of the traditional bureaucracy in instilling discipline and thereby consolidating central control and making it more efficient" (1992, p. 277). They proceed to say that "even if an individual worker is reluctant to share any positive divergence, it is likely that they will be revealed ... through the concept of continuous improvement … a powerful instrument by which management can appropriate the ingenuity of the work force" (1992, p. 285). It would seem workers are trapped by the prerogatives of management. However, Sewell and Wilkinson also found that working in teams and multi-tasking led to enhanced spheres of worker influence. Surprisingly, and much like Buroway, workers, with the tacit approval of supervisors and management, falsified productivity and quality information so long as it appeared pro duction targets were met (1992, p. 282). Once more, management's unspoken agreement to what their employees' do as captured labour time, time spent in off-task duties, enters into the effort bargain with their employer.

Other researchers such as Catherine Casey (1995) and Barbara Townley (1994) employing Foucault's notion of Panopticon arrive at much the same conclusion about the ubiquity of the *Electronic Panopticon*. In these examples, each author hopes that the end of modernity with its emphasis on produc-tionism will create new opportunities for the self. However, each also point to "capitulated selves" in the workplace. Catherine Casey, for example, notes that workers "are unlikely to create new forms of alliances and solidarities outside those formed in and by corporations. The new corporate culture is a totalizing culture" (1995, p. 197).

Research studies employing Foucault's notion of the Panopticon become trapped in much the same way as labour process theorists such as Buroway. Whether defined as captured labour time or knowledge secured from workers' experience, these approaches to the study of the workplace, be it in a factory or office, result in multiple ways to "skin a worker" (Roy, 1980). Agency is replaced by complicity and knowledge is appropriated by surveillance. In nei-ther approach do the forms of workers' actual daily resistance, nor her/his per-sonal creativity surface. All succumb in the face of insurmountable corporate, bureaucratic power. Paradoxically, both the literature emphasizing compliance and those singling out resistance account for the reproduction of large organi-zational structures and, by extension, the national social system.

Foucault's Actual Notion of Power ("Permanent Provocation") and Freedom

For Foucault, "the exercise of power consists in *guiding* the possibility of con-duct and putting in order the *possible outcome*" (Foucault, 1982, p. 221; emphasis mine). Clearly, Foucault establishes the limits of power with his double use of possibility, not its ubiquity. Let me look a little closer.

First, Foucault conveys the important point that the exercise of power is not absolute but channels behaviour. Having said that, the problem is "to know how you are to *avoid* these practices—[to go to] where power cannot play" (1991, p. 18; emphasis mine. See also, 1982, p. 222). Refusing to submit in the workplace is an exercise of freedom, for Foucault and is met by power as a guide to conduct that tries to find ways to structure possible outcomes. Therefore, the exercise of power in large organizations can never be totalizing. There are always spaces or gaps. Yet, how does one study power? He begins with the following proposition:

> taking the *forms of resistance* against different forms of power as a *starting point*. ... Rather than analyzing power relations from the point of view of its internal rationality, it consists of analyzing power relations through the *antagonism of strategies*. (1982, p. 211; emphasis mine)

In like manner, Deleuze and Guattari's (1987) seminal treatise *A Thousand Plateaus* includes an examination of power as decision-making, which incorporates connections between "all kinds of compartmentalization and partial processes but not without gaps and displacements" (1987, p. 210).

They go further when they say that within this "linear segment" they find a "suppleness of and communication between offices, a bureaucratic perversion, a permanent *inventiveness or creativity* practiced *even against administrative regulations*" (1987, p. 214; emphasis mine).

Piecing together the elements of and limits to power theorized above, one is led to conclude the following. The exercise of power in large organizations leaves pockets of spaces for employees to potentially capture as their own. It is within these "spaces" that resistance to managerial power percolates. While it may be accurate to suggest that employee resistance to managerial or administrative power is contained within modern, technologically savvy, bureaucratic life, there is also room for the spark of originality and innovation. Therefore, running against the grain of established wisdom about the increased control over humanity in the postmodern organizational workplace, the potential exists for human resistance, resourcefulness, and creativity.

Summary

To avoid the straitjacket approaches of labour process theory and the *Electronic Panopticon*, I shall begin by returning to Foucault's understanding of power as channelling behaviour, not determining outcomes. Power, for Foucault, is viewed as limiting in its capability to appropriate human skills and talent. According to Foucault, the contradictory nature of the organization's exercise of power defined as conflicting strategies leads to unintended consequences and opens up spaces for workers' resistance and, I would add, creativity and resourcefulness to penetrate.

To study power in large-scale organizations, then begins with instances of workplace resistance. Where and when these occur will be marked out below in what I refer to as **"loose time."** Second, an organization's strategies are not coherent **rationalities.** Nor can they be assumed to produce particular effects according to their planned principles. Instead, there are unintended outcomes. As such, there is the "potential to create *spaces*" and it is what happens inside these "spaces" that not only renders "conflicts at work more visible, but provide for a study of the limits of forms of power" (May, 1999, p. 776; emphasis mine. See also, May & Buck, 1998; Pile & Keith, 1997)). It is to the investigation of these "spaces" that I now turn.

Specifically, these "spaces" include captured labour time spent at work but *outside* the workers' effort bargain with the employer. Other researchers have used "quiet and interaction time" (Perlow, 1999, p. 71), while de Certeau (1988) sees "cracks that particular conjunctures open" when referring to the limits of power's reach.

Loose Time

Personally, none of the above terms captures the fact that it is a special time in the workplace we are talking about. Instead, I will employ taut and loose time to refer to the accumulation of experience about the work tasks, work groups, and organizational hierarchy and its use in not only maintaining and resisting power in the organization but potentially fostering individual creative or innovative outcomes at all levels of the organization.

Whether with relaxed supervision or computer-generated or assisted control of workflow, employees at virtually every level of the organization find time to resist managerial or administrative power while finding time to express their individuality and social creativity. At the start of the worktime spectrum, all the employees in the organization experience the time they spend at work as similar to a *taut* rope: *new, inflexible, and stressed.* Overtime, often beginning not more than four or five months into the employment relationship, these same employees experience worktime as more *flexible, habitual, and loose.* Once familiarity with the particular tasks, duties, and responsibilities settle in, employees, regardless of their location in the organization can now capture labour time as "loose time." However, not everyone in the organization experiences the exercise of power in the same manner.

THE ORGANIZATION AS BIFURCATED UNIT OF OCCUPATIONAL CONTROLS AND THE EFFORT SQUEEZE

A simplified bifurcated organizational hierarchy can be ascertained by using the definition of employee recognized by Canadian labour law as "someone who has entered into or works under a contract of service to perform specified services and/or tasks for another, the employer, in exchange for money" (Duhaime, 2010). This definition excludes those who hold managerial, financial, and related offices and those who supervise others in the organization.[3] Therefore, large organizations are constituted by a minimum of two distinct categories of workers—those employees who can be organized into trade unions and those who legally are ineligible.

On a more theoretical level, a similar distinction can be made between those in the organization such as supervisors, managers, and corporate executives who undergo occupational controls and all those lower in the hierarchy who come under the more familiar notion of the effort squeeze (see for example, Baldamus, 1961/2003). Those in the first category possess skills, education, and experience, which become occupational costs to them. Their earned income and rewards are governed by changes in the supply and demand for their labour time.

The determination of wages for semi and unskilled labour has little to do with occupational costs but with "the worker's input of *effort*, provisionally defined as the sum total of physical and mental exertion, tedium, fatigue or any other disagreeable aspect of work" (Baldamus, 1961, p. 29; italics in the original). Together, these simplified binary organizational cleavages form the "*skill–effort gap.*" Therefore, the exercise of power will be differentially experienced by these two categories of groups within the organization. However, once familiarity with the particular tasks, duties, and responsibilities settle in, employees, regardless of their location in the organization will have opportunities to capture labour time as loose time.

Methodological Strategy

Analytically, the contingency of power rests inside loose time. The manifestation of loose time, then, depends on location in the organization, that is, either as personally enabling or as resistance to power, but in either instance as potentially creative for the employee.

Returning to the discussion of the organization as a bifurcated unit, those who fall under occupational controls will experience the forms and relations of power differently from those who fall under the effort squeeze. The former experiences the practices of power as enabling; that is, loose time is often positively sanctioned. On the other hand, the operation of competing strategies in the workplace that seek to stabilize and intensify the effort squeeze, however, open up fissures or spaces that can be captured by workers as loose time. Within loose time, these workers' actions of resistance and creativity or innovativeness take form and are accorded substance.

To summarize, power is not a totalizing experience. Furthermore, the experience of loose time differs between those facing occupational controls and those undergoing the effort squeeze. The former usually understand loose time as resulting in new personal opportunities with potential benefits for the organization in increased productivity or revenue. Those inside the effort squeeze find the experience collectively and individually constraining and will find ways to resist the power they experience on a day to day level.

The methodological strategy I propose begins with employees in diverse work environments and at different levels of the organization where they are employed. By so doing, I am taking into account the differential experience of power in large organizations.

Over a roughly six-month period, from September 2007 until April 2008, interviews were completed with 24 employees: 14 women and 10 men. They included high school teachers, call centre employees, human resource consultants and managers, credit union financial advisors, and regional government administrators. In some instances, interviews were conducted at the workplace. In others, a neutral site was selected while in a few cases, interviews were done in a quiet restaurant over lunch. Each interview took approximately one hour to complete and consisted of questions dealing with their work tasks, supervisory environment, and their experience of loose time. By loose time, I mean the time in any given day or shift when each individual was able to either (1) "escape" from his or her assigned duties or tasks, (2) explain what they did during this time, and (3) if he or she found the time to investigate a problem, pursue or fulfill an objective. Methodologically, my aim was to talk to individuals about what they do to create time for themselves at work that falls outside the standard chatter, gossip or conversation engaged in daily by most employees.

Results

Power's limits within the organization to determine human conduct is differentially experienced by its employees. As a result, the episodes of loose time are also differentially encountered within the organization's hierarchy. Those holding careers with occupational controls understand loose time as encouraging personal development while those caught under the effort squeeze experience the constraining influence of power. Each category of employee uses their loose time in ways to establish their individuality and creativity while those experiencing the effort squeeze are more prone to find ways to *also* resist the exercise of power on them. The first number of passages comes from individuals who fall under the top group of employees. These will be followed by quotes from the second cluster of employees, those wedged inside the effort squeeze.

THE EXPERIENCE OF LOOSE TIME BY EMPLOYEES IN THE TOP HALF OF THE ORGANIZATION OR THOSE WITH OCCUPATIONAL CONTROLS

Corporate employees spoke about the length of time in the employment relationship it took them to feel comfortable about using loose time and how their organization enabled them to pursue interests that were mutually beneficial.

Male Financial Administrator (10 months on the job) #1—corporate:

> As you start to become more valued, because of your abilities to do jobs … once there is a trust built … you get a little more leeway … a bit more time. I no longer feel I am tied to my desk. I can actually get up and move around and talk to people. …

Male Regional Government Administrator #2—corporate:

> As an employee becomes more familiar with the organization, the supervisors, and the culture, and how things are done around here, it allows people to understand what liberties they can take. …

Several corporate employees spoke of using loose time to create opportunities to develop professionally and to reinforce social bonds with fellow employees through direct face-to-face interaction and on occasion unintentionally create business for the organization.

Male Regional Government Administrator #2—corporate:

> I've used those web-based training seminars that are offered through certain organizations. I close my door, maybe some other people come in, and we watch this for 45 minutes, they are a little bit more interactive because you can actually comment on the phone.

Female Financial Advisor #1—corporate:

> You end up building relationships but you also end up learning things that you might not have expected to learn. … If I wanted to get something done, I would

> typically email ... and I stopped doing that ... now I go upstairs and actually talk to the person ... that takes more time but things get done. ...

Female Banking Administrator #1—corporate:

> A lady that sits over here ... normally I would email her ... [this time] I talked to her about a YWCA benefit. I also needed something from her I can't remember what but she gave it to me ... now she was looking for investment dollars and so she called the YWCA ... I think the Y now invests through us.

THE EXPERIENCE OF POWER IN THE BOTTOM HALF OF THE ORGANIZATION OR AS INDIVIDUALLY CONSTRAINING

Conflicting Strategies in the Workplace

Two employees were interviewed together. Female Call Centre #1: Worker #1:

> Samuel (assumed name) ... is so laid back ... then our other manager ... when she was on the floor she kept giving bad advice to our client ... as well as the agents (call centre employees) ... they would have to go back onto the phone and say I apologize, you were misinformed, this is how it is really done. ...

Two employees were interviewed together. Female Call Centre #1: Worker #2:

> We have another manager who joined the group ... she is on top of everyone ... if you are late by 5 minutes, she will write you up. She doesn't want to speak to any of the employees ... Now, it's even more stressful than if it just started like that in the beginning, because now we have to completely change our routines, and in a call centre that could be the death for some people ...

people who aren't really good with change or who are so focused on their routine, they have to start switching it up ... and that's when you run into problems.

Female Call Centre #1: Worker #3:

We have a new site director and his whole motto is, he wants leaders to try and change the whole way of thinking around here ... because in a call centre you lose so many people ... stress ... smarter managers try to find ways to appease the workers and bring in uplifting moral strategies to try and get them to enjoy their job a little more. ...

Routinization of Work and Loose Time

Female Call Centre #2: Worker #1; after a few months on the job:

As you progress, you don't have to concentrate as much ... things become automatic. ... Between calls when they aren't worried about what you are doing (the script becomes monotonous) ... you can think ... so there is a little bit of time there ... *I was working on a novel at one point during down time.* ... (Emphasis mine)

Human Resource Consultant #2:

On the "Off Shift"—afternoons and midnights—there is more "free" time because "the wheels" aren't supervising to death. Take an automotive type company, the workers go, go, go and their parts are out by 10:00 pm. ... Well, there's 2 hours there. ... They go play euchre, read, go around and socialize and the supervisor turns a blind eye because he's got his numbers, these people get their shop time ... everyone's happy. ... The "wheels" know about it, everyone knows about it. ...

The Effort Squeeze Gets Tighter

Female Call Centre #1: Worker #4:

> The company] is always changing the rules depending
> on how much money they want coming in ... on my
> job it's a "Catch-22" ... we have to have great "stats" but
> because we have better "stats" than what our target is
> ... so [the company] looks at it as ... we're losing
> money because we are paying so many people when
> we can cut down on staff. ...

Human Resource Manager #3:

> That's the trend I see going, it's tightening up instead of
> getting looser. And the further you go down the corpo-
> rate structure, the more tightly it is controlled. ...

Loose Time, Play, and Corporate Games: Keeping Workers Happy?

Female Call Centre #2: Worker #2:

> Our section is doing so well, that they are having call
> centre Olympics ... we are doing like a bean bag
> toss. . . and this is really when people are taking calls,
> they will take you off the call, meanwhile everyone
> around you is doing calls ... it's like an extra break. ...
> [What else?] I think there is a basketball toss. They are
> designed to ... encourage you, to make work fun but
> in essence its extra time.

*Two employees were interviewed together. Female
Call Centre #1: Workers #1 and #2:*

> So they will have snack day, they will say you can get
> off the phone and go get some snacks ... or like pyjama
> day, or hat day ... which is really weird because it

reminds me of high school ... (Call centre employee 2 says) or elementary school ... yeah.

Teachers as Professional Workers: The Contradictory Nature of Their Work

Female Teacher #1 (Gym Class):

When I was in the gym class, the only thing that would lighten the load or change the routine is, I'd have kids referee ... I could do my own sort of thing. ...

Female Teacher #1:

When I'm in the classroom, the only way I could step back would be to assign group work or presentations worked really well ... that's the only way we could get away from the actual day-to-day instruction. ...

Female Teacher #1 (Special Ed):

I work in the resource room, I work with the student one on one now, I have to go and get the student out of class and bring them to my room and sit down and work on their class work ... I also interview and monitor the student throughout the year ... I have a lot of flexibility. ...

CONCLUSION

Employing the concept of loose time as the focus for the cross section of interviews completed for this research exposed several important faces of power in large organizations. First and foremost, no matter where inside the organization's hierarchy or whether the organizations were in the private or public sector, familiarity with the job led to loose time. Second, the selection of extracts from the interviews echo the bifurcated units of occupational controls and the effort squeeze. Capturing labour time for those in the top tier, for example, suggests how the experience of loose time can be self-actualizing. In the case of several financial officers and senior government administrators, the ability to physically move about the organization's offices generated opportunities for social interaction and problem solving and in one case, serendipitously facilitated more business for the organization. For others, loose time could be tied to the taking of short (45-minutes) on-line courses either alone or with one or two others behind closed doors.

Loose time resulted in increased personal interaction and communication, which facilitated problem solving and on occasion, innovativeness and creativity. Loose time, as experienced by these employees, often became linked to corporate/bureaucratic goals. Whether increasing their occupational costs through on-line training programs, or problem solving to achieve corporate efficiencies, these employees experienced loose time and the exercise of organizational power as more often than not personally rewarding.

Those stuck inside the effort squeeze, on the other hand, experienced work as constraining, even enclosing or suffocating. The results reported here from a set of interviews across a small spectrum of bottom tier jobs do describe an encompassing network of rules, games, and surveillance. However, the individual responses to power approaches Foucault's notion of power's ability to condition or direct conduct along possible avenues rather than hamstringing or "skinning" employees. The many attempts by management to make work in the call centres interesting or "fun" such as "Call Centre Olympics" or "Pyjama Day" were met with characteristic wit and opprobrium by the employees. Employees remained on the job and did as they were told while resistance to the organizations' games gave rise to individual means of expression.

Two call centre female employees illustrated Foucault's point of the "antagonism of strategies" when one spoke about two contradictory managerial prerogatives. However, in this case, contradictory managerial strategies resulted in *more stress* for some employees. Instead of opening up more space to capture loose time, these occasions were experienced negatively by many call centre employees. The contradictory messages add stress to the workplace for those who "aren't really good with change or [those] who are so focused on their routines." However, during recession, such as the one we are experiencing now, the option of voluntarily leaving the job is often closed and as a result, stress increases for many employees in the workplace.

Teachers expressed an ambiguous, often contradictory, familiarity with the changing goals of the organization. There were characteristics of occupational controls such as working one-on-one with a special needs student and elements of the effort squeeze when tied to the classroom. Some teachers sought out ways to minimize the experience of the effort squeeze by requesting assignments that allowed them to work with one or a few students.

For the teachers interviewed for this study, what was required in the classroom took on more and more the attributes of the effort squeeze. Their sense of freedom to be creative with their students in the classroom was severely restricted; hence, the desire to "escape" by doing other tasks within the organization.

The indeterminacy of power in the employment relationship echoes throughout the interviews reported in the article. It confirms Foucault's notion of power's limits to the appropriation of human skills and talents in the workplace, regardless of where one is positioned in the organization. It remains clear, however, that those who enjoy occupational controls possess many more advantages to exercise loose time as enabling and career building. On the other hand, when loose time is exercised, the organization can benefit but contributes to the occupational cost of the individual employee.

Not all the employees experiencing the effort squeeze who were interviewed spoke about the creative or innovative moments they did during their loose time. This was certainly more the case with employees supervised by occupational controls. However, as one employee in a call centre said, "I found time to work on my novel." The desire to find the time at work to be creative or innovative was found at *all* organizational levels.

Finally, the evidence gathered corroborates Foucault's notion of power in large organizations as channeling human behaviour while supporting Deleuze and Guattari's insistence on human creativity and innovativeness in the face of power. Moreover, the interview data highlighted the importance of social interaction in the workplace. Taken together, there are real limits to the exercise of power in large organizations. Social interaction that takes time from tasks, creative time that is either an occupational cost to the organization or a means of personal development, along with loose time all contribute to limiting the exercise of power in large organizations. By way of illustration, the limits to the exercise of power are represented in Figure 9.1.

FIGURE 9.1

THE LIMITS TO THE EXERCISE OF POWER IN THE WORKING ENVIRONMENT

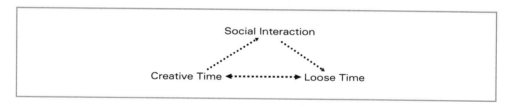

Social Interaction

Creative Time ◄┈┈┈┈► Loose Time

ENDNOTES

The author wishes to thank the Social Sciences and Humanities Research Council of Canada grant "Restructuring Work and Labour in the New Economy" under the "Innovations of the New Economy" for financial assistance.

1   Buroway notes that "cooperation revolved around 'making out,' a game in which the goal was to make a certain quota and whose rules were recognized and defended by workers and management alike" (1985, p. 10). Begun as a management initiative "to introduce some meaning [into the workplace relationship] ... 'making out' had the effect of generating consent to its rules" (1985, p. 11). In a later study, Buroway (1985) acknowledges the criticism of the loss of human agency levelled by others on his research findings. He acknowledges the importance of a broader theoretical and sociological approach to the study of shop floor struggles as a way of overcoming the straitjacket of economism. However, he concludes by insisting employees become complicit in their own exploitation in the transition from what he calls *despotic to* **hegemonic** regimes (1985, pp. 261-62).

2. However, Foucault reserved the prison as "the *only* place where power is manifested in its naked state, in its most *excessive* form" (Foucault, 1989, p. 77; emphasis mine). The factory and office were described as distinct organizations.

3. This definition of employee also excludes independent contractors.

10

Coordinated Bargaining: Stemming the Tide, Opening the Floodgates

Alan Hall

DISCUSSION QUESTIONS

1. If the federal government is likely to use the crisis and the resulting deficit to ramp up privatization, how can CUPE counter this through coordinated bargaining and other strategies?

2. If neoliberalism tends to undermine government and employer interest in centralization, should centralization be the ultimate goal of coordination efforts, and if so why? Or does this mean the need for a more frontal attack on neoliberalism itself?

3. Is there any evidence of recent shifts in government or employer thinking or responses to union demands for coordinated or centralized bargaining? What are the implications of those shifts?

4. Are there potential points of argument for persuading governments/employers to engage in collaborative coordinated bargaining including central bargaining?

5. Is membership support and commitment to coordinated strike action strong enough and sufficient enough to force the government or multiple employers to a coordinated or central bargaining table? What is needed to get the different sectors to this point?

INTRODUCTION

Labour **unions** advance the rights and conditions of their members through collective bargaining. Shaped substantially by post–World War II labour law, much of this bargaining in Canada has been conducted in a highly decentralized fashion (Schenk, 1995). This means that separate **collective agreements** are negotiated at a workplace by workplace level between an employer and a particular local union representing all or some of the workers in each specific workplace. While the same employer may have a large number of unionized workers in similar jobs at other workplaces at other locations, those workers often have to negotiate their own separate collective agreements. At the same time, many workplaces have multiple collective agreements often involving different unions representing distinct groups of workers within a given workplace, which is yet another dimension of decentralization.

Although Canada's labour laws encouraged decentralized bargaining from the outset, many unions recognized early on the enhanced bargaining **power,** organizational, and resource advantages gained through more coordinated and centralized approaches, and accordingly began to push for more coordination and centralization. For example, the United Auto Workers (UAW) and the United Steelworkers (USWA) established a system of **"pattern bargaining"** in the 1950s and 1960s that effectively standardized the conditions of employment for workers across the U.S. and Canada in the mining, auto, and steel sectors.[1] Also by the 1970s, some public sectors such as the hospitals in Ontario were establishing centralized bargaining where common agreements covering hospitals across Ontario were negotiated in one combined set of negotiations.

Interestingly enough, these initiatives were sometimes promoted by employers and not always supported by the unions. For example, there was a concerted effort to reduce **strikes** and cost instability in the Canadian construction industry during the late 1970s through coordinated and centralized bargaining, but the construction unions largely opposed these initiatives fearing the centralization would be used by employers to erode their bargaining power in the context of high inflation (Rose, 1979).

Although much of the unionized bargaining in Canada remained highly decentralized and uncoordinated, especially in comparison to Europe and Australia where national or state centralized collective bargaining had been established for the vast majority of unionized workers (Traxler, 2003a), many Canadian and U.S. unions made considerable progress during the 1960s and 1970s using coordinated and centralized bargaining to achieve significant gains in employment conditions. However, much of that progress came to an abrupt halt in the 1980s and 1990s as **neoliberalism** and **globalization** became the accepted mantras for economic and labour relations policies. In this context, coordinated and centralized bargaining came under increasing attack by employers and policy-makers in both North America and Europe. Large private sector employers in the trucking, mining, steel, and metals industries began to refuse to follow pattern bargaining, while other companies abandoned voluntary company wide agreements reverting to a plant by plant system as allowed by law (Eaton & Kriesky, 1998). Auto industry firms effectively undermined their pattern bargaining by moving to contract out the vast majority of parts production to independent suppliers, which were often smaller non-union operations (Kumar & Holmes, 1997). Many governments including the federal and provincial Canadian governments began to dismantle some of their existing centralized forms of bargaining (Karlsen, 1999), and perhaps more significantly, began to achieve the effect of decentralization by privatizing and contracting out significant amounts of public sector work to a large number of private sector employers (Camfield, 2007, p. 292; Cohen, 2006; MacPhail & Bowles, 2008).

This chapter examines the efforts of the largest union in Canada, the Canadian Union of Public Employers (CUPE), to challenge the neoliberal push to decentralization and **privatization** by developing and implementing an explicit nation-wide strategy to coordinate and/or centralize its bargaining within all its sectors including universities, schools, municipalities, hospitals, home care, nursing homes, and community services. In adopting this strategy, I argue that CUPE is not only challenging the neoliberal push away from coordination and centralization, it is seeking to extend coordination and centralization to levels well beyond what was achieved during the 1960s and 1970s. Along with an examination of CUPE's strategic efforts, this paper elaborates the conditions that are fuelling this shift and examines the advantages and challenges that are associated with coordinated and centralized bargaining, with the aim of provoking further discussion and debate regarding the steps that can and need to be taken by the labour movement more broadly to both capture those advantages and meet the challenges.[2] To add some further fuel to this latter discussion, I conclude by suggesting that there are *both* opportunities and dangers contained within the current economic crisis that need to be recognized and considered as CUPE and other unions move forward with this mandate.

To help frame this discussion, let's begin with an effort to clarify the meaning of coordinated bargaining and the different types of coordinated bargaining as evident within CUPE over the last 10 years.

CUPE AND COORDINATED BARGAINING

In 1999, the Canadian Union of Public Employees, Canada's largest union with 600,000 members, adopted an action plan that encouraged every sector in the union to move toward coordinated or centralized bargaining (CUPE, 1999). This approach has ultimately defined the main emphasis in CUPE's strategic directions in bargaining over the last 10 years (CUPE, 2005, 2007).

Some sectors in some provinces had been engaging in some form or another of coordinated or centralized bargaining for some time. For example, CUPE and other unions in the Ontario hospital sector had been engaging in voluntary centralized bargaining since 1975 (OCHU, 2009). However, most sectors such as university workers or municipal workers within CUPE in most provinces were still relying on highly decentralized single employer bargaining models, which meant that **bargaining units** with as few as five to 10 workers were negotiating separate contracts on their own, while others with histories of greater centralization were finding increasing pressure to decentralize what they had developed over previous years.

As such, the new policy was aimed both at defending existing levels of coordination and establishing higher levels and new areas of coordination across the union. This was explicitly understood within the union as a necessary response to a continuing widespread assault on the employment and working conditions of public service workers across the country. Neoliberal policies with particular reference to privatization, funding, and staffing cuts and **rationalizations** to social, health, and education services, along with the adoption of lean and mean flexible management schemes, were all identified within the union as cutting a huge trail of destruction through membership wages, job security, and other employment conditions. Greater coordination or centralization was viewed as essential in order to build the bargaining power that CUPE locals needed to resist the downward spiral of wage reductions, privatization, and job cuts.

Making the Shift

Over the next 10 years, many sectors in CUPE made significant progress in moving to coordinated or more centralized bargaining systems involving multiple employers and bargaining units. Viewed in its broadest terms, coordinated bargaining is *any collaborative attempt by distinct bargaining units to achieve common or similar bargaining outcomes through linked negotiations* (Sisson & Marginson, 2000, p. 6). Defined in this way, a move towards coordinated bargaining begins as soon as two or more distinct locals or bargaining units seek to work together in some way to improve their mutual bargaining outcomes. As happened at CUPE in most of its sectors, coordination often started at a very basic level of *information sharing* where representatives and leaders from different locals in the same sectors began exchanging information on their working and employment conditions, bargaining proposals, bargaining strategies, and progress in negotiations. This initial step was achieved by CUPE through annual coordinating bargaining conferences in each sector in each province, which brought together representatives to begin discussing common bargaining interests. As observed at a recent CUPE coordinating conference, there are still some sectors in CUPE who are operating at this early stage but most are more advanced than this.

Although information sharing is a limited level of coordination, in the sense that there are often no *formalized* or explicit processes, mechanisms, or rules for developing and achieving common proposals, information sharing is aimed ultimately at encouraging the movement to the next level where bargaining units begin to set common **benchmarks** for collective bargaining agreements, which are then taken as guides in setting short and long term bargaining goals for separate negotiating teams (Sisson & Marginson, 2000). Although some CUPE sectors moved very quickly to develop specific coordinated bargaining **targets,** benchmarking is often a crucial preliminary step used to build towards the capacity to set specific targets; that is, CUPE locals often used the benchmarking process to discuss and agree upon common standards of employment before taking on the added pressure and demands of having to meet those standards in their separate negotiations. In that sense, benchmarking allowed the leadership from different locals to develop their relationships and their trust and knowledge of each other before having to put those relationships to more significant tests within the bargaining process itself (Traxler, 2003b).

In setting and agreeing upon specific targets such as "average wage increases above inflation" or "provisions that obstruct contracting out or privatization" (CUPE, 2005, p. 9), the different bargaining units begin to strategize around *how and when* they can achieve these targets *together.* This demands that the locals within a coordinated sector seek to agree on bargaining priorities for particular negotiations. Since employers are usually unwilling to *collaborate* and negotiate jointly or centrally with other employers, especially at the beginning of this process, collective agreements are normally negotiated in separate negotiations with distinct employers. This lack of bargaining process centralization introduces numerous complications in terms of union coordination and collaboration (see p. 202, Meeting the Challenges of Coordinated Bargaining?). While actual coordination may still be limited initially to the development and promotion of common proposals, and perhaps the strategic development of common negotiation strategies and media campaigns selling those proposals, coordination within CUPE was often advanced further by trying to *synchronize* contract expiry dates with the goal of being able to engage in coordinated job actions across bargaining units. This attempt to strengthen bargaining power through joint coordinated action requires that the locals support each other in common job actions including strikes until everyone wins the same employment conditions. A successful illustration of this strategy in CUPE was evident during university negotiations in B.C. in 2000, where CUPE Locals 116, 2278, 2950, 917, 951, 3338, and 3996 from four different universities established common action days including a short but effective coordinated strike at all four institutions. A number of sectors in CUPE have achieved this level of coordination or are moving towards it. For example, CUPE Ontario's Social Service Sector (Developmental Services) were recently involved in an unprecedented round of coordinated bargaining with 50 units doing so at the same time at different tables, while the Ontario university sector is currently seeking to achieve common contract dates and hopes to be in a position to begin coordinating job actions in 2010 (OUWCC, 2008).

As noted, this effort to coordinate job action takes coordination to a much higher level in terms of planning and organization, and accordingly, takes a significant level of commitment at both the leadership *and* rank and file levels (Traxler, 2003b). The most evident advantage behind this effort to coordinate the strike weapon across multiple employers is the bargaining power gained from the more substantial threat of a sectoral wide strike. The capacity to draw on this coordinated strike weapon in a sustained way is particularly critical when the employer, and in particular multiple employers, oppose the union's efforts to negotiate common agreements. As noted, one of the challenges that CUPE and other unions have been facing within the context of neoliberalism is an increased corporate and state opposition to coordination and centralization.

As such, a key question that comes up in any discussion of coordinated target bargaining is whether the coordination is only happening on one side of the table, that is *unilateral coordination*, or whether there is *collaborative* coordination where two or more sides of the table mutually agree to coordinate negotiations in some way (Sisson & Marginson, 2000). Although pattern and other levels of coordinated bargaining can be approached in collaboration with employers (Traxler, Brandl, & Glassner, 2008), the move to collaboration is most evident when both sides representing multiple collective agreements meet together to negotiate common or *central* agreements covering all or some portion of the employment conditions for all the employees in those units. This is usually referred to as **centralized bargaining** — where formally centralized bargaining committees or agencies are empowered voluntarily or by government edict to negotiate entire or specified aspects of collective agreements covering a large number of bargaining units. Again, the Ontario Council of Hospital Unions (OCHU) is a good illustration of a longer-standing voluntary central bargaining model, where CUPE and other unions negotiate a central collective agreement for 21,000 workers representing 120 distinct bargaining units. Representing a newer development was the provincial wide school board negotiations in 2008 involving all CUPE school board locals

(105) and school boards in the province along with government facilitation, which for the first time addressed staffing levels, wage increments, and four other common issues at a central table. As this case illustrated, centralized bargaining can be conducted as a *tripartite* system where unions and employers negotiate centrally with government representatives involved as co-negotiators or facilitators. For CUPE, the 2008 agreement reached under the auspices of the Ontario School Board Coordinating Committee was seen as a significant success in addressing key issues such as wages and benefits (CUPE, 2008). As this indicates, despite a broader pattern of state and corporate opposition, CUPE is having some success in increasing the level of provincial centralization in some of its sectors and is clearly working in that direction in others despite the opposition (e.g., the university sector).

As part of its efforts to support coordinated and centralized bargaining, CUPE National has established within its constitution a number of different coordinated bargaining structures that are aimed at facilitating centralized bargaining including provincial councils of unions, provincial occupational groups, and inter-local bargaining structures such as the CUPE Ontario Health Care Workers' Coordinating Committee and the Ontario School Board Coordinating Committee (CUPE Research, 2005). The Ontario Council of Hospital Unions is a good illustration of the council structure, which in many ways allows a union within a union, including the ability to set **union dues** that can be used to fund the centralized bargaining process as well as **arbitrations** relating to provincial wide **grievance** issues. These resource issues are extremely important in coordination efforts since they enable the necessary communications and meetings between local representatives as well as providing the central capacity to defend the collective agreement provisions negotiated through coordination.

WHY COORDINATED BARGAINING? WHY CENTRALIZED BARGAINING?

All **collective bargaining** is ultimately an effort to take wages and other employment conditions out of competition. By establishing standard terms of employment across sectors and occupational groups, employers are no longer in a position to use shifting labour market conditions including the effects of globalization to intensify competition for jobs and use that competition to drive down wages and other conditions. **Coordinated bargaining** is an extension of this same logic. By presenting a wider common front on wages and other demands, that is, by negotiating common wages and employment conditions at the broadest level possible, CUPE and other unions seek to reduce the competitive economic pressures that tend to push wages and other conditions down as labour supply increases and/or demand decreases (Calmfors & Driffil, 1988; Grimshaw et al., 2007; Rose, 1986; Zweimuller & Barth, 1992).

To be successful in the face of employer opposition, collective bargaining power is the other key element that unions try to strengthen through coordinated bargaining, with particular reference to the threat of coordinated job actions (Rose, 1986; Traxler, 2003b). Provincial or sectoral centralization (e.g., hospital workers or public schools) are often seen as the long-term goal of coordination strategies because centralization offers potentially the greatest impact in terms of reduced wage competition and enhanced bargaining power (Calmfors & Driffil, 1988; Baccaro & Simoni, 2007). The basic argument is that the more workers and workplaces included in any given agreement (and in any potential job action), the less space there is in the labour market for employers to use competitive pressures to reduce wages and other conditions. And indeed, most studies show that centralized forms of bargaining tend to be more effective in taking wages out of competition as reflected by a higher level of wage equality among workers in centralized bargaining contexts (Calmfors, 1993; Kahn, 2000; Martin & Thelen, 2007; Zweimuller & Barth, 1992). Significantly, centralized bargaining also tends to reduce the likelihood of strikes, not only because of the greater threat behind the potential for sectoral wide strikes, but also because union negotiators tend to moderate their wage and other demands in the interest of achieving wage equality.

Indeed, economic historians have often noted that until neoliberalism became ascendant, many postwar employers and governments promoted centralized bargaining because it was seen as offering a level of stability in labour relations as well as predictability in wages and other labour market conditions (Traxler, 2003b). However, given the neoliberal emphasis on the importance of competition and free markets, wide ranging centralized collective agreements that prevented such competition were increasingly seen as anathemas to economic and employment growth (Sisson & Marginson, 2000; Traxler, 2003b).

Why Now?

CUPE's strategic decision to move towards more coordinated models in 1999 can be understood then as an explicit response to the adoption of neoliberal policies by Canadian governments that were greatly increasing competitive labour market pressures. This was especially evident in Ontario during the mid to late 1990s when the Mike Harris Conservative government was in power. For the public sector, the most significant change was the increasing emphasis on privatization and contracting out (Camfield, 2007; Hebdon & Jalette, 2008; Leduc Browne, 2006). This began with the sale of Crown corporations and then was increasingly expanded to include significant amounts of contracting out of public jobs to private operators, often "for profit" firms.

This was particularly significant for CUPE since much of the privatization and contracting out was implemented at the local community levels where CUPE has a large number of members. In the health area, for example, almost all rehabilitation and home care services were privatized over a short period of time (Gildiner, 2006, 2007). Long-term care was also heavily privatized as were significant areas of municipal services and utilities. As well as undermining existing bargaining units, the redistribution of these jobs to another level of private employers also had the effect of further fragmenting the entire public sector bargaining system. Most of the research evidence suggests that contracting out was particularly significant in reducing wages while leading to more significant losses in unions members overall (Thompson, 1995). Reducing the size of the state through funding cuts also greatly increased competitive labour market pressures as did the increasing use of temporary and part-time positions (Camfield, 2007; MacPhail & Bowles, 2008; Rose, 2007; Vosko, 2000).

These and other restructuring changes introduced in the name of neoliberalism explain the significant declines over the course of the 1990s in the public sector share of employment relative to the population size and the total of all jobs in the economy, both in Ontario and across the country (B.C. Stats, 2009; Stats Canada, 2009). It was also in this context that public sector wage settlements dropped quite dramatically (Rose & Chaison, 1996). However, while coordinated bargaining can be seen as an effort to protect or recover lost wages and jobs within the context of neoliberal restructuring, it should also be recognized as being part of the larger process of union resistance to restructuring, one which has the potential to build solidarity and capacity to act in a more concerted manner, both on the bargaining front *and* in other critical areas such as organizing and political action (Camfield, 2007; Eaton & Kriesky, 1998; Kochan & Piore, 1983; Rose & Chaison, 2001; Rose, 1986; Stinson & Ballantyne, 2006). When CUPE brings together workers to take common job actions in defence of working conditions outside their own workplaces, it is potentially developing a broader level of worker solidarity and consciousness that is essential to building power as a political movement rather than simply an isolated interest group.

This notion that coordinated bargaining can contribute to solidarity and renewal is supported by empirical evidence that unions are more likely to achieve and sustain higher levels of membership and union density in more coordinated and centralized systems of bargaining (Eaton & Kriesky, 1998; Rose, 1988, 2007; Traxler, 2003a). This includes research showing that union membership has declined as bargaining systems become less coordinated, which as noted, has happened quite markedly in some countries (Traxler, 2003a). Although these declines often reflect more than just a single cause, what the research shows quite consistently is that coordinated and centralized bargaining systems can contribute to worker and union solidarity by reducing inequalities in wages and other employment conditions (Blackett & Sheppard, 2003; Kahn, 2000; Martin & Thelen, 2007).

MEETING THE CHALLENGES OF COORDINATED BARGAINING? HORIZONTAL AND VERTICAL COORDINATION

As implied in an earlier section, the development of coordinated bargaining within unions can be seen as a step by step process that begins at a relatively basic level of information sharing and then works forward over time to unilateral target setting, and then ultimately, if possible, collaborative coordinated or centralized bargaining. Although there is no fixed requirement that each step is a necessary prerequisite for any other, or that the process must move from information sharing to centralized bargaining as the ultimate objective, thinking of coordinated bargaining in this way acknowledges that it usually takes time to build the common goals, relationships, and trust that are essential to making coordination work within the union and certainly across the union movement. If employers are resisting coordination, as in the current situation for the Ontario University Workers Coordinating Committee (OUWCC), then considerable time is also needed to generate the conditions and power required to push employers towards a more collaborative arrangement. Of course, it is more than just a question of time. As outlined above, coordination bargaining offers definite strengths but there are some significant challenges (Ahlquist, 2009).

When scholars and practitioners talk about the challenges of coordinated bargaining, there are two distinct coordination problems that tend to be emphasized as unions move to higher levels of coordination (Sisson & Marginson, 2000; Traxler, 2003). The first, *horizontal coordination*, is the problem of ensuring that all the representatives of the different bargaining units agree on and consistently support the bargaining goals, strategies, and tactics, and eventual outcomes. On the other hand, *vertical coordination* refers to the problem of ensuring that the members within these bargaining units also offer full support and agreement throughout the process.

Some research suggests that unions often run into trouble because they fail to adequately address both aspects of coordination (Boxall & Haynes, 1997; Ebbinghaus, 2004; Sisson & Marginson, 2000; Traxler, Brandl,

& Glassner, 2008). Other studies have suggested further that underlying this failure is the unrecognized tension between these two demands (Traxler, 2003). That is, to address the vertical problem union negotiators usually try to align their bargaining demands to the rank and file without recognizing how those alignments can often conflict with the need to address inter-bargaining unit or group interests in order to achieve horizontal coordination. These challenges are well illustrated by the events surrounding two very sim-ilar incidents in the hospital sectors.

The Cases of the HEU and OHEU

The B.C. Liberal government's introduction of Bill 29 in 2002 was a clear example of neoliberal policy in the health sector aimed at downgrading public sector working conditions. The Bill unilaterally altered the collective agree-ments of the Hospital Employees Union (HEU) in British Columbia allowing massive privatization of health and social service jobs. The HEU, which is now part of CUPE, mounted enough resistance in job actions and public pressure to bring the Hospital Employer Association of B.C. (HEABC) to province wide central negotiations. However, the resulting tentative agreement, which won some limitations on contracting out in exchange for wage concessions, was rejected by the membership. As several analysts have suggested, significant sectors of the membership within and across different locals saw no reason why they should have to take wage concessions because they were not being threatened by contracting out (Camfield, 2006; Cohen, 2006; Isitt & Moroz, 2007). This is a classic example of a vertical coordination problem in as much as significant elements of rank and file were not supportive of the larger bargaining goals of their central committee because they did not see their interests in the same way as those who were at the table.

Given the collapse of agreement, hospital administrations then moved in a massive way to contract out support services and within a year and half, 8,500 workers had lost their jobs. When the HEU was in a legal strike posi-tion the following year in 2004, the union went on strike, but after only four days the government introduced legislation (Bill 37) ordering them back to work, while at the same time imposing a collective agreement with a 15-percent wage cut along with the same concessions on contracting out that had been rejected earlier. HEU continued to strike "illegally" with considerable support from other unions including many CUPE locals, but as Isitt and Moroz (2007, p. 105) point out, there was considerable disagreement and confusion about the strike strategy between the labour leadership and the rank and file leader-ship. Although the B.C. Federation of Labour "brokered" a deal that limited the number of positions that would be contracted out during the term of the agreement, this did nothing about the 15-percent wage rollback and again a

significant proportion of the rank and file were less than satisfied with the outcome, which created splits within and between locals (Cohen, 2006, p. 637;
Isitt & Moroz, 2007). Considering the strike was illegal, there was considerable solidarity evident in the actions of the HEU and other unions in bravely
fighting against the back to work legislation. However, just as clearly there
were some significant vertical and horizontal conflicts around interests, bargaining priorities, and strategic actions that undermined that solidarity and
made all the difference in terms of the outcome.

An example of a horizontal coordination problem was evident in an earlier situation involving the Ontario hospital sector in 1981 (White, 1990).
This was the start of more aggressive neoliberal policies as governments
increasingly used the size of the government debt to argue for limits and concessions in public sector negotiations. In this situation, CUPE negotiators were
engaged in centralized bargaining representing 10,000 hospital workers across
the province and came to a tentative agreement that was seen by many locals
and some bargaining committee members as concessionary. When many local
presidents and a portion of the bargaining committee campaigned against the
deal, the settlement was soundly rejected by 91 percent of the membership.
Although a strike was opposed by the majority of the bargaining committee
and not supported by the leadership, this was followed by illegal strike when
the employers refused to renegotiate the settlement. Without adequate coordination by the union leadership, the strike collapsed in 10 days as hospital
workers began breaking ranks and returning to work. Thirty four hundred
workers were suspended, 34 were fired, and three senior union leaders were
imprisoned for participating in the strike. As in the B.C. case, this ended badly,
with the same agreement that had been rejected being imposed by an **arbitrator** (White, 1990), while the union, again as in the B.C. case, went through
considerable soul searching, conflict, and changes as a consequence.

Meeting these Challenges

Coordinating the Bargaining Units

These kinds of experiences have pushed CUPE's coordination leaders and
activists to follow certain organizational principles that have allowed them to
move forward with their agenda over time. First of all, to achieve horizontal
coordination among the bargaining units, most CUPE sectors have established
clear rules, procedures, and structures for decision-making around both bargaining priorities and job actions (Caverley & Cunningham & Mitchell, 2006;
Traxler, 2003). Significantly, those rules and structures are democratically and
voluntarily established in discussion, which is crucial in building commitment
and trust between the coordinating committee members from different locals.

One of the key values behind those rules is the effort to try to build consensus around proposals among all the coordinating committee members and the leadership from the different locals. Part of what this means is the development of strong norms around compliance regarding those rules and procedures. This is particularly crucial when attempting to coordinate a number of locals that are bargaining at separate tables at around the same time period. For example, it is understood that once the common bargaining targets are set, the separate negotiating teams will not move off those targets without consulting with and gaining the agreement of the coordinating committee and other locals. However, the emphasis on consensus over majority rules in decision-making also recognizes that this kind of commitment is much stronger when everyone fully supports the committee's positions. This also involves the need for considerable work at the local leadership level to make certain that local negotiating committees are similarly committed to the process and the targets. Although looking mainly at the European case, Traxler (2003a, b) and other researchers have suggested that one of the biggest factors affecting bargaining impact in coordinated or centralized situations is the lack of follow through at the local levels (Freeman & Gibbons, 1993; Sisson & Marginson, 2000).

Second, and although this varies somewhat among different CUPE coordinating committees, most appear to recognize the importance of trying to anticipate the sequence of management negotiating positions and actions as well as the counter positions, again especially significant if bargaining is still being done at separate tables. At the same time, when dealing with different employers, they note it is often important that coordinating committees acknowledge and recognize differences in employer positions, levels of resistance and style, and consider the implications for reaching common targets. Finally, and this is where some CUPE committee may be struggling the most, there is the need for frank discussions within the coordinating committee about divisions within the rank and file in each bargaining unit regarding interests that relate to the bargaining priorities and to develop agreed upon strategies to address these divisions (Bronfenbrenner & Juravich, 1998; Rapaport, 1999; Vielhaber & Waltman, 2008).

However, most CUPE activists involved in coordinated bargaining recognize the need for constant communication between the bargaining units as negotiations proceed, again especially when the negotiations are taking place with particular employers in different locations (Clark, 2000; Kozolanka, 2006; Meyer, 2001). CUPE uses the technique of having frequent conference call meetings as well as making significant use of e-mail exchanges. What's also significant is that they recognize the critical need to develop relations of trust and understanding between the coordinating representatives of the different bargaining units and separate bargaining team. Although some of this can be achieved through e-mails and conference calls, it is widely believed within CUPE that this can only happen in the final analysis through face to face interaction, which is why the committees advocate quite strongly for more resources to ensure regular face to face meetings with increasing frequency as they are moving into bargaining arena.

Some of the coordinating committees have also put comp thought into how the process used within those meetings can be crucial in building trust and commitment. For example, it is interesting to point to the Ontario university sector's use of a fairly open-ended participative facilitation process known as the "Art of Hosting" at its last annual meeting to set bargaining priorities. This clearly speaks to the union's awareness of the need to allow the representatives from different universities to construct their priorities through discussion and debate rather than having them imposed from above or through majority fiat (White & Gray, 2008).

Coordinating the Rank and File

Although the same principles of communication and democratic decision-making apply to vertical coordination, the key point that CUPE coordinating committees recognize here is that there has to be attention and a distinct set of actions directed towards building understanding, commitment, and involvement throughout the rank and file regarding the coordination process and its goals. This is generally understood by the committees that have been doing coordinated bargaining for some time, especially those that have learned the hard way, as in the hospital sectors, but those newer to the game acknowledge that it is often difficult to devote the time and energy at this level when they are working so hard in making the coordinating committee work (i.e., horizontal coordination). While they understand the critical need for front-end membership involvement in discussing and formulating potential bargaining priorities for the coordinating committee and action strategies, it is also at this point that they find themselves challenged by a lack of rank and file involvement, understanding, solidarity, and commitment. As such, for some, before they can move to the level of coordinating job actions, they spend time and resources promoting the value of coordinated bargaining as well as educating members about the process and challenges.

Again, they recognize the importance of face to face meetings but getting people to come to the meetings can itself be a challenge so various strategies are used to generate interest depending on resources and time. For example, the Ontario University Workers Coordinating Committee (OUWCC) used the early strategy of creating campus coalitions of CUPE locals and other unions or groups and specific campus-based actions that involved the membership and leadership of different locals as a key step in developing initial solidarity of interests across employee groups (Folk-Dawson, 2006). These coalitions were not focused on bargaining issues necessarily but rather were vehicles to demonstrate common interests to the membership and leadership and the value of collaboration (OUWCC, 2008, p. 2).

The final point to emphasize, as demonstrated graphically in the case of the B.C. hospital workers, is the need to make certain that the membership retains the final say in approving any common or central agreements reached through coordinated or central bargaining processes (Camfield, 2007). Although there is an undercurrent of complaint among activists on coordinating committees that CUPE's tradition of local autonomy weakens their capacity to coordinate, this may also be a strength in as much as it pushes the central union leadership to support voluntary active involvement and democratic decision-making involving all participating locals. The creation of several different union structures within the CUPE constitution such as the Councils of Unions which allow for significant autonomy including some control over resources, are illustrative of this capacity and may go a long way to explaining CUPE's relative success in moving towards higher levels of coordination and centralization across the country. While it is cliché to say that democracy is messy, over the long-run a commitment to membership and local power can help unions to avoid the kind of severe crises that were illustrated in the hospital sectors.

SIGNS OF PROGRESS, SIGNS OF WEAKNESS

Having suggested that there are clear signs that CUPE is meeting many of the challenges of coordinated bargaining, it would be nice to be able to end this paper by demonstrating that these efforts are reversing privatization and neoliberal policies more generally. Unfortunately, there isn't much systematic research evidence on the impact of coordinated or centralized bargaining in Canada on wages, privatization, or contracting out, whether for CUPE or any other union. Anecdotally, there are certainly examples where coordinated and/or centralized negotiations by CUPE and other unions have successfully modified and/or turned back specific management proposals on privatization. The recent success of the Ontario School Board Coordinating Committee in negotiating a strong settlement for CUPE members in 2008 is just such an example, but we have no way of knowing from these kinds of examples whether the form and level of bargaining was essential or even instrumental to those outcomes.

Still, there is some evidence that the pace of privatization has softened in Ontario and elsewhere (Cyr-Racine & Jalette, 2007; Rose, 2007). Some of this change may be more a matter of appearances in that there has been a notable decline in government rhetoric and policy statements surrounding new major initiatives in privatization under the provincial liberal regime. Still, there have been some interesting cases of "reversed privatization" (Cyr-Racine & Jalette, 2007), as in the Ontario government's 2006 decision to move privatized prisons back into the public sector. More substantively perhaps, since 2000 we've seen a gradual reversal of the steep 1990s decline in Ontario public sector employment (B.C. Stats, 2009; Statistics Canada, 2009), while the increase in temporary and part-time positions in the public sector has also slowed somewhat since 2004.

OPENING THE FLOODGATES

Whether these developments reflect the coordination and public campaign efforts of CUPE or not, I would like to conclude by suggesting that these changes also reflect the very real failure of neoliberal governments to sell the idea of full-scale privatization to a Canadian public that has continued to demonstrate a consistent commitment to things like public education and health care (Camfield, 2006). This failure has also been linked in various ways to the all too visible and very real social, economic, and environmental problems that have been created by privatization, service cuts, and globalization, both nationally and internationally (Broad, 2000; Johnston, 2006).

BOX 10.1

A GLOBAL UNION MOVEMENT

CUPE is not the only union seeking to enhance its bargaining strength through a push for more coordinated and centralized bargaining, nor are these efforts confined to the public sector. Along with defending longstanding bargaining arrangements, many private sector unions in Canada, the U.S., and Europe have sustained and expanded their efforts to encourage collaboration (Eaton, Rubinstein, & Kochan, 2008; Meyer, 2001). Private sector unions have had the additional challenge of dealing with the international movement of capital and jobs within the context of globalization, and accordingly, one very interesting development has been the attempt to coordinate bargaining across national and inter-continental boundaries. This is most evident in Europe where more significant levels of national centralized wage setting and industry wide coordinated bargaining have been retained, and where the creation of the common Economic and Monetary Union (EMU) has encouraged European governments, employers, and unions to think in terms of greater bargaining coordination across the European Union (Gennard & Newsome, 2001; Hancke & Soskice, 2003). However, North American unions have also been working to develop their capacities to coordinate bargaining at the international level. For example, the United Steelworkers union, representing over one million members in the U.S. and Canada, recently entered into a merger relationship with two U.K. unions to create the first trans-Atlantic union, called UNITE. Based in London, this new **international union** represents 3.5 million workers in the U.K., Ireland, Canada, and the U.S. One of UNITE's main objectives is to develop common approaches to collective bargaining within industry sectors and with multinational companies that operate in these four countries. At the same time, UNITE and other unions in Europe and North America are trying to assist workers in developing nations to organize and bargain to improve their conditions. One of the most interesting examples was the international expansion of a long-standing coordinating bargaining coalition of seven unions representing General Electric (GE) workers in the U.S. This U.S. bargaining coalition was originally formed in 1965 but beginning in 1997, it was expanded to include hundreds of unions across the globe. When the coalition met with U.S. GE negotiators in 1997, representatives from Brazil, Chile, and Canada were also there and a key union demand was that the company adopt minimum international **labour standards** in *every country* in which it was operating (Meyer, 2001, p. 69). As many analysts suggest, international levels of coordinated bargaining are still in their early stages, but their continued development by the major private sector unions underscores their recognition that globalization demands a global union movement (Bourque, 2008).

There are also many other signs that neoliberalism as a philosophy of governance is under increasing siege (see Box 10.1). Perhaps the most recent and most significant indicator is the recession and financial crisis that began in 2008. This crisis is a potentially pivotal point in time for public sector unions and the labour movement as a whole, with implications for the role of coordinated bargaining as a strategic direction for union renewal. On the one hand, we have media reports of world political leaders talking about the "broken" nature of our financial and economic systems and the need for *more* regulation and state intervention in the so-called free economy, which we've been told for years under the neoliberal model is best left to its own devices (e.g., Economist, 2009a, b). These political discourses, even if insincere as they surely are in many cases, offer unions and other social movements important openings to push for more permanent and significant shifts away from deregulation and other aspects of neoliberalism, in part because they challenge the idea that unregulated competition is an essential good.

Yet on the other hand, government approaches to the crisis involve the creation of huge deficits in order to pay for large-scale infrastructure projects aimed at stimulating private sector growth and employment. As the crisis subsides, it is highly likely that these deficits are going to fuel a new round of public sector cuts and probably much more privatization as governments seek to rationalize the need to reduce those deficits and corporations try to restore their rights to highly liberalized markets (Theilheimer, 2008). Whether governments return to the neoliberal rhetoric, or whether they seize on some "third way" model that acknowledges the need for increased regulation, the structural reality behind government policy will likely generate enormous pressures on the service sectors that CUPE represents, which is likely to translate into job cuts and wage concessions.

Ironically, the cuts and concessions may be so widespread, crossing both public and private sectors, as was evident in the major concessions forced on the auto sector unions in the U.S. and Canada in 2009, that this crisis may serve to unite labour around a common resistance to these concessions. If everyone is in the same sinking boat, it may be easier to organize disparate groups of workers around a coordinated or centralized platform, *and* more possible to sustain that support through coordinated job action not only within a given union or sector but across different unions and sectors. The widespread perception that the 2008 crisis was caused by greedy banks and shady Wall Street (or Bay Street) speculators is also a potentially critical factor in generating worker and public support for united union action.

Still, achieving this kind of coordination within the Canadian Labour movement will be no easy challenge given its current state of division and inter-union competition. As this paper suggests, there are enormous challenges involved in effective coordinated bargaining, even within a single union like CUPE, never mind across different unions. Nevertheless, when one considers the progress that CUPE has made over the last 10 years, despite its history of local autonomy and its complex structure of small and large union locals, the potential and possibilities of coordinated bargaining for union renewal warrants more consideration by unions and scholars than it has received thus far. Certainly among scholars, but I also would suggest even among many union activists, the renewal discourse has been focused mainly on organizing non union workers and on political action (Jackson, 2006; Kumar & Schenk, 2006; Robertson & Murninghan, 2006; Warskett, 2007; Yates, 2004). While this is understandable, we should not forget that organizing workers into unions only makes sense as a renewal strategy if unions are able to achieve and defend their collective agreements. Over the last 20 years, it has become abundantly clear that even the most powerful unions have been less and less successful in stemming the tide of concessions (Jackson, 2006). Coordinated action, in the broadest sense of both coordinated bargaining and political campaigns, may well be labour's best opportunity to challenge both neoliberalism and the aftermath of the financial crisis.

In the final analysis, it is important to remember that some of the most significant progressive changes in government policies, laws, and working and living conditions for workers were born in the context of economic and political crises such as the 1930s Depression and World War II. It is also critical to keep in mind that these shifts in policies, law, and working and living conditions did not just happen, they involved strategic actions by *collective actors*. Corporations have gained enormous power under neoliberalism, and arguably governments as vehicles for change have been weakened as have labour unions, but the labour movement cannot ignore the potential in this context to shift the pendulum towards a worker oriented agenda. Coordinated bargaining is not the only strategic means of achieving this goal, but it may well be a crucial one.

ENDNOTES

1. Common bargaining goals are established in a particular employer/union negotiation process and the first agreement reached between the union and employer is then used as a model or pattern in subsequent negotiations involving other employers and other bargaining units (Traxler, Brandl, & Glassner, 2008).

2. This paper is based largely on a review of CUPE documents and archival materials along with informal discussions with and observations of CUPE coordinating committees within Ontario.

APPENDIX: SUGGESTED WEBSITES AND FILMS BY CHAPTER

The lists of suggested websites and films below are sorted alphabetically. Numbers in parentheses refer to the chapters containing the main discussion of the content addressed by each resource.

WEBSITES

Bonham Centre for Sexual Diversity Studies

University of Toronto sexual diversity portal

(http://www.utoronto.ca/sexualdiversity) (5)

Canadian Auto Workers

The website for the largest public sector union in Canada.

(http://www.caw.ca) (2)

Canadian Centre for Policy Alternatives

Website for an independent, non-partisan research institute concerned with issues of social and economic justice.

(http://www.policyalternatives.ca) (4)

Canadian Council of Human Resources Associations

(http://www.cchra.ca) (5)

Canadian Labour Congress

The CLC federation represents most unions in Canada.

(http://www.canadianlabour.ca) (2)

Canadian Labour Law and Labour Relations Links

The website provides links to labour law and related information.

(http://www.labourrelations.org/Links/Labour_Links.html) (2)

Canadian Union of Public Employees

The website for Canada's largest union. CUPE represents 600,000 Canadian workers in a broad spectrum of public sector workplaces. This website provides links to a rich variety of information including current events, reports, and videos.

(http://www.cupe.ca) (2)

Common Frontier Canada

The website of a multi-sectoral working group that confronts and proposes an alternative to the social, environmental, and economic effects of economic integration in the Americas.

(http://www.commonfrontiers.ca/aboutus.html) (1)

Communications, Energy, and Paperworkers Union

A union website with links to their Humanity Fund and involvement in International Solidarity.

(http://www.cep.ca) (2)

Council of Canadians

This is the website for non-partisan, independent organization founded in 1985 that provides lots of information relevant to trade union and economic struggles.

(http://www.canadians.org) (1)

Cradle of Collective Bargaining

This website at McMaster University details the history and culture of unions in Hamilton, Ontario.

(http://www.humanities.mcmaster.ca/~cradle) (2)

CUPE Review of Coordinated Bargaining Structures

Review by CUPE Research Office of the different coordinated bargaining structures in CUPE.

(http://www.cupe.on.ca/aux_file.php?aux_file_id=260 (10)

Democracy Now

A daily TV/radio news program that pioneers the largest community media collaboration in the U.S. This site provides up-to-date information from a critical and progressive perspective.

(http://www.democracynow.org/) (3)

DiversityCanada Foundation

The DiversityCanada Foundation is a non-profit organization that works to promote diversity, inclusion, and harmony in Canada.

(http://diversitycanada.org/) (5)

Economics for Everyone

This website developed by Jim Stanford, economist for Canadian Auto Workers, provides very accessible information about the Canadian economy and its labour force.

(http://www.economicsforeveryone.com) (1)

HRM Guide

General guide to human resources issues in Canada.

(http://www.hrmguide.net/canada) (5)

International Confederation of Free Trade Unions

A useful website for information on anti-globalization campaigns and international trade union news.

(http://www.icftu.org) (2)

International Labour Organization

The website for this United Nations agency brings together governments, employers, and workers of its member states in common action to promote decent work and working conditions throughout the world.

(http://www.ilo.org) (10)

International Trade Union Confederation

An organization intended to promote and defend workers' rights through international cooperation

(http://www.ituc-csi.org) (2)

Jobs With Justice

This U.S. organization seeks to promote justice in workplaces and working-class communities. JWJ was founded in 1987 with the vision of lifting up workers' rights struggles as part of a larger campaign for economic and social justice.

(http://www.jwj.org) (2)

Just Labour: A Canadian Journal of Work and Society

This e-journal based at York University provides up-to-date articles on workers, their issues, and organizations.

(http://www.justlabour.yorku.ca) (8)

Labor Notes

Labor Notes is a media and organizing project of union activists.

(http://www.labornotes.org) (2)

Labour Start

An organization that uses Internet resources to spread information about labour campaigns in Canada and elsewhere.

(http://www.labourstart.org/canada/) (2)

Maquila Solidarity Network

A Canadian network promoting solidarity with labour and other groups in Mexico, Central America, and Asia.

(http://www.maquilasolidarity.org) (7)

Michael Moore's website

Michael Moore is a popular muckracking film-maker (see filmography).

(http://www.michaelmoore.com) (10)

New Unionism

A network of union activists and staffers from around the world, promoting more innovative and effective union strategies.

(http://www.newunionism.net (2)

Our Times

An on-line magazine that provides up-to-date news and articles from a union perspective, including full-text articles.

(http://www.ourtimes.ca) (2)

Rebel Graphics

This website provides a list and description of working-class videos.

(http://www.rebelgraphics.org) (8)

United Food and Commercial Workers

Union website with links to media, membership, history, and other useful information.

(http://www.ufcw.ca) (7)

United Steelworkers

Union website. Although this union started out as an industrial union, it is now found in every aspect of the Canadian workplace, from nursing homes to factories. There are numerous useful links, including to the Humanity Fund.

(http://www.uswa.ca) (2)

University of Toronto Centre for Industrial and Human Relations.

This website provides information on collective agreements as well as on labour unions and social justice groups.

(http://www.chass.utoronto.ca/cir/library/hrirwebsites.html) (10)

Walmart Watch

A website established to promote an education campaign to challenge Walmart and to inform workers, citizens, and communities about the world's largest retailer.

(http://www.walmartwatch.com) (3)

Workers Action Centre

The WAC is a worker-based organization in Ontario committed to improving the lives and working conditions of workers in low-wage and precarious employment.

(http://www.workersactioncentre.org) (6)

FILMS

Betrayed: The Story of Canadian Merchant Seamen

(concerns the history of unionization in Canada). A film by Elaine Briere. Knowledge Network and Saskatchewan Television Network. 2004. 56 min. (2)

Black Gold

(traces the global production and distribution of coffee). A film by Marc and Nick Francis. Distributed by Mongrel Media. 2005. 82 min. (8)

Capitalism: A Love Story

A film by Michael Moore. Overture Films. 2009. 2 hrs 07 min. (10)

The Corporation

(history and contemporary realities of corporate economy). A film by Mark Achbar, Jennifer Abbot, and Joel Bakan. Distributed by Mongrel Media. 2003. 145 min. (4)

Death and Profits

(workplace safety and hazards). 2002. 46 min. (7)

El Contrato

(National Film Board of Canada) A documentary on the Seasonal
Agricultural Worker Program in Canada. (7)

Enron: The Smartest Guys in the Room

(corporate malfeasance) A film by Alex Gibney et al. Distributed by
Alliance Atlantis. 2005. 1 hr 50 min. (1)

GDP: Steely Resolve

(U.S. Steel takeover of Stelco and plant closure on November 5,
2009). (Includes Interactive Web project—globalization and
unemployment.) (2)

Germinal

(1993, Dir. Claude Berri) With French subtitles. Starring Gerard
Depardieu. Hard struggle of miners to form an early union. In the
end the miners lose this fight—but the viewer knows full well
that the battle isn't over. (2)

The Global Assembly Line

(Lorraine Gray) (6)

Harlan County USA

(1976, Dir. Barbara Kopple) A realistic and brutal portrayal of the
challenge of fighting back, in an epic Kentucky coal strike. Reveals
the highly non-neutral role played by government and its agencies.
Kopple also directed the equally powerful American Dream (1992)
about another epic but losing strike (at the food processing
company Hormel). Both films won Academy Awards. (2)

The Hasty Man Drinks His Tea with a Fork

(our speeded up lives in the modern economy). 2003. 83 min.
French with subtitles. (8)

Immigrant Workers Fight To Unionize Their Workplace

(John Bonnar) (6)

I.O.U.S.A.

(proliferation of debt-based economy in U.S.) A film by Patrick
Creadon and Christine O'Malley. Distributed by CinemaVault.
2009. 85 min. (3)

Imperfect Union (series)

(1989 history of Canadian unions). (2)

Let's Make Money

(guide to understanding the global economic crisis). A film by Erwin Wagenhofer. Distributed by Mongrel Media. 2008. 110 min. (1)

Margaret's Museum

(1995, Dir. Mort Ransen) Another film about the struggle of coal miners, with a Canadian connection. (2)

Maxed Out

(proliferation of debt-based economy in U.S.) Distributed by Mongrel Media. 2006. 90 min. (3)

Modern Times

(1936, Dir. Charlie Chaplin) Last (and most powerful) appearance of Chaplin's "Little Tramp" character. Shows the consequences when rationalization of labour in the interests of profit maximization is taken to its logical extreme. (2)

The Necktie

(alienating impact of work and prospect of hope). 2009. 17 min. Animated. (8)

The New Rulers of the World (4) "Quel numéro, What number?" or, "The Electronic Sweatshop"

(Sophie Bissonnette) (6)

Shipbreakers

(exploitation and abuse of workers in India). 2004. 72 min. (5)

The Take

(Argentinian workers take over abandoned factory). A film by Avi Lewis and Naomi Klein. Barna-Alper Productions and Klein Lewis Productions. 2004. 1 hr 27 min. (10)

24 Days in Brooks

(follows the strike by workers—including many immigrant workers—at Lakeside Packers, Alta., one of the largest slaughterhouses in Canada). 2007. 42 min. (2)

Wal-Mart: The high cost of low price

(examination of impact of Wal-Mart on local and global economies). A film by Robert Greenwald. Brave New Films. 2005. 97 min. (3)

Wal-Town

(Canadian students seek to raise public awareness about Walmart business practices). A film by Sergio Kirby. Distributed by National Film Board of Canada. 2006. 66 min. (3)

Work for All: Stop Racism in the Workplace (series).

2006. 202 min. (6)

Zeitgeist (4)

The following is a list of films available through the National Film Board of Canada website:

GLOSSARY

Numbers in parentheses refer to the chapters in which the boldfaced key term appears.

A

Arbitration A process through which an employer and a union settle a matter in dispute that they are not able to resolve through negotiation but without engaging in a work stoppage. (2, 3, 10)

Arbitrator A "neutral" third party (usually jointly selected by the union and the employer) who is responsible for making a binding ruling on the issue presented to him or her. (10)

B

Bargaining agent The union that holds the legal certification to represent and negotiate on behalf of a group of workers. (2)

Bargaining unit A specified group of workers, in one or more employers or worksites, who are covered by a particular collective agreement. (2, 10)

Benchmarks (in collective bargaining) A set of measurable standards used to evaluate bargaining outcomes. (10)

Business unionism A more conservative philosophy of trade unionism, in which unions focus exclusively on winning economic gains for their members through collective bargaining, and avoid participating in broader social and economic debates and struggles. (2)

C

Career choices or who gets what jobs/careers are dependent on one's family, class, upbringing and related cultural capital; however, other factors must be taken into account including gender, sexual orientation, age, race/ethnicity, and region in Canada.

Centralized bargaining Unions and employers representing multiple collective agreements meet together to negotiate common or *central* agreements covering all or some portion of the employment conditions for all the employees in those units. (Introduction; 10)

Certification The process through which a union organizes members and wins official recognition from both the employer and the government's labour regulator (e.g., a labour board). (2, 3)

Closet This term is used as a metaphor to describe someone who has opted not to reveal an invisible characteristic. It is often used in relation to gays and lesbians who are "in the closet." (5)

Collective agreement A contract between an employer and a union that specifies the wages, pensions, and benefits, hours of work, representation, union security, and other terms and conditions of work in a unionized workplace. (2, 10)

Collective bargaining The process through which an employer and a union negotiate the terms and conditions of employment for all the members of the bargaining unit. (Introduction; 2, 10)

Coordinated bargaining Any collaborative attempt by two or more distinct bargaining units to achieve common or similar bargaining outcomes through linked negotiations. (10)

D

Diversity management This is a proactive approach to ensuring diversity is celebrated and valued. (Introduction; 5)

Dual earner-female career model A dominant arrangement in which men and women are both workers in the paid labour market but women continue to assume the responsibility for the work of social reproduction. (4)

E

Emotional labour Work characterized by the requirement that workers elicit positive feelings toward clients or customers, that they contain their own emotions, and that they maintain a smile and positive outlook regardless of the circumstances and tasks at hand. (3)

F

Feminist political economy This popular theoretical perspective in the social sciences draws attention to the historical organization of the economy (global capitalism), the power structure implied by this organization, and our personal relationships to the economy (worker, owner). Gender (and intersecting inequalities such as age, race, sexual orientation) is understood to be pivotal in understanding and challenging these complex power relationships. (8)

Fixed term work This refers to work for a specified length of time and includes contract, casual, and seasonal work. In addition, work constructed through an employment agency is often structured for a specific time period. (8)

Flexibilization or flexibility of employment This term refers to contemporary management practices aimed at reducing labour costs by reducing the permanent (core) full-time labour force to its smallest size while drawing on on-call, part-time, or casual workers only during peak demand periods. (3, 8)

Fordism Named after Henry Ford, the term fordism refers to a form of production characterized by mass production, protected market, and standardized work structures. (6)

G

GLBT This is an acronym for gay, lesbian, bisexual, transgender. (5)

Globalization The global integration of national economies achieved through the increased mobility of goods, services, labour, and investment across national boundaries. (Introduction; 1, 3, 10)

Globalized workplace Once work is globalized the conditions of employment (pay, benefits, educational requirements, rates of unionization, and so on) are influenced not only by realities in the national context but also by global patterns. (8)

Grievance A verbal or written process that sparks a dispute resolution process between the employer and the union. A grievance is filed when the union believes that the rights of an individual or the collective as established in the collective agreement have been violated. (2, 9, 10)

Guest worker programs Also called migrant worker programs or temporary worker programs, guest worker programs refer to the state's regulatory framework for the importation of workers under specific conditions of employment, with specifically defined rights, in specifically defined places of employment for a specifically defined time. (Introduction; 7)

H

Hegemonic relations The concept as developed by Italian Marxist intellectual Antonio Gramsci refers to a power relationship based on consensus between the dominant and subordinate groups. (4, 6, 9)

HIV/AIDS HIV is a virus that may lead to immunological problems including the disease known as AIDS. (5)

Hours polarization Refers to an increase at both ends of the spectrum or a growing gap between the numbers working long hours and the numbers working too few hours, resulting in increasing income inequalities. (3)

I

Integration paradigm This is a way of understanding diversity that promotes equality and capitalizes on difference as an asset. (Introduction; 5)

Inter-cultural learning This refers to the mutual learning process and outcomes associated with experiences of different national, racial, ethnic, or regional cultures. (7)

International unions Unions that are based in one country, but represent workers in another country. About one-quarter of Canadian union members (and half of private-sector union members) belong to U.S.-based international unions. (2, 10)

Invisible characteristic This is an aspect of a person that is not readily apparent. (Introduction; 5)

J

Job sharing In contrast to work sharing, job sharing is a government, employer, and/or union mandated policy that requires workers during periods of economic downturn to share the available work among the workforce so as to avoid (further) layoffs and dismissals. (8)

Just-in-time management practices The expansion of economic globalization along with technological innovation have prompted a variety of new management practices aimed at reducing costs and increasing profitability. Just-in-time refers, for example, to the reduction of warehousing costs so that product is delivered just in time for processing. Consistent with this approach is a flexibilization of the workforce. (6, 8)

L

Labour standards Refers to conventions, agreements, and recommendations for standards of working conditions to ensure that workers' rights are taken into account and to guard against unjust and inhumane labour practices. Labour standards are enshrined in provincial, national, and international labour law. (Introduction; 3, 10)

Leisure This concept is frequently used to refer to the wide range of non-obligatory or discretionary activities that humans engage in. Leisure may assume a variety of forms, including passive leisure (watching television, reading a book), active leisure (engagement in sports or other physical activities) and social leisure (activities that include social relationships). (Introduction; 8)

Life chances Real "options" or choices available to people. These can be achieved from family's social class background and by the redistributive mechanisms of the state. (1)

Life course perspective This sociological approach draws attention to the overall life cycle and seeks to locate research in terms of the overall structure of individual lives within a particular societal or cultural context. (Introduction; 8)

Lockout A work stoppage initiated by the employer that restricts the workers from entering the workplace. This may occur when the parties have reached the expiration of their collective agreement and have entered into collective bargaining but are unable to reach an agreement. (2)

Loose time Refers to the accumulation of experience about the work tasks, work groups

and organizational hierarchy and its use in not only maintaining and resisting power in the organization but in potentially fostering individual creative or innovative outcomes at all levels of the organization. (Introduction; 9)

M

Mandatory retirement This term refers to the legal requirement that all employees retire when they reach age 65. Throughout the developed economies, this requirement has been steadily eroded and in its place other policies (for example, the employee's ability to continue to perform the work) have been applied rather than chronological age. (8)

McDonaldization This term refers to the increasing rationalization of the routine tasks of everyday life. (3)

McJobs This term is used to refer to jobs characterized by low wages, few or no benefits, few opportunities to advance or learn, low rates of unionization, non-standard hours. These jobs are described as insecure and precarious. (3)

Multiple job holding This term is applied to those individuals who are employed at more than one job at one time. This may include simultaneously working several part-time jobs or combining part-time and full-time employment. (4, 8)

N

Neoliberal ideologies A set of ideas underlying economic policies that promotes privatization of national economy, liberal trade policies, and greater openness to foreign investments. (6)

Neoliberalism Theories and policies of economic and political governance that emphasize deregulated markets and enhanced competition, achieved principally through reductions in legislative and social security protections, international and regional free trade agreements, and the transfer of public services into private hands. Neoliberalism elevates the notion of the free market and advocates individualism and individual rights over collectivism or group rights. (Introduction; 1, 2, 3, 4, 10)

New Economy This refers to the continual development of new goods, technologies, and social relations under capitalism. Features of the new economy include flexibility in production systems and labour markets, global production networks, globalization, and neoliberal policies. (Introduction; 1, 3)

Non-standard employment This term refers to the wide variety of work that is framed outside the "traditional" 40-hour/5-day workweek. Non-standard employment may be part-time, seasonal, contract work, work obtained through a temporary help agency, or own-account self-employment. Workers in non-standard employment may work for one or more employers at the same time. (Introduction; 3, 4, 6, 8)

Non-work This term is used to cover the wide variety of human activities that are not encompassed by paid or unpaid work (domestic labour). Related terms include non-obligatory activities and leisure. (Introduction; 3, 8)

O

Outsourcing Refers to the contracting out of business to an external provider. When businesses outsource work to providers outside the nation, this may be referred to as *offshoring*. (3)

P

Part-time work This term is applied to paid employment at less than the usual number of hours for full-time work. While the specific hour definition varies, typically part-time work involves employment for fewer than 30 hours per week. Part-time work may be permanent (with no set term of employment) or precarious (based, for example, on an on-call arrangement). (Introduction; 3, 6, 8)

Passing This term is used to describe someone who attempts not to reveal some characteristic. Often used in relation to Black people who attempt to pass as White, but is also used with other groups such as a gay man who may attempt to appear heterosexual. (5)

Paternalism Attitudes or policies of governments, organizations, or individuals that appear to be fatherly or benevolent, but are intrusive and do not respect or allow for peoples' rights or responsibilities. (3)

Pattern bargaining The negotiation of a collective agreement between a particular bargaining unit union and employer, which is then used as a model or pattern in subsequent negotiations involving other employers and other bargaining units. (2, 10)

Popular education While the term is subject to broad historical interpretations, in contemporary educational studies it is associated with the theories of Paulo Freire who developed an educational method that was rooted in the experiences of oppressed social groups and linked to collective interpretation, problem-solving, and action. (7)

Post Fordism Work arrangements characterized by deregulation, the rise of global markets, subcontracting and temporary work patterns. (6)

Power Signifies compliance to the will of others holding offices positioned higher than oneself inside the bureaucratic hierarchy. Foucault established the limits of power's reach inside large organizations while Deleuze and Guattari argue the potential for resourcefulness and creativity. (Introduction; 3, 6, 9, 10)

Precarious work A form of employment usually characterized by temporary, part-time, contract-based, or indirect (e.g., through an employment placement agency) work, and where workers are faced with sub-standard working conditions (including low pay, no benefits, no access to vacation and holiday pay, etc.). Precarious jobs break from more traditional employment relationships, which generally offer full-time stable employment, higher wages, non-wage benefits, and more stable and consistent work hours. (Introduction; 3, 6)

Privatization The transfer of ownership and control of services and programs operated by the government to the private sector. (Introduction; 4, 10)

R

Racial fixities The ascription of behaviours and characteristics on the basis of biological traits. (6)

Racialization The process and practice of attributing biological and social differences to groups of people. (6)

Racialized gendering of jobs Where certain jobs are done predominantly by women or by men and are assumed to require a predefined performance of femininity or masculinity. (6)

Racism The ideology and practice of inferiorizing groups of people who are racialized. (6)

Rationality The acceptance of rules, efficiency, and practical results as the right way to approach human affairs. (9)

Rationalization of society A widespread acceptance of rationality and a process by which interactions are increasingly based on efficiency rather than on emotions, customs, or traditions. (10)

S

Semiperipheral A middle-level status in the world economy characterized by the export of both natural resources and innovative manufactured goods where the state plays a pivotal role in whether the country moves up or down in the world economy. (1)

Seniority A ranking system that orders a group of workers in a union typically based on their tenure working for an employer. The most common seniority system is one where the day a worker starts working is set as the seniority date. The names of the workers along with their seniority date are then compiled in order from most senior to junior. Most union contracts ensure that access to new opportunities, and protection against layoff, is determined at least partly on the basis of seniority. The goal of these provisions is to prevent employers from weakening union solidarity through favouritism, or through persecution of union activists. (3)

Social choices refers to material life chances that are dependent on income derived from paid employment for the Canadian population as a whole.

Social reproduction The work that is involved in the daily and generational reproduction of the population. It includes the dynamics that produce and reproduce people in material, social, and cultural ways. (4)

Social unionism A philosophy of trade unionism that recognizes that unions must be active in broader social and political debates, in order to most effectively advance the interests of their members. (2)

Standard employment relationship Refers to full-time, full-year, long-term employment. This was considered to be the standard for middle and working-class White men in the postwar period. (3)

Stigma This is a seriously negative quality placed on someone's character by others. (Introduction; 5)

Strike A work stoppage initiated by the employer, when the collective agreement has expired and collective bargaining cannot come to an agreement. In a strike, union members collectively withdraw their work from the workplace until a satisfactory resolution is attained through bargaining. (2, 10)

Supply chains Refers to the system of moving a product or service from supplier to customer by linking organizations, technologies, resources, activities, and information. (3)

T

Targets in collective bargaining Specific long or short-term bargaining objectives such as a 5-percent wage increase, a restriction on contracting out bargaining unit work, or the creation of an early retirement plan. (10)

Time crunch This term is used throughout the sociology of work literature to refer to the intense stress reported by women and men who are combining the conflicting demands of family obligations (household work, childcare) and paid employment. (8)

Transnational labour While not an entirely new phenomenon, this term refers to the increasing globalization of labour markets such that workers now more frequently and in greater numbers cross national borders in search of and to perform work. (7)

U

Union An organization that is empowered to negotiate for the collective workplace interests of its members. (Introduction; 1, 2, 3, 5, 6, 7, 9, 10)

Union dues The financial contribution that workers pay to their union, to support the union's own expenses and operations. (2, 10)

Union security Provisions of a collective agreement that provide for mechanisms (such as automatic check-off and transfer of union dues), which enhance the stability and power of the union. (2)

Unpaid work A term used to refer to the wide variety of productive activities that are not compensated by wages. Most significant in this category is household work, including domestic labour, childcare, and elder care. (Introduction; 3, 8)

V

Volunteerism This concept refers to personal efforts that are donated, with no (apparent) expectation of direct compensation, to a community, agency, or social group. Traditionally, volunteers were not under any compulsion to provide their unpaid labour and were seen to be motivated by a commitment to public or community service. (8)

W

Walmartization A term referring to profound transformations in regional and global economies through the sheer size, influence, and power of the big box department store, Walmart. (Introduction; 3)

Work normally refers to paid employment; housework, for example, is work but is not usually considered paid employment unless a domestic worker or cleaning service is hired to do the tasks.

Workplace learning Workplace learning is typically composed of organized training as well as informal learning gleaned from on-the-job learning. It may also include forms of tacit learning (learning that people do that they do not consciously recognize they have done). (7)

Worksharing This term refers to employment arrangements wherein several (usually two) workers share one employment position. For example, a full-time position might be redefined into two part-time positions. Unlike regular part-time work, a work-sharing arrangement implies that wages, benefits, job security, and training opportunities that normally accrue to the full-time position continue on a pro rata basis for the work sharers. (8)

REFERENCES

Introduction

Dyer-Witheford, N. (1999). *Cyber-Marx: Cycles and circuits of struggle in high-technology capitalism*. Chicago: University of Illinois Press.

Mills, C. Wright. (1951). *White collar*. New York: Oxford University Press.

Munro, M. (2010, February 24). Climate scientists fight for renewed research funding. *The Gazette*, A11.

Sayer, L. C. (2005, September). Gender, time and inequality: Trends in women's and men's paid work, unpaid work and free time. *Social Forces, 84*(1), 285–303.

Zaretsky, E. (1986). *Capitalism, the family and personal life* (rev. ed.). New York: Harper and Row Publishers.

Chapter 1

Anastakis, D. (2005). *Auto Pact: Creating a borderless North American auto industry, 1960-1971*. Toronto: University of Toronto Press.

Berger, J., Motte, A., & Parkin, A. (2007). *The price of knowledge 2006-07*. Canadian Millennium Scholarship Foundation.

Bourdieu, P. (with Jean-Claude Passeron). (1990). *Reproduction in education, society and culture*. London: Sage.

Canadian Council on Social Development. (2005). The state of Canada's social programs. *Perceptions, 27*(3/4), 2–29.

Canadian Social Trends. (2008). Ottawa: Statistics Canada (Catalogue No. 11–008).

CBCNews. (2009, January). *Nortel: Canada's technology shining star becomes financial black hole*. Retrieved from http://www.cbc.ca/money/story/2009/01/14/f-nortel-backgrounder-january09.html

Conference Board of Canada. (2005). *The world and Canada: Trends reshaping our future*. Ottawa.

Dahrendorf, R. (1980). *Life chances: Approaches to social and political theory*. Chicago: University of Chicago Press.

Domhoff, G. W. (2006). *Power in America: Wealth, income and power*. Retrieved from htttp://sociology.ucsc.edu/whorule-samerica/power/wealth.html

Dunn, J. (2002). *Are widening income inequalities making Canada less healthy?* Toronto: Making Connections Project. Retrieved from http://www.healthnexus.ca/projects/index.htm#hdp

Evans, M. (2008, December). *Why Nortel is still important to Canada*. Retrieved from http://seekingalpha.com/article/112533-why-nortel-is-still-important-to-canada

Forsyth, D. (1999). *End of an era? International challenges to the Auto Pact: Members briefing*. The Conference Board of Canada, 4 pages.

Gerlsbeck, R. (2008, December). Squeezed: Canada's middle class is in financial trouble. That's in good times. What happens in a recession? *MoneySense*.

Glenday, D., et al. (1997). *Good jobs, bad jobs, no jobs: The transformation of work in the 21st century*. Toronto: Harcourt Brace.

_____ 1989. Rich but semiperipheral: Canada's ambiguous position in the world economy. *Review: Fernand Braudel Centre, 12*(2), 209–261.

Goodman, A., & Shephard, A. (2002). *Inequality and living standards in Great Britain: Some Facts*. London: The Institute for Fiscal Studies: Briefing Note No. 18.

Government of Canada. *Key economic events: 1965—Canada–US Auto Pact.* Retrieved from http://www.canadianeconomy.gc.ca/ english/economy/1965canada_us_auto_ pact.html

Johnston, D. C. (2007, March 29). Income gap is widening, data shows. *New York Times.*

Kerstetter, S. (2009). *The Affordability gap: Spending differences between Canada's rich and poor.* Ottawa: Canadian Centre for Policy Alternatives.

Niosi, J. (1996). Periphery in the centre: Canada and the North American economy. In W. G. Martin (Ed.), *Semiperipheral states in the world economy.* New York: Greenwood Press.

Porter, J. (1979). *The measure of Canadian society: Education, equality and opportunity.* Toronto: Gage.

Robbins, R. (1999). *Global problems and the culture of capitalism.* Allyn and Bacon.

Chapter 2

Akyeampong, E. (2002, August). Unionization and fringe benefits. *Perspectives on Labour and Income,* 3–9.

Akyeampong, E. (1999, August). Unionization: An update. *Perspectives on Labour and Income.*

Bureau of Labor Statistics, U.S. Department of Labor. (2009). *Union members summary.* Washington: Bureau of Labor Statistics.

Card, D. E., & Freeman, R. B. (1993). *Small differences that matter: Labor markets and income maintenance in Canada and the United States.* Chicago: University of Chicago Press.

Emmanuel, A. (1972). *Unequal exchange: A study of the imperialism of trade* (B. Pierce, Trans.). New York: Monthly Review Press.

Friedman, M. (1968). The role of monetary policy. *American Economic Review,* 58(1), 1–17.

Godard, J. (2005). *Industrial relations: The economy and society* (3rd ed.). Toronto: Captus Press.

Gonick, C., Phillips, P., & Vorst, J. (Eds.). (1996). Labour gains, labour pains: 50 years of PC 1003. *Socialist Studies Annual, 10.* Winnipeg: Fernwood.

Harvey, D. (2005). *A brief history of neoliberalism.* Oxford: Oxford University Press.

Hebdon, R. (2008). *Industrial relations in Canada.* Toronto: Thomson Nelson.

Heron, C. (1996). *The Canadian labour movement: A short history.* Toronto: Lorimer.

Human Resources Development Canada, Strategic Policy, Analysis, and Workplace Information Directorate. (2007). *Union membership in Canada—2007.* Ottawa, HRDC.

Jackson, A. (2009). *Work and labour in Canada: Critical issues.* Toronto: Canadian Scholar's Press.

Jackson, A. (2006). Rowing against the tide: The struggle to raise union density in a hostile environment. In P. Kumar & C. Schenk (Eds.), *Paths to union renewal: Canadian experiences.* Peterborough: Broadview Press.

Klein, N. (2007). *The shock doctrine: The rise of disaster capitalism.* New York: Metropolitan Books.

Kumar, P. (2008). Is the movement at a stand-still? *Our Times, 27(5).*

Kumar, P., & Schenk, C. (Eds.) (2006). *Paths to union renewal: Canadian experiences.* Peterborough: Broadview Press.

Morissette, R., Schellenberg, G., & Johnson, A. (2005, Summer). Diverging trends in unionization. *Perspectives on Labour and Income.* Statistics Canada.

Pupo, N. (Ed.) (2009). Unionization and the economic and social well-being of Canadians. *Just Labour: A Canadian Journal of Work and Society, 15.*

Resnick, P. (1989). From semiperiphery to perimeter of the core: Canada's place in the capitalist world-economy. In *The masks of proteus: Canadian reflections on the state.* Montreal: McGill-Queen's University Press.

Stanford, J. (2008a). *Economics for everyone: A short guide to the economics of capitalism.* Halifax: Fernwood Publishing.

Stanford, J. (2008b). Staples, deindustrialization, and foreign investment: Canada's economic journey back to the future. *Studies in Political Economy, 82,* 7–34.

Stanford, J., & Vosko, L. (Eds.). (2004). *Challenging the market: The struggle to regulate work and income.* Montreal: McGill-Queen's University Press.

Statistics Canada. (2008, August). Unionization. *Perspectives on Labour and Income.*

Verma, A., & Fang, T. (2002, September). Union wage premium. *Perspectives on Labour and Income, 3*(9).

Visser, J. (2006). Union membership statistics in 24 countries. *Monthly Labor Review, 129*(1), 38–49.

Vosko, L. F. (Ed.). (2006). *Precarious employment: Understanding labour market insecurity in Canada.* Montreal: McGill-Queen's Press.

Chapter 3

Adams, R. (2005, Autumn). Organizing Wal-Mart: The Canadian campaign. *Just Labour: A Canadian Journal of Work and Society, 6/7,* 1–11.

Adams, T. J. (2006). Making the new shop floor: Wal-Mart, labour control, and the history of the postwar discount retail industry in America. In N. Lichtenstein (Ed.), *Wal-Mart: The face of twenty-first century capitalism.* New York: The New Press.

Appelbaum, R., & Lichtenstein, N. (2007). A new world of retail supremacy. Supply chains and workers' chains in the age of Wal-Mart. *International Labor and Working-Class History, 70,* 106–125.

Banach, N. (2005, February 8). UCLA examines "Wal-Martization." *The Daily Bruin Online.*

Barboza, D. (2008, January 5). In Chinese factories, lost fingers and low pay. *The New York Times.*

Bernard, A. (2009, February). Trends in manufacturing employment. *Perspectives on Labour and Income.* Statistics Canada, Catalogue No. 75-001-X, 5–13.

Bonacich, E., & Wilson, J. B. (2008). *Getting the goods: Parts, labor, and the logistics revolution.* Ithaca: Cornell University Press.

Bonacich, E., & Wilson, J. B. (2005). Hoisted by its own petard: Organizing Wal-Mart's logistics workers. *New Labor Forum, 14*(2), 67–75.

Broad, D., & Antony. W. (2006). Capitalism rebooted? The new economy may not be all that new. In D. Broad & W. Antony (Eds.). *Capitalism rebooted: Work, welfare and the new economy.* Halifax: Fernwood Publishing.

CBC News. (2009, April 9). *Unionized Quebec Wal-Mart workers get 1st contract.* Retrieved April 15, 2009, from http://www.cbc.ca/canada/montreal/story/2009/04/09/mtl-walmart/sthyacinthe-unionized-0409.html

CBC News. (2008, December 19). *Wal-Mart to fight ruling that lets Gatineau store unionize.* Retrieved

April 15, 2009, from http://www.cbc.ca/canada/contreal/story/2008/12/19/ot- 081219-wal-mart.html/

CBC News. (2008, December 9). *Union certified at Wal-Mart store in Saskatchewan.* Retrieved April 15, 2009, from http://www.cbc.ca/canada/saskatchewan/story/2008/12/09/wal-mart.html

CBC News. (2005, February 14). *Wal-Mart to appeal union decision in Saint-Hyacinthe.* Retrieved April 15, 2009, from http://www.cbc.ca/Canada/story/2005/02/13/walmart-quebec050213.html

Dicker, J. (2005). *The United States of Wal*Mart.* New York: Jeremy P. Tarcher/Penguin.

D'Innocenzio, A. (2006, April 18). A new Wal-Mart? World's largest merchant proposes to help local competing businesses. *The Hamilton Spectator,* p. A12.

Dickerson, M. (2008, March 8). Wal-Mart plants seeds of alliance with Latin farmers. *Los Angeles Times.* Retrieved from http://www.latimes.com/news/nationworld/world/latinamerica/la-fi-walmart8mar08,1,6049189.story?ctrack=5&cset=true

Duffy, A., & Pupo, N. (1992). *Part-time paradox: Connecting gender, work and family.* Toronto: McClelland & Stewart.

Ehrenreich, B. (2001). *Nickel and dimed: On (not) getting by in America.* New York: Metropolitan Books.

Ewing, J. (2005, April 11). Wal-Mart: Struggling in Germany. *Business Week.* Retrieved from http://www.businessweek.com/print/magazine/content/05_15/b3928086_mz054.htm?chan=gl

Featherstone, L. (2004). *Selling women short: The landmark battle for workers' rights at Wal-Mart.* New York: Basic Books.

Fedrix, E. (2009, October 29). Dying for a sale: Walmart now peddling caskets. *The Hamilton Spectator,* p. A15.

Fishman, C. (2007, December 19). The Wal-mart you don't know. *Fast Company,* 77. Retrieved from http://www.fastcompany.com/magazine/77/walmart.html

Fishman, C. (2006). *The Wal-Mart effect: How the world's most powerful company really works—and how it's transforming the American economy.* New York: The Penguin Press.

Flavelle, D. (2009, March 5). Food sales gain traction. *Toronto Star,* pp. B1, B7.

Flavelle, D. (2006, August 13). Ontario grocers ready for a battle. *Toronto Star.* http://www.thestar.com

Forbes. (2009). The world's richest people. *Forbes.com.* Retrieved May 7, 2009, from http://www.forbes.com/lists/2006/10/Rank_1.html

Fortune 500. (2009). *CNN Money.com.* Retrieved May 7, 2009, from http://money.cnn.com/magazines/fortune/fortune500/2009/snapshots/2255.html

Freeman, R. (2003, November 28). Wal-Mart "eats" more U.S. manufacturers. *Executive Intelligence Review.* Retrieved from http://www.larouchepub.com/other/2003/3046wal-mart_pricing.html

Global 500. (2009). Retrieved February 22, 2010, from http://money.cnn.com/magazines/fortune/global500/2009/index.html

Gougeon, P. (2009). Minimum wage. *Perspectives on Labour and Income.* Statistics Canada, Catalogue No. 75-001-X, January, 1–5.

Greenhouse, S., & Barbaro, M. (2006, October 2). Wal-Mart to add wage caps and part-timers. *The New York Times.*

Hanley, W. (2009, September 4). Wal-Mart aims to silence workers: Corporation using trademark law in attempt to control website's content. *The Hamilton Spectator*, p. A11.

Kabel, M. (2007, August 16). Wal-Mart factory inspectors find drop in worst labour violations. *The Hamilton Spectator*, p. A11.

Kabel, M. (2007a, October 25). Wal-Mart targets Canada, China, Mexico. *The Hamilton Spectator*, p. A17.

Lancaster House Labour Law On-Line. (2009, December 2). *Supreme Court decides Wal-Mart case on narrow grounds: Quebec law different from rest of Canada.* Retrieved from http://www.lancasterhouse.com

Lichtenstein, N. (2007). Supply chains, workers' chains, and the new world of retail supremacy. *Labor: Studies in Working-Class History of the Americas*, 4(1), 17–31.

Lichtenstein, N. (Ed.). (2006). *Wal-Mart: The face of twenty-first century capitalism.* New York: The New Press.

Lin, J. (2008, September). Trends in employment and wages, 2002 to 2007. *Perspectives on Labour and Income.* Statistics Canada, Catalogue No. 75-001-X, 5–15.

Marotte, B. (2005, February 26). Wal-Mart intimidated unionists, board rules. *The Globe and Mail*, p. A9.

Morissette, R. (2008, February). Earnings in the last decade. *Perspectives on Labour and Income.* Statistics Canada, Catalogue No. 75-001-X, 12–24.

Morissette, R., & Johnson, A. (2005, January). *Are good jobs disappearing in Canada?* Statistics Canada, Catalogue No. 11F0019MIE-No. 239. Minister of Industry. Retrieved from http://www.statcan.gc.ca/pub/11f0019m/11f0019m2005239-eng.pdf

Murray, G., & Cuillerier, J. (2009, November). The sky is not falling: Unionization, Wal-Mart and first-contract arbitration in Canada. *Just Labour: A Canadian Journal of Work and Society,* 15, 78–98.

New Rules Staff. (2005, March). Wal-Mart tries to skirt Maryland size cap law. *New Rules Project.* Institute for Local Self Reliance. Retrieved from http://www.newrules.org/retail/news/walmart-tries-skirt-maryland-size-cap-law

Owram, K. (2009, February 27). Wal-Mart closing six club stores. *The Hamilton Spectator*, p. A18.

PBS Video. (2004). Frontline: *Is Wal-Mart good for America?* WGBH Educational Foundation.

Peritz, I. (2005, February 11). Unionized Wal-Mart employees fear second Quebec store to shut. *The Globe and Mail*, p. A7.

Pier, C. (2007). *Discounting rights: Wal-Mart's violation of U.S. workers' right to freedom of association.* New York: Human Rights Watch.

Pupo, N., & Duffy, A. (2000). Canadian part-time work into the millennium: On the cusp of change. *Community, Work and Family*, 3(1), 49–69.

Ribeiro, S. (2005, January 16). The costs of "Walmartization." *Znet.* Retrieved from http://www.zmag.org/znet/viewArticle/7074

Rinehart, D. (2007, November 15). Scrubbing from the top down: Wal-Mart walks the environmental walk, makes suppliers clean up their acts. *The Globe and Mail*, pp. E1, E4.

Ritzer, G. (1996). *The McDonaldization of society: An investigation into the changing character of contemporary social life* (rev. ed.). Thousand Oaks, CA: Pine Forge Press.

Rubin, B., & Brody, C. J. (2005). Contradictions of commitment in the new economy: Insecurity, time and technology. *Social Science Research, 34*(4), 843–861.

Schaefer, L. (2006, July 28). World's biggest retailer Wal-Mart closes up shop in Germany. *DW-World.De—Deutsche Welle.* Retrieved from http://www.dw-world.de/dw/article/0,2112746,00.html

Scoffield, H. (2008, May 27). New national refrain: Can I help you? *The Globe and Mail*, pp. B1, B6.

Scott, H. (2004). Reconceptualizing the nature and health consequences of work-related insecurity for the new economy: The decline of workers' power in the flexibility regime. *International Journal of Health Services, 34*(1).

Statistics Canada. (2008). CANSIM table, 282-0008.

Statistics Canada. (2008a, August). Unionization. *Perspectives on Labour and Income.* Statistics Canada, Catalogue No. 75-001-X, 1–10.

Statistics Canada. (2007). CANSIM Table 281-0027, Catalogue No. 72-002-X.

Thomas, M. P. (2009). *Regulating flexibility: The political economy of employment standards.* Montreal & Kingston: McGill-Queen's University Press.

Usalcas, J. (2009, February). The labour market in 2008. *Perspectives on Labour and Income.* Statistics Canada, Catalogue No. 75-001-X, 23–28.

Usalcas, J. (2008, March). Hours polarization revisited. *Perspectives on Labour and Income.* Statistics Canada, Catalogue No. 75-001-X, 5–15.

Wells, D. (2007). Too weak for the job: Corporate codes of conduct, non-governmental organizations and the regulation of international labour standards. *Global Social Policy, 7*(1), 51–74.

Williams, C. L. (2006). *Inside toyland: Working, shopping, and social inequality.* Berkeley: University of California Press.

Chapter 4

Battle, K. (2008). *A bigger and better child benefit: A $5,000 Canada child tax benefit.* Ottawa: Caledon Institute of Social Policy.

Battle, K. (2006, April/May). Modernizing the welfare state. *Policy Options*, 47–50.

Beaujot, R. (2000), *Earning and caring in Canadian families.* Peterborough, ON: Broadview Press.

Beck, U. (2000). *The brave new world of work.* Cambridge: Polity. Bezanson, K. (2006). *Gender, the state and social reproduction.* Toronto: University of Toronto Press.

Braedley, S., & Luxton, M. (2010). Introduction. In S. Braedley & M. Luxton (Eds.), *Neoliberalism and everyday life.* Montreal and Kingston: McGill-Queen's University Press.

CBC Television. (2008, October 7). *The National with Peter Mansbridge.*

CCPA. (2009). *Exposed: Revealing truths about Canada's recession.* Canadian Centre for Policy Alternatives.

CCSD. (2009). *Families: A Canadian profile.* Retrieved May 25, 2009, from http://www.ccsd.ca/factsheets/family/

Clarke, J. (2008). Living with/in and without neo-liberalism. *Focaal, 51*(1), 135–147.

Connell, R. W. (2010). Understanding neoliberalism. In S. Braedley & M. Luxton (Eds.), *Neoliberalism and everyday life.* Montreal and Kingston: McGill-Queen's University Press.

Elson, D. (1998). The economic, the political and the domestic: Businesses, states and households in the organization of production. *New Political Economy, 3*(2).

Elson, D. (1995). *Male bias in the development process.* Manchester. Manchester University Press.

Feller, B. (2008). *Bush, candidates urge Congress to support bailout.* Retrieved September 30, 2008, from http://www.reportonbusiness.com/servlet/story/RTGAM.20080930.wbush0930/BNStory/Business/home

Galabuzzi, G. (2006). *Canada's economic apartheid: The social exclusion of racialized groups in the new century.* Toronto: Canadian Scholars Press Inc.

Guardian Weekly. (2008, October 31). Weekly Review. *The Guardian Weekly,* pp. 26–28.

Harvey, D. (2006). Neo-liberalism as creative destruction. *Geogr. Ann., 88B*(2), 145–158.

Harvey, D. (2005). *A brief history of neoliberalism.* New York: Oxford University Press.

International Monetary Fund. (2009, April). *Global financial stability report: Responding to the financial crisis and measuring systemic risks.* Retrieved May 6, 2009, from http://www.imf.org/external/pubs/ft/gfsr/2009/01/pdf/text.pdf

Klein, N. (2007). *The shock doctrine: The rise of disaster capitalism.* Toronto: A.A. Knopff.

Law Commission of Canada. (2004). *Is work working? Work laws that do a better job.* Ottawa: Law Commission of Canada.

Lott, J. R. (2007). *Freedomnomics: Why the free market works and other half baked theories don't.* Washington: Regnery Publishing Inc.

Luxton, M. (2006). Friends, neighbours and community: A case study of the role of informal caregiving. In K. Bezanson & M. Luxton (Eds.), *Social reproduction: Feminist political economy challenges neo-liberalism.* Montreal and Kingston: McGill-Queen's University Press.

Mahon, R. (2006). The OECD and the reconciliation agenda: Competing blueprints. In J. Lewis (Ed.), *Children in context: Changing families and welfare states.* London: Edwin Elgar.

Marshall, K. (2009, April). The family work week. *Perspectives on Labour and Income.* Ottawa: Statistics Canada.

McBride, S. (2006). Domestic neoliberalism. In V. Shalla (Ed.), *Working in a global era.* Toronto: CSPI.

New York Times. (2009, May 7). Credit crisis: The essentials. *New York Times,* pp. 1–11. Retrieved May 9, 2009, from http://topics.nytimes.con/topics/reference/timestopics/subjects/c/credit_crisis/

OECD. (2006). *Starting strong: Early childhood education and care.* Paris: OECD.

Peck, J., & Theodore, N. (2007). Variegated capitalism. *Progress in Human Geography, 31*(6), 731–772.

Pilieci, V. (2009, April 11). "He-cession" hits men's jobs harder. *Winnipeg Free Press.* Retrieved April 20, 2009, from http://www.winnipegfreepress.com/business/he-cession-hits-mens-jobs-harder-42843302.html

Rice, M., & Prince, J. (2000). *Changing politics of Canadian social policy.* Toronto: University of Toronto Press.

Rudd, K. (2008, October 6). The children of Gordon Gekko. *The Australian.* Retrieved May 13, 2009, from http://www.theaustralian.news.com.au/story/0,25197,24450662-7583,00.html

Scoffield, H. (2008, September 30). Canadian economy booms in July. *The Globe and Mail.* p. A1.

Scott, J. (2008). *Paid and unpaid work: A retreat in gender role egalitarian attitudes.* Paper presented at the annual meeting of the American Sociological Association Annual Meeting, Sheraton Boston and the Boston Marriott Copley Place, Boston, MA. Retrieved May 23, 2009, from http://www.allacademic.com/meta/p242289_index.html

Statistics Canada. (2009, June 2). Average income after tax by economic family types 2003-2007. *The Daily.* Ottawa: Statistics Canada.

Statistics Canada. (2007). *Women in Canada: Work chapter updates.* Ottawa: Statistics Canada.

Stewart, L. (2008, November 7). New world, same old ideology. *The Guardian Weekly,* p. 18.

Stiglitz, J. E. (2008, July). The end of neo-liberalism? *Project Syndicate Commentary.* Retrieved from http://www.project-syndicate.org

UNICEF. (2008). *The child care transition.* Florence, Italy: UNICEF Innocenti Research Centre.

Vosko, L. (2004). Precarious employment: Towards an improved understanding of labour market insecurity. In L. Vosko (Ed.), *Precarious employment: Understanding labour market insecurity in Canada.* Montreal and Kingston: McGill-Queen's University Press.

Vosko, L. (2000). *Temporary work.* Toronto: University of Toronto Press.

World Bank. (2009, April 24). *World development indicators database.* Retrieved May 6, 2009, from http://siteresources.worldbank.org/DATASTATISTICS/Resources/GDP.pdf

Yalnizan, A. (2009). *Exposed: Revealing the truths about Canada's recession.* Ottawa: Canadian Centre for Policy Alternatives.

Chapter 5

Amaeichi, J., & Bull, C. (2007). *Man in the middle.* Holmes, PA: ESPN Books.

Bagley, C., & Tremblay, P. (1998). On the prevalence of homosexuality and bisexuality, in a random community survey of 750 men aged 18-27. *Journal of Homosexuality, 36*(2), 1–18.

Beatty, J., & Kirby, S. (2006). Beyond the legal environment: How stigma influences invisible identity groups in the workplace. *Employee Responsibilities and Rights Journal, 18*(1), 29–44.

Beatty, J., & Kirby, S. (2004). *Feeling misunderstood: The emotional experiences of people with invisible identities.* Paper presented at the Academy of Management Annual Conference, New Orleans, LA.

Clair, J., Beatty, J., & Maclean, T. (2005). Out of sight but not out of mind: Managing invisible social identities in the workplace. *Academy of Management Review, 30*(1), 78–95.

Conyers, J., & Kennedy, R. (1963). Negro passing: To pass or not to pass. *Phylon: The Atlanta University of Race and Culture, 24*(3), 215–223.

Croteau, J., Anderson, M., & VanderWal, B. (2008). Models of workplace sexual identity management: Reviewing and extending concepts. *Group and Organizational Management, 33*(5): 532–565.

DeJordy, R. (2008). Just passing through: Stigma, passing, and identity decoupling in the workplace. *Group and Organization Management, 33*(5), 504–531.

Dovidio, J., Major, B., & Crocker, F. (2000). Stigma: Introduction and overview. In T. Heatherton, R. Kleck, M. Hebl, & J. Hull (Eds.), *The social psychology of stigma.* New York: Guilford Press.

Goffman, I. (1963). *Stigma: Notes on the management of spoiled identity.* New York: Prentice-Hall.

Herek, G., Jobe, J, & Carney, R. (Eds.) (1996). *Out in force: Sexual orientation and the military.* Chicago: University of Chicago Press.

Kinsey, A., Pomeroy, W.B., & Martin, C.E. (1948). *Sexual behavior in the human male.* New York: Saunders.

Mathews, C., & Harrington, N. (2000). Invisible disability. In D. Braithwaite & T. Thompson (Eds.), *Handbook of communication and people with disabilities: Research and application.* Mahwah, NJ: Erlbaum.

Paetzold, R., Dipboye, R., & Elsbach, K. (2008). A new look at stigmatizations in and of organizations. *Academy of Management Review, 33*(1), 186–193.

Park, A. (2008, April). Making diversity a business advantage. *Harvard Management Update.*

Pettrak, J. et al. (2001). Factors associated with self-disclosure of HIV serostatus to significant others. *British Journal of Health Psychology, 6*(1), 69–79.

Ragins, B. (2008). Disclosure disconnects: Antecedents and consequences of disclosing invisible stigmas across life domains. *Academy of Management Review, 33*(1), 194–215.

Thomas, D. (2004). Diversity as strategy. *Harvard Business Review, 82*(9), 98–108.

Thomas, D., & Ely, R. (1996). Making differences matter: A new paradigm for managing diversity. *Harvard Business Review, 74*(5), 79–90.

Woods, J. (1993). *The corporate closet: The professional lives of gay men in America.* New York: The Free Press.

Chapter 6

Abraham, M. (2008). Globalization and the call center industry. *International Sociology, 23*(2), 197–210.

ACTEW. (2007). Contingent work: Employment facts from ACTEW. Toronto: ACTEW.

Armstrong, J., & Ng, R. (2005). Deconstructing race, deconstructing racism—A conversation by Jeannette and Roxana Ng (with a postscript by Roxana Ng). In J.A. Lee & J. Lutz (Eds.), *Situating race and racism in time, space and theory: Critical essays for activists and scholars.* Montreal & Kingston: McGill-Queen's University Press.

Bakker, I. (1996). Introduction: The gendered foundations of restructuring in Canada. In I. Bakker (Ed.), *Rethinking restructuring: Gender and change in Canada.* Toronto: University of Toronto Press.

Breitbach, C. (2001). *Gender and the globalization of the US meatpacking industry.* Retrieved May 5, 2008, from http://www.maxwell.syr.edu/moynihan/programs/gandg/pdfs/meatpacking.pdf

Buchanan, R., & Koch-Schulte, S. (2000). *Gender on the line: Technology, restructuring and the reorganization of work in the call centre industry.* Ottawa: Status of Women Canada.

Carnoy, M. (1999). *Sustaining flexibility: Work, family, and community in the information age.* New York: Russell Sage.

Cranford, C. J., & Vosko, L. F. (2006). Conceptualizing precarious employment: Mapping wage work across social location and occupational context. In L. F. Vosko (Ed.), *Precarious employment: Understanding labour market insecurity in Canada.* Montreal and Kingston: McGill-Queen's University Press.

Das Gupta, T. (2006). Racism/anti-racism, precarious employment, and unions. In L. F. Vosko (Ed.), *Precarious employment: Understanding labour market insecurity in Canada.* Montreal and Kingston: McGill-Queen's University Press.

deWolff, A. (2006). Privatizing public employment assistance and precarious employment in Toronto. In L. F. Vosko (Ed.), *Precarious employment: Understanding labour market insecurity in Canada.* Montreal and Kingston: McGill-Queen's University Press.

deWolff, A. (2000). *Breaking the myth of flexible work: Contingent work in Toronto.* Contingent Workers Project, Toronto.

Francesconi, M., & Gosling, A. (2005). *Career paths of part-time women.* Working Paper 19. Manchester: Equal Opportunities Commission.

Galabuzi, G. (2006). *Canada's economic apartheid: The social exclusion of racialized groups in the new century.* Toronto: Canadian Scholar's Press.

Gannagé, C. (1986). *Double day, double bind: Women garment workers.* Toronto: Women's Press.

Gannagé, C. M. (1999). The Health and safety concerns of immigrant women workers in the Toronto sportswear industry. *International Journal of Health Services, 29*(2), 409–429.

Guard, J. (2003). *Manitoba's call centre explosion: A preliminary overview.* Paper presented at the Conference on Organizing Call Centres: From the Workers' Perspective, Toronto.

Hall, S. (1996). Gramsci's relevance for the study of race and ethnicity. In D. Morley & K.H. Chen (Eds.), *Stuart hall, critical dialogues in cultural studies.* London & New York: Routledge.

Hall, S. (1980). Race, articulation and societies structured in dominance. *Sociological Theories, Race and Colonialism.* Paris: UNESCO, 305–345.

Hipple, S. (2001). Contingent work in the late-1990s. *Monthly Labor Review, 124*(3), 3–27.

MacIvor, H. (1996). *Women and politics in Canada.* Peterborough: Broadview Press.

Mastracci, S.H., & Thompson, J.R. (2005). Nonstandard work arrangements in the public sector: Trends and issues. *Review of Public Personnel Administration, 25*(4), 299–324.

McLean, L.R., & Barber, M. (2004). In Search of comfort and independence: Irish immigrant domestic servants encounter the courts, jails and asylums in nineteenth-century Ontario. In M. Epp, F. Iacovetta, & F. Swyripa (Eds.), *Sisters or strangers? Immigrant, ethnic, and racialized women in Canadian history* (pp. 133–160). Toronto: University of Toronto Press.

Miles, R. (1993). *Racism after "race relations."* London: Routledge.

Miles, R. (1989). *Racism.* London: Routledge.

Millar, J., Ridge, T., & Bennett, F. (2006). *Part-time work and social security: Increasing the options.* Department for Work and Pensions: Centre for the Analysis of Social Policy, University of Bath. Retrieved December 8, 2009, from http://research. dwp.gov.uk/asd/asd5/rports2005-2006/ rrep351.pdf2004

Mirchandani, K., & Chan, W. (2007). *Criminalizing race, criminalizing poverty: Welfare fraud enforcement in Canada.* Halifax: Fernwood Publishing.

Mirchandani, K., Ng, R., Coloma-Moya, N., Maitra, S., Rawlings, T., Shan, H.,

Siddiqui, K., Slade, B. (2010). Transitioning into contingent work: Immigrants' learning and resistance. In P. Sawchuk & A. Taylor (Eds.), *Challenging transitions in learning and work: Reflections on policy and practice*. Rotterdam: Sense Publishers.

Mirchandani, K., Ng, R., Coloma-Moya, N., Maitra, S., Rawlings, T., Siddiqui, K., Shan, H., Slade, B. (2008). The paradox of training and learning in a culture of contingency. In D. Livingstone, K. Mirchandani, & P. Sawchuk (Eds.), *The future of lifelong learning and work: Critical perspectives*. Rotterdam: Sense Publishers.

Murji, K., & Solomos, J. (2005). Introduction: Racialization in theory and practice. In K. Murji & J. Solomos (Eds.), *Racialization: Studies in theory and practice*. Oxford: Oxford University Press.

Ng, R. (2002). Freedom from whom? Globalization and trade from the standpoint of garment workers. *Canadian Woman Studies, 21*(4), 74–82.

Ng, R., Man, G., Shan, H., & Liu, W. (2006). *Learning to be good citizens: Informal learning and the labour market experiences of professional Chinese immigrant women*. Paper presented at the Canadian Association for the Study of Adult Education (CASAE), York University, Toronto.

Ng, R., & Mirchandani, K. (2008). Linking global trends and local lives: Mapping the methodological dilemmas. In K. Gallagher (Ed.), *The methodological dilemma: Creative, critical and collaborative approaches to qualitative research*. New York: Routledge.

Padavic, I. (2005). Laboring under uncertainty: Identity renegotiation among contingent workers. *Symbolic Interaction, 28*(1), 111–134.

Phoenix, A. (2005). Remembered racialization: Young people and positioning in differential understandings. In K. Murji & J. Solomos (Eds.), *Racialization: Studies in theory and practice*. Oxford: Oxford University Press.

Rawlings, T. (2005). *Post-Fordist workplace model in a learning environment for vulnerable workers*. Paper presented at the Canadian Association for the Study of Adult Education (CASAE), University of Western Ontario, London, ON.

Statistics Canada. (2008a). *2006 census: Ethnic origin, visible minorities, place of work and mode of transportation*. Retrieved June 10, 2008, from http://www.statcan.ca/Daily/English/080402/d080402a.htm

Statistics Canada (2008b). *Census snapshot: Canada's changing labour force, 2006 census*. Ottawa.

Statistics Canada. (2007). *2006 census: Immigration, citizenship, language, mobility and migration*. Retrieved June 10, 2008, from http://www.statcan.ca/Daily/English/071204/d071204a.htm

Statistics Canada. (2006, March). *Women in Canada: A gender-based statistical report* (5th ed.). Ottawa. Retrieved June 16, 2008, from http://www.statcan.ca/ english/ freepub/89-503-XIE/0010589-503-XIE.pdf

Steedman, M. (2003). *The changing face of the call centre industry in Canada*. Paper presented at the Conference on Organizing Call Centres: From the Workers' Perspective, Toronto.

Szabó, K., & Négyesi, A. (2005). The spread of contingent work in the knowledge based economy. *Human Resource Development Review, 4*(1), 63–85.

Teelucksingh, C., & Galabuzi, G.-E. (2005). *Working precariously: The impact of race and immigrants status on employment opportunities and outcomes in Canada*. Toronto: The Canadian Race Relations Foundation.

Theodore, N., & Mehta, C. (1999). *Contingent work and the staffing industry: A review of worker-centered policy and practice*. Chicago, Illinois: Ford Foundation.

Toronto Training Board. (2005). *Ten ways of seeing precarious employment*. Retrieved May 13, 2008, from http://ttb.on.ca/downloads/Precariouspercent20Employmentpercent20NEW.pdf

Usalcas, J. (2005). Youth and the labour market. *Perspectives: On Labour and Income, 6*, 1–10.

Vosko, L. F. (Ed.). (2006). *Precarious employment: Understanding labour market insecurity in Canada*. Montreal and Kingston: McGill-Queen's University Press.

Vosko, L. F., Zukewich, N., & Cranford, C. (2003). Precarious jobs: A new typology of employment. *Perspectives on Labour and Income, 4*(10), 16–26.

Yanz, L., Jeffcott, B., Ladd, D., Atlin, J., & Network, M. S. (1999). *Policy options to improve standards for women garment workers in Canada and internationally*. Ottawa: Status of Women Canada.

Zietsma, D. (2007). *The Canadian immigrant labour market in 2006: First results from Canada's labour force survey*. The Immigrant Labour Force Analysis Series. Statistics Canada.

Chapter 7

Basok, T. (2002). *Tortillas and tomatoes*. Montreal: McGill-Queens University Press.

Binford, L. (2002). Social and economic contradictions of rural migrant contract labor between Tlaxcala, Mexico, and Canada. *Culture and Agriculture, 24*(2), 1–19.

Bolaria, B. (1992). Farm labour, work conditions, and health risk. In *Rural sociology in Canada*. Toronto: Oxford University Press.

Burawoy, M. (1976). The functions and reproduction of migrant labor: Comparative material from Southern Africa and the United States. *The American Journal of Sociology, 81*(5), 1050–1087.

Cecil, R., & Ebanks, G. (1991). The human condition of West Indian migrant farm labour in Southwestern Ontario. *International Migration, 29*(3), 384–404.

Chacón, J., & Davis, M. (2006). *No one is illegal: Fighting racism and state violence on the U.S.-Mexico Border*. Chicago: Haymarket Books.

Hinnenkamp, K. (2004). *The experience of Mexican seasonal agricultural workers in Canada: A collaborative multimedia project*. Toronto: J4MW. Retrieved from http://www.justicia4migrantworkers.org

Preibisch, K. (2004). *Globalizing work, globalizing citizenship: Migrant worker alliances in southwestern Ontario*. Paper presented at University of Guelph.

Preibisch, K., & Binford, L. (2007). Interrogating racialized global labour supply: An exploration of the racial/national replacement of foreign agricultural workers in Canada. *Canadian Review of Sociology and Anthropology, 44*(1), 5–36.

Satzewich, V. (1991). *Racism and the incorporation of foreign labour: Farm labour migration to Canada since 1945*. New York: Routledge.

Sharma, N. (2006). *Home economics: Nationalism and the making of migrant workers in Canada*. Toronto: University of Toronto Press.

Sharma, N. (2001). On being not Canadian: The social organization of "migrant workers" in Canada. *Canadian Review of Sociology and Anthropology, 38*(4), 414–439.

Smart, J. (1998). Borrowed men on borrowed time: Globalization, labour migration and local economies in Alberta. *Canadian Journal of Regional Science, 20*(12), 141–156.

Stasiulis, D., & Bakan, A. (2005). *Negotiating citizenship: Migrant women in Canada and the global system.* Toronto: University of Toronto Press.

Toronto Star. (2009, November 4). "Guest worker" abuses blasted.

United Food and Commercial Workers Union of Canada. (2002). *National report: Status of migrant farm workers in Canada.* Ottawa: UFCW. Retrieved from http://www.ufcw.ca/cgi-bin/download.cgi/Ntional+ReportENG.pdf?id = 231&a = v&name = National+ReportENG.pdf

Vogel, R. (2007, January). Transient servitude: The U.S. guest worker program for exploiting Mexican and Central American workers. *Monthly Review,* 1–23.

Weston, A., & Scarpa de Masellis, L. (2003). *Hemispheric integration and trade relations: Implications for Canada's seasonal agricultural workers program.* Ottawa: North-South Institute.

Chapter 8

Ashton, J., & Elliott, R. (2007). Study, work, rest and play: juggling the priorities of students' lives. *Australian Journal of Early Childhood, 32*(2): 15–27.

Bailyn, L. (2006). *Breaking the mold: Redesigning work for productive and satisfying lives* (2nd ed.). Ithaca and London: ILR Press.

Beaujot, R., & Andersen, R. (2007). Time-crunch: Impact of time spent in paid and unpaid work, and its division in families. *Canadian Journal of Sociology, 32*(3), 295–315.

Bonney, N. (2005). Overworked Britons? Part-time work and work-life balance. *Work, Employment and Society, 19*(2), 391–401.

Bosch, G. (2001). Working time: From redistribution to modernization. In P. Auer (Ed.), *Changing labour markets in Europe: The role of institutions and policies* (p. 115). Geneva: International Labour Office.

Boulin, J-Y., Lallement, M., Messenger, J. C., & Michon, F. (Eds.). (2006). *Decent working time: new trends, new issues.* Geneva: International Labour Office.

Bradbury, B. (1982). The fragmented family: Family strategies in the face of death, illness, and poverty, Montreal, 1860-1885. In J. Parr (Ed.), *Childhood and family in Canadian history* (pp. 109–128). Toronto: McClelland and Stewart.

Chai, C. (2009, April 4). Extra effort pays off. *Toronto Star,* p. B8.

Copp, T. (1974). *The anatomy of poverty: The condition of the working class in Montreal 1897-1929.* Toronto: McClelland and Stewart.

Coulter, R. (1982). The working young of Edmonton, 1921-1931. In J. Parr (Ed.), *Childhood and family in Canadian history* (pp. 143–159). Toronto: McClelland and Stewart.

Cruikshank, J. (2007). Lifelong learning and the new economy: Rhetoric or reality? *Education Matters, 47*(2), 32–36.

Duffy, A. (forthcoming). Families in tough times. In N. Mandell & A. Duffy (Eds.), *Canadian families* (4th ed.). Toronto: Nelson.

Duffy, A., Glenday, D. G., & Pupo, N. (1998, Fall). Seniors in the part-time labour force: Issues of choice and power. *International Journal of Canadian Studies, 18,* 133–152.

Duffy, A., & Pupo, N. (1992). *The part-time paradox: Connecting gender, work and family.* Toronto: McClelland & Stewart.

Fast, J., & Frederick, J. (2004). *The time of our lives: Juggling work and leisure over the life cycle.* Statistics Canada. Ottawa: Minister of Industry. Catalogue no. 89-584-MIE-No. 4.

Fast, J., Frederick, J., Zukewich, N., & Franke, S. (2001). The time of our lives. *Canadian Social Trends, 63,* 20–23.

Gillin, C.T., MacGregor, D., & Klassen, T. (Eds.). (2005). *Time's up! Mandatory retirement in Canada.* Toronto: James Lorimer & Company, Ltd.

The Globe and Mail. (2009, March 18). Economic fallout: And the surveys say. . . . *The Globe and Mail,* p. B15.

The Globe and Mail. (2008, August 15). Quebec workers no strangers to long hours. *The Globe and Mail,* p. C5.

Grevatt, M. (2007). Workers need 30-hour week more than ever. *Workers World.* Retrieved from http://www.workers.org/2007/us/flint-0412 Hayden, A. (1999). *Sharing the work, sparing the planet: Work time, consumption & ecology.* Toronto: Between the Lines.

Heisz, A, & LaRochelle-Cote, S. (2006). Work hours instability. *Perspectives on Labour and Income, 7*(12), 17–20.

Heisz, A., & LaRochelle-Cote, S. (2003). *Working hours in Canada and the United States.* Research Paper. Statistics Canada. Catalogue no. 11F0019MIE-No. 209.

Hillbrecht, M., Zuzanek, J., & Mannell, R. (2007). Time use, time pressure and gendered behaviour in early and late adolescence. *Sex Roles, 58,* 342–357.

Hochschild. A. (1997). *The time bind: When work becomes home and home becomes work.* New York: Henry Holt.

Holmgren, K., Dahlin-Ivanoff, S., Bjorkelund, C., & Hensing, G. (2009). The prevalence of work-related stress, and its association with self-perceived health and sick-leave in a population of employed Swedish women. *BMC Health 9*(73), 73–83.

Humm, C. (2009). Occupational hazard: Working nights can seriously damage your health—in fact it has now been classified as a carcinogen. *Nursing Standard, 20*(1), 20–23.

Hurst, M. (2008, April). Who gets any sleep these days? Sleep patterns of Canadians. *Canadian Social Trends,* 39–45.

Jackson, A. (2005). *Work and Labour in Canada.* Toronto: Canadian Scholars' Press Inc.

Keown, L-A. (2007, Summer). Time escapes me: Workaholics and time perception. *Canadian Social Trends,* 30–33.

Keune, M., & Galgoczi, B. (Eds.). (2006). *Collective bargaining on working time: Recent European experiences.* Brussels: ETUI-REHS.

Kopun, F. (2009, March 25). Recession stress cuts short maternity leave. *Toronto Star,* p. A6.

Krahn, H., & Lowe, G. S. (1988). *Work, industry and Canadian society.* Toronto: Nelson Canada.

Lewis, S. (2003). The integration of paid work and the rest of life: Is post-industrial work the new leisure? *Leisure Studies,* 333–335.

Livingstone, D. (2001, Winter). Expanding notions of work and learning: Profiles in latent power. *New Directions for Adult and Continuing Education, 92,* 19–30.

Maher, J., Lindsay, J., & Franzway, S. (2008). Time, caring labour and social policy: Understanding the family time economy in contemporary families. *Work, Employment and Society 33*(3), 547–558.

Manrai, L. A., & Manrai, A. K. (1995). *Journal of Business Research, 32,* 115–128.

Marshall, K. (2007, May). The busy lives of teens. *Canadian Social Trends,* 5–15.

Martin, J. E., & Sinclair, R. R. (2007). A typology of the part-time workforce: Differences on job attitudes and turnover. *Journal of Occupational and Organizational Psychology, 80*(2), 301–320.

Mattingly, M. J., & Bianci, S. M. (2003). Gender differences in the quantity and quality of free time: The U.S. experience. *Social Forces, 81*(3), 999–1030.

Menzies, H. (2005). *No time: Stress and the crisis of modern life.* Vancouver: Douglas and McIntyre.

Messenger, J. C. (Ed.). (2004). *Working time and worker preferences in industrialised countries: Finding the balance.* London: Routledge.

Nebenzahl, D. (2010, March 20). Canadians falling asleep on the job. *Toronto Star,* p. B8.

Perrons, D., Fagan, C., McDowell, L., Ray, K., & Ward, K. (Eds.). (2006). *Gender divisions and working time in the new economy: Changing patterns of work, care and public policy in Europe and North America.* Northhampton, MA: Edward Elgar.

Popplewell, B. (2009, March 10). Staying at home so others don't have to. *Toronto Star,* pp. B1, B4.

Presser, H. (2000). Nonstandard work schedules and marital instability. *Journal of Marriage and the Family, 63*(1), 93–111.

Ravenscroft, N., & Gilchrist, P. (2009). The emergent working society of leisure. *Journal of Leisure Research, 41*(1), 23–50.

Reynolds, J. (2004). When too much is not enough: Actual and preferred work hours in the United States and abroad. *Sociological Forum, 19*(1), 89–120.

Rinehart, J. W. (2001). *The tyranny of work: Alienation and the labour process* (4th ed.). Toronto: Harcourt Canada.

Rojek, C. (2001). Leisure and life policies. *Leisure Sciences, 23,* 115–125.

Roxburgh, S. (2002). Racing through life: The distribution of time pressures by roles and role resources among full-time workers. *Journal of Family and Economic Issues, 23*(2), 121–145.

Rubin, B. A., & Brody, C. J. (2005). Contradictions of commitment in the new economy: Insecurity, time, and technology. *Social Science Research, 34,* 843–861.

Saloniemi, A., & Zeytinoglu, I. U. (2007). Achieving flexibility through insecurity: A comparison of work environments in fixed-term and permanent jobs in Finland and Canada. *European Journal of Industrial Relations, 13*(1), 109–128.

Schor, J. B. (1992). *The overworked American.* New York: BasicBooks.

Sennett, R. (1998). *The corrosion of character: The personal consequences of work in the new capitalism.* New York: W.W. Norton & Company.

Shields, M. (2006). Unhappy on the job. *Health Reports, 17*(4), 33–37.

Shillingford, N. (2009). We must demand a 30-hour workweek. *Socialist Alternative.* Retrieved from http://www.SocialistAlternative.org/news/article14.php? Id=1062

Sjoberg, G. (1965). *The preindustrial city: Past and present.* New York: Free Press.

Statistics Canada. (2006a, July 26). General social survey: Time use patterns of older

Canadians. *The Daily.* Retrieved from http://www.statcan.ca/Daily/English/060726/d060726a.htm Statistics Canada. (2006b, October 17). Health reports: Job satisfaction, stress and depression. *The Daily.* Retrieved from http://www.statcan.ca/Daily/English/061017/d061017a.htm

Statistics Canada. (2006c, July 19). General social survey: Paid and unpaid work. *The Daily.* Retrieved from http: //www.statcan.ca/Daily/English/060719/d060719b.htm

Statistics Canada. (2004, September 20). Non-profit institutions and volunteering: Economic contribution, 1997 to 1999. *The Daily, 9–12.*

Statistics Canada. (2003). *2001 census: Analysis series—Where Canadians work and how they get there.* Ottawa: Minister of Industry. Catalogue no. 96F0030XIE2001010.

Strazdins, L., Clements, M. S., Korda, R. J., Broom, D. H., & D'Souza, R. M. (2006, May). Unsociable work? Nonstandard work schedules, family relationships, and children's well-being. *Journal of Marriage and Family, 68,* 394–410.

Tausig, M., & Fenwick, R. (2001). Unbinding time: Alternative work schedules and work-life balance. *Journal of Family and Economic Issues, 22*(2), 101–119.

Toronto Star. (2009, April 2). Daimler work weeks to shrink. *Toronto Star,* p. B4.

Turcotte, M. (2007). Time spent with family during a typical workday, 1986 to 2005. *Canadian Social Trends, 83,* 2–11.

Twenge, J. M., Campbell, S. M., Hoffman, B. J., & Lance, C. E. (2010, March 1). Generational differences in work values: Leisure and extrinsic values increasing, social and intrinsic values decreasing. *Journal of Management (OnlineFirst).*

U.S. Department of Labor, Bureau of Labor Statistics. (1997, February). Workers are on the job more hours over the course of the year. *Issues.*

Usalcas, J. (2008). Hours polarization revisited. *Perspectives on Labour and Income, 9*(3), 5–15.

Van Echtelt, P. E., Glebbeek, A. C., & Lindenberg, S. M. (2006). The new lumpiness of work: explaining the mismatch between actually and preferred working hours. *Work, Employment and Society, 20*(3), 493–512.

Vosko, L. F. (2000). *Temporary work: The gendered rise of a precarious employment relationship.* Toronto: University of Toronto Press.

Wallace, J., & Young, M. C. (2010). Work hard, play hard? A comparison of male and female lawyers' time in paid and unpaid work and participation in leisure activities. *Canadian Review of Sociology, 47*(1), 27–47.

Warburton, J., & Smith, J. (2003). Out of the generosity of your heart: Are we creating active citizens through compulsory volunteer programmes for young people in Australia. *Social Policy and Administration, 37*(7), 772–786.

Wight, V. R., Raley, S. B., & Bianchi, S. M. (2008). Time for children, one's spouse and oneself among parents who work nonstandard hours. *Social Forces, 87*(1), 243–272.

Zaretsky, E. (1986). *Capitalism, the family and personal life* (rev. ed.). New York: Harper and Row Publishers.

Chapter 9

Baldamus, W. (1961/2003). *Efficiency and effort: An analysis of industrial administration.* London. Tavistock.

Derberoglu, D. (2002). *Labor and capital in an age of globalization: The labor process and the changing nature of work in the global economy.* New York: Rowman and Littlefield.

Braverman, H. (1998). *Labor and monopoly capitalism.* New York: Monthly Review Press

Brown, R. K. (1988). The employment relationship in sociological theory. In D. Gallie (Ed.), *Employment in Britain.* Oxford: Basil Blackwell.

Buroway, M. (1979). *Manufacturing consent.* Chicago: University of Chicago.

_____. (1985). *The politics of production.* London: Verso.

_____. (2001). Donald Roy—Sociologist and working stiff. *Contemporary Sociology, 30*(5), 453–458.

Casey, C. (1995). *Work, self and society: After industrialism.* London: Routledge.

de Certeau, M. (1988). *The writing of history.* New York: Columbia University Press.

Deleuze, G., & Guattari, F. (1987). *A thousand plateaus: Capitalism and schizophrenia.* Minneapolis: University of Minnesota Press.

Duhaime. (2010). *Employee.* Retrieved from http://duhaime.org/LegalDictionary/E/Employee.aspx

Foucault, M. (1980). *Power/knowledge, selected interviews and other writings, 1972-1977* (C. Gordon, Ed.). Brighton: Harvester.

_____. (1982). The subject and power. In H. Dreyfus & P. Rabinow (Eds.), *Michel Foucault: Beyond structuralism and hermeneutics.* Chicago: University of Chicago Press.

_____. (1989). *Foucault live: Collected interviews 1961-1984* (F. Lotringer, Ed.; J. Johnston, Trans.). New York: Semiotext(e).

_____. (1991). Politics and the study of discourse. In G. Burchell, C. Gordon, & P. Miller (Eds.), *The Foucault effect: Studies in governmentality.* London: Harvester Wheatsheaf.

Glenday, D. (1997). Lost horizons, leisure shock: Good jobs, bad jobs, uncertain future. In *Good jobs, bad jobs, no jobs: The transformation of work in the 21st century* (pp. 8–34). Toronto: Harcourt Brace.

Gorz, A. (1985). *Paths to paradise: On the liberation from work.* London: Pluto Press.

_____. (1987). *Farewell to the working class: An essay on post-industrial socialism.* London: Pluto Press.

May, T. (1999). From banana time to just-in-time: Power and resistance at work. *Sociology, 33*(4), 767–783.

May, T., & Buck, M. (1998). Power, professionalism, and organisational transformation. *Sociological Research Online, 3*(2). Retrieved from http://www.socresonline.org.uk/socresonline/3/2/5.html

Perlow, L. A. (1999). The time famine: Toward a sociology of work time. *Administrative Science Quarterly, 44*(1), 57–81.

Pile, S., & Keith, M. (1997). *Geographies of resistance.* London: Routledge.

Roy, D. (1959-60). "Banana time" job satisfaction and informal interaction. *Human Organization, 18,* 158–168.

_____. (1980). Review of Michael Buroway, manufacturing consent. *Berkeley Journal of Sociology, 24,* 329–39.

Sewell, G., & Wilkinson, B. (1992). Someone to watch over me: Surveillance, discipline, and the JIT labor process. *Sociology, 26*(2), 271–289.

Townley, B. (1994). *Reframing human resource management: Power, ethics and the subject at work.* London: Sage.

Wardell, M. L., Steiger, T., & Meiksins, P. (Eds). (1999). *Rethinking the labor process.* Albany: State University of New York.

Weber, M. (1968). *Economy and society: An outline of interpretive sociology* (G. Roth & C. Wittich, Eds.) (2 vols.). New York: Bedminster Press

Chapter 10

Ahlquist, J. (2009, December). *Building strategic capacity: The political underpinnings of coordinated wage bargaining.* Institute for Research on Labor and Employment, University of California, 1–46.

Baccaro, L., & Simoni, M. (2007). Centralized wage bargaining and the "Celtic tiger" phenomenon. *Industrial Relations, 46*(3), 426–455.

B.C. Stats. (2009, January). *British Columbia Public Sector Employment.* Issue 09-01. Retrieved from http://www.bcstats.gov.bc.ca

Blackett, A., & Sheppard, C. (2003). Collective bargaining and equality: Making connections. *International Labour Review, 142*(4), 419–457.

Bourque, R. (2008, Spring). International framework agreements and the future of collective bargaining in multinational companies. *Just Labour: A Canadian Journal of Work and Society, 12,* 30–46.

Boxall, P., & Haynes, P. (1997). Strategy and trade union effectiveness in a neo-liberal environment. *British Journal of Industrial Relations, 35*(4), 567–591.

Broad, D. (2000). *Hollow work, hollow society.* Halifax: Fernwood Publishing.

Bronfenbrenner, K., & Juravich, T. (1998). It takes more than house calls: Organizing to win with a comprehensive union building strategy. In K. Bronfenbrenner et al., *Organizing to win: New research on union strategies.* Ithaca, NY: ILR Press.

Calmfors, L. (1993). *Centralization of wage bargaining and economic performance: A survey.* OECD Economic Department Working Paper No. 131.

Calmfors, L., & Driffil, J. (1988, April). Centralization of wage bargaining. *Economic Policy, 14*–61.

Camfield, D. (2007). Renewal in Canadian public sector unions: Neoliberalism and praxis. *Relations Industrielles/ Industrial Relations, 62*(2), 282–304.

Camfield, D. (2006). Neoliberalism and working-class resistance in British Columbia: The hospital employees' union struggle, 2002–2004. *Labour, 57,* 9–41.

Caverley, N., Cunningham, B., & Mitchell, L. (2006). Reflections on public sector-based integrative collective bargaining: Conditions affecting cooperation within the negotiation process. *Employee Relations, 28*(1), 62–75.

Clark, P. (2000). *Building more effective unions.* Ithaca, NY: ILR Press.

Cohen, M. (2006). The privatization of health care cleaning services in Southwestern British Columbia, Canada: Union responses to unprecedented government actions. *Antipode,* 626–644.

CUPE. (2008, February 25). *Bargaining GR8 in 08.* Ontario School Board Coordinating Committee: Provincial Discussion Table.

CUPE. 2007. *Securing the future.* Strategic Directions Program for CUPE: 2007-2009. Adopted by the CUPE National Convention, 2007.

CUPE. (2005). *Gaining ground: Moving forward from 2003.* Strategic Directions Program for CUPE: 2005-2007. Adopted by the CUPE National Convention, 2005.

CUPE. (1999). *CUPE Action Plan.* Retrieved February 24, 2009, from http://cupe.ca/PolicyCampaign.

CUPE Research. (2005). *CUPE coordinated bargaining structures in CUPE.* Presented at Social Services Convention, 2005.

Cyr-Racine, C., & Jalette, P. (2007). What have unions got to do with reverse privatization. *Journal of Collective Negotiations, 31*(4), 303–318.

Eaton, A., & Kriesky, J. (1998). Decentralization of bargaining structure: Four cases from the US paper industry. *Relations Industrielles/Industrial Relations, 53*(3), 1–18.

Eaton, A., Rubinstein, S., & Kochan, T. (2008). Balancing acts: Dynamics of a union coalition in a labor management partnership. *Industrial Relations, 47*(1), 10–35.

Ebbinghaus, B. (2004). The changing union and bargaining landscape: Union concentration and collective bargaining trends. *Industrial Relations Journal, 35*(6), 574–587.

Economist. (2009a, February 14–20). Gloom offensive: The politics of the recession, 37–38.

Economist. (2009b, March 14–20). The state and the economy: Back in the driving seat, 55.

Folk-Dawson, J. (2006, November 17). *Coordinated bargaining in the university sector.* Presentation to the CUPE National University Workers Meeting.

Freeman, R., & Gibbons, R. (1993). *Getting together and breaking apart: The decline of centralized collective bargaining.* Working Paper No. 4464. National Bureau of Economic Research, Cambridge, MA.

Gennard, J., & Newsome, K. (2001). European coordination of collective bargaining: The case of the UNI-Europa graphical sector. *Employee Relations, 23*(6), 599–613.

Gildiner, A. (2007). The organization of decision-making and the dynamics of policy drift: A Canadian health sector example. *Social Policy and Administration, 41*(5), 505–524.

Gildiner, A. (2006). Measuring shrinkage in the welfare state: Forms of privatization in a Canadian health care sector. *Canadian Journal of Political Science, 39*(1), 53–75.

Grimshaw, D., Jaehrling, K., van der Meer, M., Mehaut, P., & Shimron, N. (2007). Convergent and divergent country trends in coordinated wage setting and collective bargaining in the public hospitals sector. *Industrial Relations Journal, 38*(6), 591–613.

Hancke, B., & Soskice, D. (2003). Wage setting and inflation targets in the EMU. *Oxford Review of Economic Policy, 19*(1), 149–160.

Hebdon, R., & Jalette, P. (2008). The restructuring of municipal services: A Canada-United States comparison. *Environment and Planning, 26*(1), 144–158.

Isitt, B., & Moroz, M. (2007, Spring). The hospital employee's union strike and the privatization of medicare in British Columbia, Canada. *International Labor and Working Class History, 71*, 91–111.

Jackson, A. (2006). Rowing against the tide: The struggle to raise union density in a hostile environment. In P. Kumar & C. Schenk (Eds.), *Paths to union renewal: Canadian experiences*, (pp. 61–78). Peterborough, ON: Broadview and Garamond Press.

Johnston, J. (2006). Who cares about the commons. In J. Johnston, M. Gismondi, & J. Goodman (Eds.), *Nature's revenge: Reclaiming sustainability in the age of corporate globalization*. Peterborough, ON: Broadview Press.

Kahn, L. (2000). Wage inequality, collective bargaining and relative employment from 1985-1994: Evidence from fifteen OECD countries. *Review of Economics and Statistics, 82*(4), 564–579.

Karlsen, G. (1999). Decentralized–centralism: Governance in education from Norway to British Columbia, Canada. *Canadian Journal of Educational Administration, 13*, 1–17.

Kochan, T., & Piore, M. (1983). Will the new industrial relations last? Implications for the American labor movement. *The Annals of the American Academy of Political Science, 473*, 177–198.

Kozolanka, K. (2006). Taming labour in neo-liberal Ontario: Oppositional political communication in a time of crisis. *Canadian Journal of Communication, 31*(3), 561–580.

Kumar P., & Holmes, J. (1997). Canada: Continuity and change. In T. Kochan, R. Lansbury, & J. MacDuffie (Eds.), *After lean production: Evolving employment practices in the world auto industry*. Ithaca: ILR Press.

Kumar, P., & Schenk, C. (2006). Union renewal and organizational change: A review of the literature. In P. Kumar & C. Schenk (Eds.), *Paths to union renewal: Canadian experiences* (pp 29–60). Peterborough, ON: Broadview and Garamond Press.

Leduc Browne, P. (2006). *Public pain, private gain: The privatization of health care in Ontario: A report to the Ontario health coalition*. Canadian Centre for Policy Analysis.

MacPhail, F., & Bowles, P. (2008). Temporary work and neoliberal government policy: Evidence from British Columbia, Canada. *International Review of Applied Economics, 22*(5), 545–563.

Martin, C., & Thelen, K. (2007, October). The state and coordinated capitalism: Contributions of the public sector to solidarity in post-industrial societies. *Work Politics, 60*, 1–36.

Meyer, D. (2001). Building union power in the global economy: A case study of the coordinated bargaining committee of General Electric unions. *Labor Studies Journal, 26*(10), 60–76.

OCHU. (2009). OCHU RPN Committee Report 2008-2009, April Convention 2009.

OUWCC. (2008, March 3). Ontario University Workers Coordinating Committee, OUWCC '08 Conference and Action Plan, CUPE.

Rapaport, D. (1999). *No justice, no peace: The 1996 OPSEU strike against the Harris Government in Ontario*. Montreal and Kingston: McGill-Queen's University Press.

Robertson, D., & Murninghan, B. (2006). Union resistance and union renewal in the CAW. In P. Kumar & C. Schenk (Eds.), *Paths to union renewal: Canadian experiences* (pp. 161–185).Peterborough, ON: Broadview and Garamond Press.

Rose, J. (2007). Canadian public sector unions at the crossroads. *Journal of Collective Negotiations, 31*(3), 143.

Rose, J. (1986). Legislative support for multi-employer bargaining: The Canadian experience. *Industrial and Labor Relations Review, 40*(1), 3–18.

Rose, J. (1979). A Canadian view of labor relations in construction. *Industrial Relations, 18*(20), 156–173.

Rose, J., & Chaison, G. (2001). Unionism in Canada and the United States in the 21st century: The prospects for revival. *Relations Industrielles/Industrial Relations, 56*(1), 34–55.

Rose, J., & Chaison, G. (1996). Linking union density and union effectiveness: The North American experience. *Industrial Relations, 35*(1), 78–105.

Schenk, C. (1995). Fifty years after PC 1003. The need for new directions. In C. Gonick, P. Phillips, & J. Vorst, *Labour gains, labour pains: 50 years of PC 1003* (pp. 193–214). Winnipeg and Halifax, Society of Socialist Studies and Fernwood Publishing,

Sisson, K., & Marginson, P. (2000). *Coordinated bargaining: A process for our times.* Working Paper No. 14/00. Industrial Relations Research Unit, University of Warwick.

Statistics Canada. (2009, February 20). Public sector employment. *The Daily.* Retrieved from http://www.statcan.gc.ca/daily

Stinson, J., & Ballantyne, M. (2006). Union renewal and CUPE. In P. Kumar & C. Schenk (Eds.), *Paths to union renewal: Canadian experiences* (pp. 129–144). Peterborough, ON: Broadview and Garamond Press.

Theilheimer, I. (2008). *Public service will face squeeze with economic crisis: Recession could be used to justify privatization and cuts.*

Retrieved May 15, 2009, from http://www.publicvalues.ca

Thompson, M. (1995). The industrial relations effects of privatization: Evidence from Canada. In G. Swimmer & M. Thompson (Eds.), *Public sector bargaining in Canada: Beginning of the end or the end of the beginning* (pp. 164–177). Kingston, ON: IRC Press.

Traxler, F. (2003a). Bargaining (de)centralization, macroeconomic performance and control over the employment relationship. *British Journal of Industrial Relations, 41*(1), 1–27.

Traxler, F. (2003b). Coordinated bargaining: A stocktaking of its preconditions, practices and performance. *Industrial Relations Journal, 34*(3), 194–209.

Traxler, F., Brandl, B., & Glassner, V. (2008). Pattern bargaining: An investigation into its agency, context, and evidence. *British Journal of Industrial Relations, 46*(1), 33–58.

Vielhaber, M., & Waltman. (2008). Changing uses of technology: Crisis communication responses in a faculty strike. *Journal of Business Communication, 45*(3), 308–330.

Vosko, L. (2000). *Temporary work: The gendered rise of a precarious employment relationship.* Toronto: University of Toronto Press.

Warskett, R. (2007). Remaking the Canadian labour movement: Transformed work and transformed labour strategies. In V. Shalla & W. Clement, *Work in tumultuous times: Critical perspectives* (pp. 380–400). Montreal and Kingston: McGill-Queen's University Press.

White, E., & Gray, D. (2008, November 1). Adventures in coordinated bargaining: New organizing models bear fruit for Ontario university sector workers. *Briarpatch Magazine.*

White, J. (1990). *Hospital strike: Women, unions and public sector conflict.* Toronto: Thompson Education Ltd.

Yates, C. (2004, Fall/Winter). Rebuilding the labour movement by organizing the unorganized: Strategic considerations. *Studies in Political Economy, 74,* 171–9.

Zweimuller, J., & Barth, E. (1992). *Bargaining structure, wage determination and wage dispersion in six OECD countries.* Institute for Research on Labor and Employment, Working Paper Series, Paper, iirwps'047-92, University of California, Berkeley, CA.

INDEX